FACING EXISTENTIAL CONTRADICTIONS

SELF-EXAMINATION AS A TOOL FOR PEACE AND HAPPINESS VOLUME 1

Jacques L. Koko, Ph.D.

Balboa Press books may be ordered through booksellers or by contacting:

Balboa Press
A Division of Hay House
1663 Liberty Drive
Bloomington, IN 47403
www.balboapress.com
1 (877) 407-4847

Cover Art by Jacques L. Koko

Print information available on the last page.

ISBN: 978-1-9822-0887-5 (sc)
ISBN: 978-1-9822-0885-1 (hc)
ISBN: 978-1-9822-0886-8 (e)

Library of Congress Control Number: 2018908504

Balboa Press rev. date: 07/31/2018

In memory of Dr. Wayne Dyer, a good friend and mentor! You will not be forgotten! I hope you find some time out of your everlasting rest to read or leaf through this book I respectfully dedicate to you.

For Anne, my wonderful mother, the wisdom of my inspirations!

To Barbara, my wife, and to our children, Julie, Jacques Jr., and Marie!

CONTENTS

ACKNOWLEDGMENTS

Dear Mother!

Based upon your experience raising me, you once told me that the title of "mother" is the most beautiful and meaningful label an earthborn being could ever carry, but while living with you, I have also learned that "mother" is the most comforting and supportive name a child can call on earth—with the exception of divine identities.

Mother, my life is from you, and it leans on you like on a mountain. I lean on you through existential contradictions. You stand by me in times of darkness and pain. You dwell with me in the shadows of long nights. You give me strength in periods of weakness and suffering. When I suffer, you condole with me. When I cry, you console me. When I doubt, you give me hope and faith. When I stumble, you hold me firm. When I am hungry and thirsty, you make me eat and drink. When I am naked, you wrap me with your arms and get me dressed. When I am sick, you help me recover. When I am sad, you make me happy. When I am tired or sleepy, you make me rest. When I am disoriented, you give me advice and guidance. When I am lost, you become my only refuge. You also stand by me in times of success and joy. When I smile and laugh, you rejoice with me. You vigilantly help me escape successfully from the traps of existential contradictions and conflicts. You make me transform my self-conflicts into opportunities for growth or progress on the road to happiness. Like a good mediator, you guide and inspire me at the crossroads of contradictions. Mother, you have provided me with your mediation in times of contradictions or conflicts! On several occasions, you have served as an inspiring mediator between me and others! The wisdom of your intervention has been my inspiration during my self-conflicts! How could I repay you for always being such a supportive and gracious mother? Every time I rely on your advice, I transform and transcend my conflicts! Acknowledging you as the pillar of my life makes me reconnect with my roots! You show me the paths to peace of mind and heart.

Mother, you are a pillar of my life on all accounts. Like a pillar, you support my life and existence. You make me stand strong. Yes! You are my stronghold days and nights. All the while, my life dives in the ocean of your wisdom and protection. My life would be missing its roots without you, my solid foundation. My life was modeled inside of you. In nine months, you patiently cocreated me. I am the flesh of your flesh. I can only imagine that day you gladly or reluctantly accepted to conceive me. I wonder how you handled those dizzy days of fecundation and implantation. I read your journal about those mysterious months of gestation. I read about your sleepless nights and uneasy changes in your body. I heard about your pain in labor and delivery. Mother, I am grateful to you for giving me life and for nurturing it.

I know you are still mindful of your joy upon my arrival into life. I now hold in my hands some memorable pictures with a shiny smile on your smooth face. This evidence meaningfully tells it all about your love for me. As I look at the pictures, I admire how you carefully hold me like an egg in your hands. You cover me nicely under the protective feathers of your arms. You press me gently against your warm chest. The serenity of your look reflects your meditative attitudes on the gift of my life. The peace on your face expresses your faith in God and in my life. The patience in your eyes echoes your wisdom of existence.

As I contemplate such pictures, I meditate on how you provide me with pillars for my life. This makes me appreciate how a mother is like a springboard of life; she jumpstarts life and nurtures it. You make me stand firm and strong with your advice. In times of discouragement, your instructions give me words of encouragement. When impetuous winds of distress blow up and the waves of pain spill over into the boat of my existence, you hold me. The wind of suffering and pain shakes me up, but it does not knock me down. The waves spill over into my boat, but you do not allow my boat to sink. Like a scaffold, you raise me up and support me. You make me stand by, training me to embrace core values and virtues of life. Your instructions illuminate the orientation of my existence every day. Your coaching guides my life into the right direction and onto the paths of peace.

Mother, you challenge me to be at peace with myself in order to be at peace with others. My peace of mind and heart would radiate into happiness for me and others. Mother, I thank you for exposing my life to such a challenge of inner-self peace! I thank you for teaching me that happiness sums up into the peace of mind and heart. Amazing Mother, I am forever indebted to you. How could I repay you for all your goodness to me? It is with gratitude that I dedicate these pages to you and to motherhood.

CHAPTER 1

Self-Examination in the Midst of Existential Contradictions

Dear reader,

I must warn you that this book features human contradictions. It exposes Suru's existential contradictions. Suru stands here for the name of the main character of the book, but this book is not fiction. I purposefully call all main actors by different names to keep their identities confidential. I also use false names (including country and city names) for the locations of scenes for the same concerns of confidentiality. This book is the first volume in a series I plan to write to conceptualize what I call *existential contradictions.* I do not expect you to agree with me on everything I say. The words I write reflect subjective human experiences. This book is merely a saga of existential contradictions. It mirrors a subjective phenomenology of existence. It presents a subjective psychology of some dynamics of anthropological contradictions. It unveils an anthology of relative ontological contradictions. It profiles human stories. It is the fruition of years of self-examination. In the following pages, I carefully try to unravel the puzzle of existential contradictions and happiness.

The potential to be happy is within each one of us. Yet happiness keeps challenging us with myriad existential contradictions. Every human being is a nexus of contradicting potentials. We all have the potential to be good, but our limitations often challenge our potential to be good. The key question revolves around the meaning of happiness and how we unlock such a potential in the midst of daily existential contradictions. To that end, you have already probably taken some important steps in your life. You are adding another significant step here and now by expressing your interest in this book and have made a meaningful decision by selecting it to read. Maybe you have been trapped by existential contradictions just as Suru has.

Sometimes, existence makes you become so attached to the things and people around you that you find detachment bitter and even unbearable. You faithfully respect and trust someone, but that person unexpectedly disappoints you. You are in a relationship where you care about someone deeply and wish that person could care about you in return, but that person does not care about you. You are shocked that a spouse who loves you becomes abusive to you, so you consider the options of dialogue, third-party intervention, counseling, family therapy, or divorce. You meet the love of your life, who cares about you and whom you care about. Unfortunately, your parents or relatives do not want to see you around that person due to some differences in culture, ethnicity, race, or religion. You love your children so much and wish they would listen to you and heed your advice, but they don't; instead, they cause you stress daily. You respect and love your parents dearly, but they do not want to respect your freedom. You are very happy in a relationship, but you lose your partner or spouse to a sudden disease or accident. You enjoy life, but death takes away a friend or loved one and warns that you might be its next target. You take good care of yourself to be healthy, but you still get sick, and medication designed to help you could hurt you if you abuse it. You want peace but get war and chaos instead. You get trapped as a refugee or an internally displaced person or an innocent victim in a war that you never wished for or expected, and you find it difficult to leave everything behind you, including your land and community, and run away for safety or head to the unknown. You leave work excited to go home and rest in your gorgeous house, but by the time you reach home, you hear that your beautiful house got caught in a wildfire or was unexpectedly taken away by a tornado or was wiped off the map by a flood, hurricane, or tsunami. Your business is doing well, but a sudden crash in the market turns it upside down or puts it unexpectedly on the verge of collapse, and you lose all the gains you made or everything you have worked hard for over the years.

At times, things might not make much sense to you, but you have to find meaning in them. Sometimes you may grapple with understanding others. At times, you might not understand even the people you trust. You might feel like even your friends are against you sometimes, but you need to trust them. You may not be able to always understand, but you need to always have faith. You cannot live or exist without it.

Some moments you struggle greatly with understanding yourself. You do your best to anticipate and prevent mistakes, but you still make them. You often think other people are the source or cause of your problem, but in many cases the problem is within yourself. You tend to blame others or yourself for your mistakes instead of accepting them as a reminder of human limitations, but you cannot always get it right. You will make mistakes, and you will be wrong sometimes. Even if you carefully think before your next step, you may still slip up moving forward. If you do not make a mistake here, you will make one there. If you make no mistake today, you will likely make one tomorrow. If you record no mistake in the present, you will certainly record some in the future, per a Latin saying, *"errare humanum est"* (making mistakes is a human attribute). You want to always win, but you often lose. Existence teaches you cannot always be the winner.

You struggle sometimes with doing the good things you intend to do. You even fail in doing them at times. You may get caught up or trapped in things you do not want. Maybe you want to always be positive or optimistic, but you get negative or pessimistic sometimes and settle down in negative feelings instead of moving past them. Maybe you want to always tell the truth but catch yourself lying sometimes. Or you want to always show love to people but get trapped in hatred every once in a while. Or perhaps sometimes you get jealous of others instead of being happy with them and for them. People may also get jealous of you sometimes instead of celebrating with you, and you find yourself cursing them instead of blessing them.

You may judge others but not be ready to get a taste of your own medicine. You may tend to condemn others instead of showing compassion and forgiveness. Maybe you're under the impression you know somebody well, and you find out you do not know that person at all. You may think you know a lot about a situation, but it turns out you do not know much or even anything about it. You think you are wise—only to find out you are foolish. Maybe in the workplace, you respect your supervisor and everyone, but your supervisor disrespects you at times. In performing your duties and through your interactions, you display honesty and deontology, while your supervisor requires loyalty or a cult of personality. You might work hard to satisfy the people you serve, but all you harvest from them is frustration and dissatisfaction. You wish you could get some credit for your good deeds, but you get no credit for them. You expect promotion in the workplace but get demoted instead, or anytime you hope for credits, you get discredited. Or unexpectedly, you lose your job or have to quit. You might want to do well and succeed, but what you get in the process is failure. You might prepare very well for an exam and expect to pass yet end up failing. Or due to structural and systemic reasons, you have to keep paying interest on a loan whose principal you think you have completed paying—at least as you figure it with elementary math.

Some days, you do what you are supposed to do, but other days, you do things you should not be doing. You speechlessly witness your strength becoming your weakness. You lose control over a situation you thought you had control over. At times, you feel cold when you are supposed to be warm and vice versa. You are often quiet when you should talk and noisy when you should be silent. You laugh when you need to cry and cry when you need to laugh. Sometimes you speed up when you are supposed to slow down. You keep going even when your safety and health require that you stop or take a break. Or you tend to move backward when you should move forward. You sit down instead of standing up. You stay awake instead of sleeping and vice versa. You selfishly spend and waste your time, money, and energy even when you have good reasons to save them.

Sometimes people reject you when you expect them to welcome you, even your own people; you feel like a stranger in your own home. Some moments you are harsh when you are expected to be nice and nice when you are supposed to be harsh. You become reluctant, doubtful, or distrustful when you thought you would be confident. You are hopeless when you should be hopeful. You want to get something, but you do not know how to ask for it. You hope to find something, but you do not know how to seek it. You want a door to open, but you do not know how to knock on it. You ask but do not receive. You seek but do not find. You knock repeatedly, and yet the door does not open.

Sometimes you might disappear when everyone counts on you

to appear. Maybe people put you on a pedestal and look up to you, but you fall so low that you disappoint them. You highly think of yourself, but existence makes you discover your shortcomings and lowliness. You know firsthand how it feels to be a victim, yet you keep victimizing others. You know how it feels to be defamed, yet you keep defaming people. You would not want anybody to abuse or mistreat you, yet you abuse or mistreat others. You would not want anyone to cheat on you, yet you cheat on others. You would not want to be hurt, but you hurt others. You tend sometimes to demonize others instead of finding the image of God in them. You struggle sometimes with sharing with people what you have and who you are; you try to keep it all for yourself.

People are hungry next to your table of abundance, but you would not feed them. They are thirsty next to your water fountain, but you would not give them a drink. Some could die from hunger or thirst, but you could also die from greed, for eating or drinking too much. Homeless, refugees, and strangers keep knocking at your door, but you would not welcome them in your home. Not too far from your closets full of clothes, some people are naked, but you would not clothe them. Many people are sick around you, but you would not allow them health care. People are in prison or marginalized around you, but you would not pay any attention to their conditions. You preach tolerance and forgiveness, but you are not always so tolerant or forgiving of others. You say so much about change, but you do so little to bring it. You are so vocal in wishing peace, but you are not so keen on working for it. You advocate for unity but engineer division at times. You tend to build or erect walls instead of bridges between people. Your words fly high and fast, but sometimes your actions go low and slow. You intend to help people, but you end up hurting them in some cases. You do harm sometimes as you try to do good. You wish existence was easier, but it gets hard sometimes. You wish you had more time for rest or fun, but you have to work hard daily to earn your living.

You wish people could treat you based on your personal and moral character, but they look at your ethnic, racial, national, or religious origin. They quickly judge the book of your existence by its cover without first reading its content. Society tends to compartmentalize us into rigid groups. We often create or use standards to judge you and your group without looking at the dynamics of individual personalities. We tend to apply the same standards to all groups across the spectrum without carefully taking into account the weight of cultural differences or contexts. We might be aware of contradictions inherent to such paradigms of social grouping—or even make notable efforts to counter them sometimes—but the facts remain. We are often inclined to look at others through those same social lenses. You hope people would always understand you, but they do not seem to sometimes.

You are nice to others, but they are mean to you sometimes. You love them, but they display hate for you. You help everyone but get ingratitude in return. You do many good deeds but do not get rewarded accordingly. You smile at people, and what you get back from them is anger and mockery sometimes. You send everyone your best wishes, but you find out that not everyone wishes you well. You show compassion to all; it turns out that some people do not feel sorry for you. You make sure you take care of everybody but yourself. You care about everyone, but no one seems to care about you. You get arrested without deserving it. You tell your story, but no one listens to you. You only present the facts as they are, yet people criticize you bitterly. You tell some truth, but no one believes in what you say. You are innocent but judged as guilty. You get condemned for the wrong you did not do. You are a victim, but you are treated as an offender. You treat others fairly and expect to be treated fairly; instead, they treat you unfairly.

You want to be treated as a human subject, but they dehumanize you and force you into categories of an object.

You want people to respect or appreciate you, but not everyone respects or appreciates you—just as you also struggle sometimes in respecting and appreciating everyone. You want people to agree with you, but not everyone agrees with you, just as you may disagree with people sometimes. Sometimes you value what may not have any value in other people's sight. Sometimes we embrace or worry about so many things instead of focusing on one thing and doing it well. At times, we tend to focus more on what is accessory instead of focusing on what is necessary or needed. How do you approach all such contradictions? What do you do in the midst of existential contradictions?

By existential contradictions, the book means any conflicts that divide self into opposing parts, contradicting motions, thoughts, or actions standing against each other or against the self. Existential contradictions imply conflicts splitting subjectivity. They unveil a self with conflicts inside and outside. In these pages, the two words of *contradiction* and *self-conflict* can be used interchangeably to mean the same thing.

Existential contradictions encompass all contradictory motions, conditions, or situations more or less inherent to human existence, whether they are natural, cultural, social, structural, or systemic. Such contradictions also include what the book coins to be conceptual conflicts of *misrepresentation*. By conceptual conflicts, the book intends to mean conflicts that are over a misunderstanding or a misrepresentation of the conventional meaning or definition of the concepts we use in daily communications.

We often use the same words in our conversations, but unfortunately, we do not always mean the same thing. We do not always mean what we say. As a result, we create confusions and even contradictions over the meanings of concepts. Conceptual conflicts of misrepresentation can resonate in poor choices of words, lack of understanding the conventional meanings of concepts, manipulations, and lies.

Once upon a time, a notorious political leader was confronted with handling a hostage crisis for his country. When the news media asked him about the development of the situation, he suggested his government was talking to the kidnappers for the release of the hostages, but he concurrently insisted his government was not negotiating with the hostage takers. Unfortunately, the news media did not do enough pushing back to understand how one could talk in that situation without negotiating by the same means or at the same time. When you understand that negotiation means talk, you do not believe in that political leader's manipulative statement. Ironically, many followers would delightfully swallow that kind of statement without any further questioning. People would all believe in that leader's statement, except you. You might be all alone with the correct understanding. What do you do in that situation? You should stand for what you believe in. That example illustrates what the author means by conceptual conflicts.

Suru once had an interesting conversation with a good friend. That friend's name was Ewo. Ewo once suggested he was exchanging text messages with someone but was not communicating with that person. Suru summoned Ewo to clarify what he meant. Ewo explained that he had not spoken with that person since they had only exchanged text messages. Suru disagreed with what Ewo meant. Ewo did not equate texting with communicating; Suru's friend failed to take one for the other one. When you understand texting as a means of communication, you cannot believe in Ewo's suggestion.

Many of the conflicts we deal with daily are over meaning. We often say something, but we mean something else. However, words quite are meaningful. They create and shape cultural dynamics; they can construct or destroy, and they can unite or divide. Their power to do either thing is in their meaning. Let us be mindful to say what we mean.

Another illustration could be found in our depiction of the colors of human race in terms of black and white. We often identify ourselves with such colors without any questioning. Sometimes, we even fight over such identifications, but let us think of it. Is there anybody as black as darkness? Is there anyone as white as snow? Perhaps, human race is more or less brown or peach and any other color between these two. Maybe we are not black or white.

Suru's daughter, Ele, made him aware that the human race is not black and white. Ele's outstanding questions have taught her father to question the status quo, the conventional or the standard. In kindergarten, as she was learning patterns of colors, Ele once wondered why society painted human race as black and white. At first, Suru did not want to engage in such a conversation with his daughter. He thought it was too early to expose her to racial issues. But Ele did not back down; instead she pressed her father on it. She argued there was nothing like black or white in human race. Suru still did not pay much attention to what she had to stay, and the day went by without Ele getting any answer from him to her enquiry. He could tell Ele was not happy with his attitude vis-à-vis her concern. On that evening, her lack of excitement at the dining table clearly confirmed her malaise.

Later on that day, as Suru was wrapping up his day in self-examination before going to bed, Ele's enquiry on the colors of human skin navigated his mind over and over again. He suddenly felt bad he did not engage with his daughter on that question. He gathered that Ele's concern was relevant. She was being reasonably curious.

For that matter, he contributed to Ele's sense of curiosity. He always encouraged her to ask questions relentlessly. He always told her there was no bad question. Suru often insisted he would always welcome Ele's questions at any given time, no matter what and how. He thought he should had paid more attention to what she had to say. All such thoughts made him feel guilty. He felt guilty he did not satisfy his daughter's curiosity. He was not happy his silence on the issue was responsible for Ele's unhappy feelings. At the end of that day neither Suru nor Ele was happy. In the process of his self-examination, Suru resolved to find a way to engage with Ele on that issue.

The next day, early in the morning, he noticed Ele was quiet and reserved at breakfast. She barricaded herself within hermetic walls of silence; she was sober in words. Suru managed to figure out what was bothering his daughter. He guessed it had to do with his previous attitude. He thought Ele's silence was triggered by his silent response to her question a day before. He tried to make her say something. But he was not able to have her open her mouth for a word. He did not succeed in making Ele break the walls of her silence. The morning rush did not help either. Suru had to hurry up to go drop Ele and her brother and sister at school and go to work on time. He really felt bad about the entire situation.

After dropping his children at school, Suru felt Ele's sad face hunted him all day long. As a matter of course, his entire day was affected, including his performance at work. His productivity was low because he was low in energy. He regretted bitterly his attitude toward Ele's concern on the colors of human skin. He wished he had paid more attention to her concern and handled her question as she would like him to. On that day Suru used his time of self-examination at noon to design strategies to repair the damage and put back a smile on Ele's face. Having his daughter recover her happy face was Suru's immediate goal.

In the evening, before her father even had the opportunity to take the initiative, Ele came up with the same question on the colors of human skin. Immediately, upon arriving home, back from school, she asked Suru the same question while dropping her bag. He decided to take her enquiry seriously this time. He paid more attention to what she had to say. Ele continued by stressing there was nobody black or white on earth. In the process of saying that, she stretched her left hand and reached out to two markers resting on a desk nearby. She presented the markers to Suru, asking him to identify their colors. They were black and white. One of the markers was black like darkness. The other one was white like snow. Upon his answer, Ele presented her father with three other markers she was holding in her left hand. They were brown, peach, and pink. One marker was brown like chocolate. The other one was peach like the fruit. The last one was just like a pink rose.

She looked at Suru straight in the eyes, and concluded that human skin resembled more the colors she had in her left hand. She said, "Human beings are either brown, peach, or pink, and not black or white, at least according to my understanding of conventional colors learnt in kindergarten." As Suru listened, Ele made one additional move to enforce her conclusion. She took out of Suru's closet his black and brown shoes, belts, and ties, and urged him to distinguish between the black and the brown matter-of-factly. Of course, Suru obeyed and did it.

Ele's conclusion made her father speechless. She opened his eyes. Suru was simply amazed by his little daughter's fact-finding reasoning. He thought Ele just gave him a meaningful lesson on the colors of human race. Ele was a good fact-finder. His agreement with her was matter-of-course. He pictured human race as brown, peach, or pink instead of black or white. At that moment Suru humbly realized that he could learn meaningfully from his kindergartener. Out of their innocence and candid curiosity, kindergarteners and children can teach us a lot about human nature and society. Wisdom dwells in every human mind and heart no matter the age or culture or color. Throughout that process, Ele taught Suru that every question deserved attention. She reminded him that every human concern should be taken seriously. Every question matters.

Later on, Suru decided to follow up. He wanted to make sure Ele was not a victim of racial slurs or experiencing any issue of crisis of identity. Their discussion got the heat and taste of spicy arguments. To lower the temperature of their communication, Suru joked and said, "The colors of black and white are not bad for our skin after all, for black is beautiful and white is great." In a further attempt to appease Ele, he added, "Black is so beautiful that even those who would discriminate against it as a skin color would adore wearing it as their favorite shoes, ties, trousers, shirts, dresses, hats, or belts." And he continued, "White is so great that even those who would discriminate against it as a skin color would enjoy wearing it as their favorite dresses, shirts, or hats."

Ele was not amused by her father's joke. She and Suru were not on the same page. You could tell she was not amused, looking at her facial expression. Ele made a straight face as Suru joked. To show her father that she was very serious in what she meant, the straight-faced Ele countered Suru and said, "Brown is even more beautiful and sweet just like the chocolate melting in the mouth." She added, "Peach is sweet as well, and pink is awesome."

It turned out Ele was not comfortable with the traditional racial tags of black and white with their underlying assumptions and implications for social interactions. History shows that the concepts of black and white create and entertain antagonistic cultural dynamics in society.

Words create, shape, or carry sensitive cultural baggage. Conflict enjoys the ride of the vehicle of culture by all odds. Ele's sentiments resonated powerfully in her father's mind and heart. They brought back to Suru's mind and heart all the literature he read on racial issues, including on skin colors and their impact on human society. This process awoke Suru to a self-examination on the issue. Ele's fact-finding made her father have a second thought that challenged conventional thinking on the colors of human skin.

Suru endorsed Ele's enquiry as she framed it: "Are we even black or white?" "After all, human skin is not so black or white as we pretend it to be." Suru thought Ele was certainly right in her thinking. He thought nobody was so black or white. We are more or less brown, peach and pink. His endorsement of Ele's perspective triggered a series of existential questions in his head: Why do we pretend so much to be what we are not? Why do we let colors define so much who we are? Why do we lock our identity within categories of colors? Why do we allow such categories to define our behaviors? Why do we allow colors to affect our relationships? Why do we engage in conflict over colors? Why do we pretend so much instead of being? Why can't we just be who we are by nature? Aren't we all human beings by nature? What if we focus on that common denominator that binds us together and let it regulate our relationships?

Ele caught Suru ruminating such questions. He shared them with her. Both the father and his daughter kept trying hard to find answers to those existential questions. But to Suru's surprise, Ele had a tentative answer to all of such questions. Her answer was simple but thoughtful: "If we could matter-of-factly stick to being who we are instead of pretending, human society would be a better place to live."

Suru thought her daughter's answer was meaningful. If we are able to express our identities and cultures as they are, we get to know one another as we are. In the process of getting to know who we are, we learn to respect one another, and tolerate our differences. In that same process we become aware of how our differences represent assets, we learn to transcend them constructively. Our conflicts then provide opportunities for learning, growing, and improving our relationships. It becomes obvious to us that we are because others are. We need them to be who we are. When we love them, we love ourselves. When we hurt them, we hurt ourselves. We are all one in humankind regardless of our cultures.

We should not be fighting over colors that do not even depict our skin. Yet, we do fight over them in fact. How would you explain those facts? I would simply call them existential contradictions. We daily face existential contradictions in our social environment. Existential contradictions intrusively and relentlessly permeate human existence.

Their existential nature easily makes such contradictions inescapable to human condition. They may be different from one individual to another one, but they dynamically hunt every human life somehow. They may involve—but are not limited to—natural disasters, social rejection, discrimination, lies, interpersonal conflicts, intrapersonal conflicts, failure, suffering, illness, death, or other misfortunes.

Existential contradictions nurture antagonisms within the self. They create dissatisfaction or disagreement of self with self and with others. They bring troubles into our hearts and minds. Existential contradictions subject self or ego to the wind of instability and disharmony. Existential contradictions can put us at the crossroads between hatred and love, greed and generosity, attachment and detachment, professional reality and vocation or calling, authority and service, bitterness and sweetness, disobedience and obedience, disrespect and respect, or dishonesty and honesty, to briefly mention a few examples. Such contradictions are always present, moving within and beyond us. We cannot escape from them reaching and immersing into our existence, but we can willingly transform or transcend them for sustainable and rewarding periods of peace and happiness in our existence.

When transformed or transcended, existential conflicts vacate our physiology for the sake of our peace of heart and mind. Unaddressed, they jeopardize our peace of heart and mind, trap us into feelings of unhappiness, and eventually contaminate or condition happiness in our social surrounding. Unaddressed self-conflicts may negatively affect the happiness of our immediate social environment in the same way the decay or decomposition process of a bad orange, apple, potato, or tomato can contaminate or affect other oranges, apples, potatoes, or tomatoes in the same basket.

The critical question remains how we effectively face existential contradictions for peace and happiness. Unequivocally, these pages do not pretend to provide a comprehensive answer to such an existential question, but they take you through cycles of subjective existential contradictions and peace. They remind us that existence is not unipolar. Existence is multipolar—or at least bipolar. These pages warn you about the traps of self-conflict. They alert you about how to open your mind and heart to peace through a perpetual process of self-examination or self-evaluation.

Self-examination implies a process of self-mediation. Self-mediation is a mediation conducted by self between self and self. It challenges you to look at existential contradictions as opportunities for growing on the path to happiness. It shows you how you can shift constructively from self-conflict to peace of mind and heart. It guides you in how to transition from instability or disharmony to stability, harmony, and happiness.

When the cyclones of existential contradictions churn the boat of your life and make it capsize in the deep waters of the ocean of existence, you will either float or sink. Self-examination provides you with appropriate skills to float on the waves of contradictions. It develops your ability to navigate and withstand tribulations. Self-examination gives you what it takes to float alive on the waves of existential contradictions. Regardless of what happens, the waves will safely welcome you if you put on the life jacket of self-examination. Obviously, the waves will end up throwing you on a shore somewhere. You can only hope they throw you ashore alive. Self-examination maximizes your chances to stay alive in the process.

This book is the fruit of self-examinations across contexts and over the years. What do you think of when you hear the phrase *self-examination*? The first time Suru curiously asked his wife, Lafia, that question, her answer was straightforward. As a very good nurse practitioner, Lafia thought of self-examination as a process of self-examining your body to prevent or detect potential life-threatening diseases such as breast cancer. She is not wrong. Suru would admit that Lafia is exceptionally good at self-examining her body religiously and daily. I can understand your viewpoint if you think of self-examination as Lafia did. You would not be wrong in thinking so, but parallel to that understanding of self-examination stands another one. How often do we take time to examine our mind, thoughts, and actions in the same way we examine our bodies? How should we think of self-examination in the context of this book? What is self-examination here? That series of questions deserves answers that emerge from real-life stories.

During Suru's first years in elementary school, his mother would often walk him to school in the morning. Suru's mother was named Iya. On their way to school, Iya and Suru had to cross a relatively busy road. Prior to reaching that road, they both would usually be chatting elatedly, but once they reached the road, Iya would become silent. She would focus and require silence from her son as well. Every time they reached that road, Suru's mother would stop silently. She would take her time to check the traffic coming from her right side and the traffic coming from her left side. After making sure there was no traffic coming from either direction, she would hold Suru's hand as they crossed the road. After crossing the road, they would happily resume their conversation.

One day, after they crossed the road, Suru naively asked his mother a question. He wondered why Iya always stopped and checked her left and right side before crossing the road. Iya's answer was up front. She indicated she did not want them to take the risk of being run over. In case of an accident, their lives would become miserable; they could even lose their lives. They would not be happy losing their lives.

Suru thought his mother's answer was relevant to their safety. Safety, in this case, implies their happiness. Thinking of it, everybody should stop and check the traffic before crossing a road to continue their journey. By analogy, self-examination is a brief and silent stop we make to check the existential traffic of our lives in order to move happily forward in existence. In the same way stop signs are for traffic regulation, self-examination authorizes frequent stop signs in our existence to regulate it. Self-examination allows us to stop and take an evaluative look at our existence. Existential evaluation requires us to stop briefly or pause to examine the left, the right, the front, the back, the up, and the down of our existence. Just as stop signs foster harmony on the road, self-examination brings harmony to human existence. Just like a stop sign, self-examination reminds us we do not have to reach a red light in our existence before we stop for evaluation. We should often stop to evaluate our existence.

That simple analogy implies that self-examination is a method of self-reflection and self-evaluation. To some extent, self-examination encompasses the notion and practice of soul-searching, but it is larger in scope or magnitude. It is a self-evaluation of the impacts of your thoughts and actions (including attitudes and behaviors) on yourself (on your mind and body) and on your social environment (on your social surrounding and on others around you). It involves a quiet contemplation and review process of your interactions with your mind, your body, and your social environs. It allows you to discern your thoughts, attitudes, and behaviors in order to identify those thoughts, attitudes, and behaviors that grant you and your social environment peace of mind and heart. It directs you to side with thoughts, attitudes, and behaviors that give you and others such peace and capitalize on them. Self-examination allows you to conduct a meaningful content analysis of your thoughts, actions, and feelings.

Compassion and respect for self and for others would be main criteria for identifying your peace-bearing thoughts, attitudes, and actions. Self-examination would make you reject and stay away from any thoughts, attitudes, or behaviors that bring worries or troubles upon you and others. Self-examination portrays and performs a spiritual introspection for the peace of mind and heart. It generates a unique negotiation process involving oneself negotiating with itself over what grants peace of mind and heart to self. I previously noted that this process could also be called self-mediation.

Self-examination awakens the potential for peace within self. In self-examination, self manages to remember and think deeply about self in relation to others for happiness. Self-examination ultimately proceeds as a sagacious mental training that prepares self to understand that every human mind and heart goes through a fairly perpetual existential cycle of consolation and desolation. Self-examination allows us to understand that human existence is a playground for contradictions. It certainly helps us identify happiness in the nexus of existential contradictions.

The ideal location or setting for self-examination should be quiet and relaxing. Self-examination should be done in silence, away from all noise. We live in a world of noise and noise pollution. Noise pollution is harmful. Too much noise can intoxicate our hearts and minds. Self-examination endorses the love of silence. The body's posture in self-examination should also be relaxing. It can be different depending on the individual. Sometimes Suru would enjoy self-examination in the Buddha's sitting posture. Other times, he would do self-examination on his knees or in other related positions, but you can sit on a mat, chair, or couch for your self-examination. Ideally, Suru would do self-examination twice a day: at noon and before bedtime. It would take him between fifteen to thirty minutes in a silent or remote corner of his office or bedroom. At noon, Suru formatively reviews his morning hours to make sure he is on the right track to meet the goals he set for his day during his morning meditation. In the process, he identifies his thoughts or actions of peace, and he expresses gratefulness for them. He also identifies his worrisome thoughts and actions of instability, and he resolves to improve by taking steps to move away from them.

At night, before going to bed, Suru repeats and applies the same process to the entire day. Subsequently, he makes resolutions for the next day to continue in the path of thoughts and actions of peace recorded during the day and to break the course of thoughts and actions of worries. At the end of the week, he repeats and applies the same process to the entire week in what he calls *weekly self-examination*. At the end of the month, he repeats and applies the process to the entire month in the form of what he calls *monthly evaluation*. At the end of the year, Suru repeats and applies the same process to the whole year in what he considers to be *annual self-evaluation*.

Self-examination may be demanding as a method. For the least, it requires rigor and discipline. Yet, its experiment is worth the price you pay for it. Suru has learned how to fit self-examination in his daily schedule, including in his busiest timetable. The practice redeems his days in peace of mind and heart. Any day he happens to fail to do his self-examination, Suru sees the difference in terms of troubles in comparison to days when he does his self-examination.

In the midst of our demanding days filled with thoughts and activities, finding a moment for self-examination is not a bad idea; it is not a waste of time. Self-examination has the potential to break down the stressful rhythm or cycle of our activities for rejuvenation, improvement, and peace. It reduces stress levels. Self-examination provides you with an opportunity for self-reflection and self-education. It is a process of auto-criticizing of self. It makes you look at yourself in the mirror of your conscience. It helps you learn how to critically measure yourself against yourself for happiness. Acquiring happiness or peace of heart and mind requires some level or degree of self-examination. I do not think you will regret trying to self-examine yourself at your pace.

In the beginning, your practice of self-examination might be difficult as it is with the start of every good training process, but if you keep on trying and doing it on a regular basis, it becomes a much easier reflex in your life, a routine integrated into your calendar. Per a Latin saying, "*fabricando fit faber*" (by making, you become a maker), the more you engage in self-examination, the more familiar it becomes—and the easier it becomes. Just as your physician or doctor would examine you to diagnose your health issues in order to eventually help you, you need to examine your heart and mind to ultimately obtain peace of heart and mind. Self-examination allows you to judge for yourself the right thing to do for peace of mind and heart. Self-examination whispers the right course of action to your mind and heart.

Have you ever asked yourself these closed-ended questions? How often do we take time to enjoy a good shower and feel the water running on our bodies? How often do we take time to enjoy long night sleeps or daytime naps? How often do we take time to enjoy or savor the taste or flavor of what we eat for lunch or dinner? How often do we take time to relax our bodies and clean up our minds using meditation, yoga, or techniques of self-evaluation? How often do we take time to examine our being, our thinking, and our doing? How often do we take time to appreciate our strengths and capitalize on them constructively in our being, thinking, and doing? How often do we take time to contemplate and challenge our weaknesses or limitations? Think about it for a minute, and what you will find is challenging.

We often take care of so many things and so many people, but we tend to forget to take care of our bodies and minds. If we happen to take care of our bodies in some cases, we often fail to take care of our minds. Self-examination is a review process of *the* how of our being, our thinking, and our doing. Such a review is for learning, growth, transformation, and happiness. It provides us with a golden opportunity for self-care. It fosters a self-regeneration of the body and mind.

Self-examination allows human beings to take care of their hearts and minds for peace. Most existential contradictions would likely escalate into violence due to a lack of self-care, or in the absence of self-care, of our bodies and minds. In the midst of existential contradictions, your happiness depends largely on your siding with thoughts, attitudes, and behaviors of peace, through the practice of self-examination. Even if self-examination were a mistake, it would be worth making such a mistake. In self-examination, we find a synthesis that transcends and reconciles the thesis and antithesis of our contradictions. Put together, existential contradictions reveal parts or details of existence. They raise our awareness about the core components that make up our existence. Yet they should not trump our attempt to think of life as holistic. Self-examination enables human beings to grasp the potential holism of life by transcending its contradicting parts or elements peacefully.

This book reflects and translates piece by piece Suru's practice of self-examination over the years. Throughout the lines of Suru's stories, the book unveils the transformative potential of self-examination for peace and happiness. In Suru's experience, the human journey to peace or happiness is a long one. His journey certainly remains a long and challenging one. Every time he thinks or feels like he has conquered peace or happiness for good, he ends up being wrong. He ends up losing his peace; his happiness escapes and challenges him to keep on running after the goal. And when he succeeds in catching up with it, peace dwells within his mind and heart for some time and escapes again. He keeps longing for peace and happiness. His road to happiness is filled with contradictions. His search for peace seems endless; it is like a lifelong journey.

Every time the roadblocks of contradictions show up, they abruptly force the train of Suru's existential journey to stop for a moment. Fortunately, self-examination transforms that stop into the opportunity of a much-needed station for the train of his existence. At that station, he pauses and takes the time to evaluate the direction of his existential movement to find his lost peace.

For as long as we live, peace will come and go until we reach the perfect peace in eternal happiness. Eternal happiness is reached only after death—when we rest in peace. Self-examination provides us with a tool for spiritual growth in peace and constructive progress toward happiness. Existential peace might not last forever, but it can be sustained for a relatively extended period before the next round of contradictions. Self-examination contributes to making human peace endure. Self-examination has the potential to provide us with sustainable happiness and consistent peace of mind and heart.

Suru is often trapped by his contradictions. He often seems to be a slave of contradictions. Contradictions often keep him away from the heaven of peace. Amid contradictions, he calls on self-examination for help. He finds refuge in self-examination. He dwells in self-examination for peace. Self-examination serves as his transition to peace and happiness. Self-examination takes him to the kingdom of peace of mind and heart. Self-examination sets him free from the chains of daily contradictions.

Existential contradictions ultimately translate tensions between our bodies and spirits and our hearts and minds. Human bodies or hearts can get weak at times, but our spirits remain strong. The spirit might need to be awakened. Self-examination provides us with a good ground for awakening the spirit. Once it is awake, the spirit energizes the body and supplements its weaknesses. Through self-examination, we can resort to the strength of our spirit to empower our bodies in its times of weakness.

Self-examination is a cradle of happiness. It fecundates felicity. Self-examination deters contradictions from trumping our happiness. Existence often throws us amid contradictions inherent to zero-sum situations, but self-examination first digs us out of the holes of such situations and then helps us transcend them by lifting our hearts and minds up to peace. Self-examination cleanses and sanitizes the self for peace of mind and heart.

In a quest for a happy existence, self-examination opens us to profoundly understand the meaning of happiness. Self-examination raises our awareness that our attachment to things or people does not define or determine our existence. Life is not reduced to what we may be attached to or the things or people around us. Self-examination would reveal that happiness is not much about financial success or attachment. Self-examination opens the gates of happiness to self. The practice of self-examination patiently trains us in how to put on outfits of happiness. Self-examination slowly tailors our existence to habits of happiness. Its practice progressively entertains us with the rhythm of happiness. Consistent self-examination eventually immerses us in the ocean of happiness.

You may also be reading these pages for correlated reasons. Perhaps, someone in your life alerts you to existential contradictions or assists you in facing and transforming them. That helpful person may be providing you with what I call *pillars of happiness*. In Suru's case, his mother, his wife, and his daughter all provide him with such pillars of happiness. They alert him to existential contradictions. They help him transition from self-conflicts to peace.

Chances are high that your mother, your sister, your wife, your girlfriend, or your daughter help you in the same way. They have the ability to do so. If you are aware of this, recognize and celebrate such women every day of your existence. If you are not aware of it, pause here for a moment and take some time to think about it. You may be able to identify or find at least one such women. Push your way to her in gratitude and acknowledge her for providing you with a pillar of happiness.

A pillar is a support system. It represents a stronghold for the structure it supports. Any structure cannot be without its supports. It is hard to image how we can be without our mothers, our wives, our girlfriends, or our daughters. We cannot come to life without our mothers. To some extent, we cannot live without their support. Daily existential experiences demonstrate that such women provide pillars of life and happiness as mothers, wives, girlfriends, and daughters. They bring us to life, they nurture us, they protect us, they care for us, they love us, and they stand by us strongly. They help us address daily life dilemmas or conflicts. They help us grow and change. They contribute tremendously to our life and happiness.

There is nothing we can do without some sort of help from women! As strange as that statement may look or sound to the patriarchy, it is the truth of this matter. Women are hidden queens behind almost every decision coming from their so-called kings. In some ways and to some degree, women enable most of such decisions under more or less normal or natural circumstances. Women are present in every piece of every human life—from its beginning through its end. They do more in our daily lives than the patriarchy can imagine. They have more merit than the patriarchy thinks. They deserve more credit than the patriarchy tends to give them. If they are able to run our households so effectively, they can certainly run our countries successfully. They are more capable than how the patriarchy portrays them. As a society, we certainly owe them more recognition. Suru has experienced and witnessed what I mean by these words, and this book testifies to it to some degree.

This book is the first in a series that will substantially review subjective and existential experiences of self-conflict transformation. It will contemplate Suru's contradictions in relation to his natural and social environment. It will highlight Suru's interactions with a mother, a wife, and a daughter in their ability for problem-solving and conflict transformation.

The book intends to pay a tribute to the charisma and goodness in such women's being and doing in routine existential conflicts that trap a son, a husband, and a father. It also intends to echo the message that there is nothing a man can be and do without a woman's succor or support. Men exist because women exist. Women are prerequisites for men's existence. This book hails the merits of motherhood. It venerates the grandeur of the assets of womanhood for conflict transformation. Such assets nestle in our mothers, sisters, wives or girlfriends, and daughters. In that perspective, the following pages emphasize or celebrate some amazing things a mother, a wife, and a daughter can do for you in times of existential contradictions. Those women could assist in providing you with pillars that contribute to transforming your contradictions into peace of mind and heart. To a large extent, the scenarios in this volume (and in the ones to follow) revolve around Suru's acquaintance and connections with his mother, his wife, and his daughter, three genial women in his life.

At different stages of his life, Suru was fortunate to be exposed to Iya, Lafia, and Ele. That exposure would smoothly mutate into some meaningful acquaintance of them. They all happened to provide Suru with pillars of happiness in times when he needed them most. He is forever grateful to them. This book presents some stories of his encounters and interactions with them. It is a reminiscence of meaningful experiences with those gracious human beings you will meet on these pages. They are Suru's godsends, the pillars his life rests on. They are not perfect, but they are good human beings. Their stories reverberate human stories and maybe yours as well; their stories shape and reshape human experiences and vice versa. Their stories and our stories are intertwined. Such stories are worth sharing with all human beings who long for the peace of mind and heart. You will understand more of what I mean as you read the following pages.

I believe that these human stories somehow resound in you. These stories reflect those of women helping others around the globe find peace and happiness in the midst of daily existential contradictions.

Mothers, wives, and daughters are so good to humankind. I hope the stories on these pages inspire you. I hope reading these stories will enthusiastically unveil the faces of all such women who provide you with pillars of happiness daily. It is not always that we are mindful that we are given invaluable assets in their presence by our sides, but we should be more aware that our mothers, wives, and daughters are exceptional advisers, mentors, and mediators. We do not have to wait until Mother's Day or Valentine's Day before we celebrate them. We need to acknowledge them more often, here and now, in every day of our existence.

More specifically, this book exposes you to a series of observations on achieving peace of mind and heart, based on Suru's life experiences with his mother, his father, his wife, his children, and his other relatives and friends. Most of the stories emerge out of a self-examination of Suru's existence. Therefore, the book mainly relies on self-examination as the main method for data collection and analysis. It is an evaluation of cyclical self-conflicts in Suru's life. It is his recollection of learning experiences with his mother, his father, his wife, his children, and his other relatives and friends about their existential travels from frequent zones of turbulence to temporary heavens of stability. Such learning experiences about the transformation of self-conflicts mirror how women give us life and the resources our existence needs to blossom into happiness.

Much of the book deals with contradictions, inner divisions, or conflicts over everyday concerns. It all starts with an existential question about happiness. It then goes on to assert that happiness has no secrets; instead, it has pillars. Pillars of happiness are depicted as spiritual resources, good manners, and matters of common sense that contribute to transforming self-conflict for peace of heart and mind. In general, these concern personal and spiritual relations with nature, society, and God. Some specifically address family relations and workplace issues. Others broadly deal with matters of environmental and social relationships. All imply the need for self-control and self-improvement through a reconnection to our inner-self sources.

Much is said about listening, planning, dreaming, passion, patience, meditation, finding and embracing one's vocation, working hard, service, generosity, compassion, forgiveness, courage, loyalty, humility, detachment, healthy eating and sleeping habits, physical activities, and silence. It turns out that a mother, a wife, and a daughter can become significant mediators in unveiling such pillars of peace to our hearts and minds. Self-examination becomes a critical tool for peace of mind and heart. Through self-examination, you engage in a self-mediation process with yourself.

Self-mediation allows you to mediate between you and you over contradictions or self-conflicts. It allows you to distinguish between what makes you happy and what does not make you happy. It helps you comprehend what makes you happy and what makes you unhappy. You take action accordingly to counteract whatever does not make you happy by doing, promoting, or cultivating what makes you happy. The process of self-examination raises your awareness about self-conflicts and disposes you to counter and transform them. This implies that self-mediation prompts the counteraction and transformation of self-conflicts. The author's writing style in the book translates some resourceful conversations between Suru and his mother, his wife, and others. The book earnestly portrays stories that touch them personally.

As the stories unfold with ups and downs, the underlying message of this book transpires. For a happy life, we have to creatively develop habits that transform our existential contradictions into opportunities for peace of mind and heart. Self-examination triggers the creation of such habits. Existence is full of contradictions. They come and go and come back again. Some may go for good, but others will keep coming back to us throughout existence.

Happiness is where you find that state of peace of heart and mind. Anytime the book uses the word *happiness* or the adjective *happy,* it refers to *peace of mind and heart.* Similarly, whenever the book mentions *peace of mind and heart*, it implies *happiness.* The book uses *happiness* and *peace of mind and heart* interchangeably. On earth, human happiness is not permanent due to the limitations of human nature and existence. Human existence is full of contradictions. Our happiness remains constantly challenged by self-conflicts or contradictions.

Human happiness requires a perpetual cycle of inner-conflict transformation. You create happiness in how and what you think and do; life often makes it appear and disappear, but we have the potential to make happiness sustainable over a long period. How do we make it sustainable? By addressing our self-conflicts or contradictions. How do we identify and transcend our contradictions? How could we transform self-conflicts? Through the process of self-examination.

Suru's mother, Iya, once told him how she used self-examination to preserve her marriage with her husband, Baba. In the early years of their marriage, Iya and Baba experienced some contradictions over how to raise their children. The negative impacts of such contradictions did not spare the harmony in their relationship. Their life together hit some low points during that period. Fortunately, in the midst of such contradictions, Iya did her best to preserve their marriage. Using daily self-examination, she would carefully identify her attitudes or behaviors in their relationship that made both her and Baba happy. She would capitalize on those attitudes or behaviors and perform them often to make her husband happy. She would intentionally avoid attitudes and behaviors that frustrated Baba. She would also purposefully reminisce about positive feelings they experienced during their first dates at the beginning of their love story. She tried to factor them into her interactions with her husband as much as she could. She would try to remind Baba of those mutual feelings they enjoyed à deux. She actively believed that both her and her husband had the potential to eventually recover or recreate those positive feelings in their relationship. Her efforts would eventually pay off, and her patient dream would become reality on a happy day.

After ten years of marriage, as they celebrated their anniversary, Iya and Baba decided to evaluate their relationship. In that process, they also renewed their vows of an unconditional love for one another. When the time came for the renewal of their vows, Baba, absorbed by the good mood of the occasion, emotionally suggested that his wife should ask him anything she would want him to do for a happy relationship and life together. He promised he would do anything Iya asked him to do.

As if she had been waiting for that moment, his wife would rise on that occasion to take the credit for keeping their marriage together. Iya used that opportunity to confide to Baba how she spent years doing self-examination to redeem their marriage. As a result, her demand was straightforward. She told Baba she would appreciate it if he could pay her back in the same coin by doing his self-examination daily.

Upon hearing Iya's confession and demand, Baba was filled with admiration and gratitude for his wife. He gave her a big hug and covered her lips with loving kisses. He took an oath to pay Iya back in the same coin. And he kept his promise to do his self-examination daily. His daily practice of self-examination would even inspire Baba to quit smoking cigarettes and drinking alcohol. Self-examination allowed him to notice that he was often confused and keen to yell at his wife after consuming alcohol. On the other hand, he was calm and nice to Iya whenever he took a break from alcohol. He also noticed how Iya was always frustrated when he came around with a cigarette. She would always warn him he was running the risk of lung cancer and exposing everyone around him to that same risk. Yet every time he took a break from smoking, his wife would happily praise him. And the house felt better.

Following repeated self-examinations about smoking and drinking, Baba prayed about it and ended up quitting both. Baba and Iya were very happy about it. Their entire family celebrated such a great achievement. Their marriage lasted a long time. Iya and Baba ended up spending nearly five decades together. It all ended when Baba sang his Nunc Dimittis. Only Baba's death physically split them apart. Yet Iya would remain in a loving spiritual communion with Baba. Baba is now physically far from Iya's eyes, but he remains close to her heart and mind.

In the wake of existential contradictions, would your heart and mind settle down on rock or sand? The wisdom of happiness would exhort you to root them firmly in the rock of self-examination. Torrential rains of contradictions will pour down, rivers of contradictions will flood over, and winds of contradictions will blow vehemently against your existence, but it will not collapse because it is rooted in the rock of self-examination. In the absence of self-examination, your existence may run the risk of collapsing in the heavy rains of existential contradictions and their flooded rivers and vehement winds.

Self-examination trains you to get back your peace whenever you lose it. It makes you learn which direction to head to recover your lost peace. When we transform our self-conflicts, we gain our peace of heart and mind, our happiness. Once we get it, we feel challenged to work to make it last. Self-examination can train us to make happiness sustainable. When we lose it—or when we do not have it—we should work hard to find it or get it back. We can always get it back on our own or with the help of its mediators in our social environment.

Suru's mother, his father, his wife, and his children have consistently inspired and challenged him again and again to transform and transcend existential contradictions for peace of mind and heart. Using a combination of their stories and stories from other relatives and friends, this book shows how the transformation of one self-conflict triggers the emergence of another inner-conflict or contradiction. When the latter is thought of as transformed, another one erupts to confirm that existential contradictions are always present and require attention and transformation. If they are not transformed constructively, they escalate, spread, and become destructive to the self and others.

A constructive transformation of self-conflict results in peace of mind and heart. Once we are in peace with ourselves, we are likely to be in peace with others. Chances are high our peace will impact our social environment constructively. We are happy and likely to make others happy. We need to make peace inside and out. We ought to make sure conflict does not destroy us inside and out. Most conflicts, if not all, surge from some lack of inner-self peace or happiness or internal instability. Self-examination helps make peace inside and outside of us. Thus, self-examination should be the first stage in any process of problem-solving, conflict transformation, dispute-system design, or peacemaking. In times of conflict, each party tends to blame only the other party; each party tends to focus solely on the opponent. We tend to focus so much on conflicts and wars outside of us, but not so much on conflicts and wars within us. To achieve whole peace we ought to take care of conflicts within and outside of us. Self-examination would allow each party to focus on the self while paying attention to the other party. Self-examination allows each party to identify their respective contribution to conflict and conflict transformation by asking the following questions:

"How did I contribute to the ongoing conflict?"

"What do I do to transform it constructively?"

Self-examination would foster a constructive transformation of existential contradictions for peacemaking.

In the process of reading this book, you will find out that your social environment can contaminate you with disharmony or harmony. If you live in a stable environment, it will likely submerge you with peace. However, if your life environment is unstable, it will likely flood you with disharmony. It serves your happiness that you contribute to creating a stable environment around you. Yet your main contribution to building a stable environment around you is to start building a stable environment within you. A reconciliation of ego with itself certainly triggers the reconciliation with alter ego or others. You can constructively contaminate your external environment from within you. The disharmony within you could also spill over around you. In short, your internal environment contaminates your external environment and vice versa.

Valued reader, I wish I could make my final remark confidential—just for me and you and only between us. Those who know Suru well would agree with the next sentence. It is not Suru's habit to open his heart and mind to everyone as he did in this book. Many friends consider Suru a private individual. He sees himself as a very private person. He enjoys his privacy and respects the privacy of others. In general, he opens up only to those he knows well and trusts. Here he is now! He does not know you well, yet he decides to trust you with contradictions that echo his life. Suru's existence is filled with contradictions. He is full of them. He is immersed within them. He is faced with them. He is surrounded by them. Contradictions are part of his life. They shape and reshape his existence. Suru wonders whether he can ever get rid of them, yet he can willingly transform them constructively—regardless of how often he may need to do so. This process could be a lifelong routine.

Suru has come to a place of accepting his contradictions. He has learned to patiently recognize and identify them. He has slowly and humbly learned how to address and coordinate them for harmony. His peace of heart and mind depends on how he deals with them. Suru shares these self-examinations with you because he believes the most important things you need to pay attention to in life are the motions swinging within you. Your happiness is activated from inside of you. As you climb up the hill of life, you will fall at times. When you fall, you face two choices. One choice requires that you accept the challenge of getting up and continuing up the hill with the goal of reaching the happy heaven at the top of the hill. The other choice makes you give up and roll downhill. In the end, you land in the valley of death.

If the journey of life is like climbing a mountain, we ought to keep our eyes fixed on the ultimate goal at the top of that mountain; we ought to keep on trying to move up, regardless of the challenges. We either face the challenge if we value our lives, or everything we build will go downhill, including our lives. All the progress we made will be lost forever.

In his self-examinations, Suru opens his mind and heart to you in the hope that you will open your mind and heart to yourself while reading these pages. Suru has decided to unveil his humble existential struggles in the hope that you will see where he is in his existential travel. He hopes you will not judge him too harshly. He knows he still has a long way to go in his journey toward achieving peace with himself and with others. The path of transformation for happiness is a lifelong learning process. Suru hopes you will candidly look at where he comes from to assess how far he has come and see the road he still needs to travel on his journey of transformation for peace. He hopes this enlightens you about how far a human being can go in longing for happiness. Perhaps the stories in this book will inspire your quest for peace in the midst of existential contradictions.

Once again, you do not have to agree with everything I say in this book. My perspectives certainly bear limitations. They are humble human viewpoints. They reflect my humble conceptualization of human experiences. No human achievement is perfect. Our feelings, thoughts, views, and deeds always have limitations. I understand you may disagree with me on some accounts. If you disagree with my perspectives, I humbly accept your disagreement and gladly look forward to welcoming your perspectives. It is fine if you disagree with my views. This book is also about that. This book is about contradictions. Contradictions nestle in disagreements. There is always room for disagreements in everything we feel, think, say, and do. There is always room for disagreement with me, you, and them. Happiness requires that we allow room for disagreement with us and with them. Yes, we can disagree. We are allowed to disagree. We should disagree. Disagreement is existential contradiction.

Dear reader, I spent years yearning and longing for the conception and arrival of this book. I have been pregnant with this book for so long. My heart and mind have been anointing it tirelessly through its gestation. I have been waiting impatiently for the day of its labor and delivery. Fortunately, the labor and delivery has been a safe process. I am pleased to finally deliver it safely into your precious hands. Be blessed and inspired as you travel through the pages of this book. I hope they inspire you and give you some peace of heart and mind.

When you are down, I hope these pages remind you that the time will also come for you to be up. When you are up, remember you will certainly be down sometimes. What is now lost may be found in the future. Whatever the night is, a day will follow it. And the day will not last forever; a night will also follow it at some point. People might like you today and might not tomorrow. They might not like you today but might in the future. If someone does not like you or appreciate you, someone else will. If a person does not love you, another person does or will.

When you are last, be mindful that the time will come when you will become first—as long as you do not give up. And when you are first, be mindful that you can become last sometimes. Sometimes you win, other times you lose. That is the cycle of existential contradictions. Existence certainly needs sunshine, but it also requires rain. In existence, there is up because there is down and vice versa. There is top because there is bottom and vice versa. There is front because there is back and vice versa. There is left because there is right and vice versa. There is north only because there is south and vice versa. If there is east, then there is west and vice versa. A yes will always remain an alternative to a no and vice versa.

Greatness comes out of smallness. And per Aristotle's philosophy, the end will always be in the beginning. In the midst of existential contradictions, it could be difficult to find peace—and the path to peace could become nebulous—but with the tool of self-examination, peace is likely to find you. Self-examination brings peace your way or within your reach. Enjoy your reading trip as you leaf through this book! Godspeed!

CHAPTER 2

Happiness or Peace of Heart and Mind

Suru started the fourth quarter of 2013 as someone you would think of as a happy human being. At least you would think his life was heading in a happy direction. And he had good reasons to think so. He was happily married to Lafia, the love of his life, a wonderful woman. Lafia was Suru's sweetheart, his secret garden, his best friend, and his private spring. Their union generated three lovely children in their daughters and son, the finest fruits they could ever bear. They all felt graciously blessed with good health by the divine protection.

In August 2013, they purchased and moved into their dream house. Suru was fond of his job as a university professor. Lafia was equally passionate about her profession as a nurse practitioner. Overall, the music of their quiet lives reflected a good harmony. The notes sounded coordinated in a nearly perfect symphony under the splendid supervision of a divine conductor. Nearly everything seemed orchestrated for their happiness. It felt like they were born to be happy, but a dark day in October changed the course of events.

On October 7, 2013, Suru got a phone call from Lafia. He thought it was a regular phone call. Lafia and Suru were both at work. It was their routine to check in on each other at work. On that day, it was not the regular phone call Suru was used to.

When he picked up the phone to listen to his sweetheart, Suru was caught by surprise. From the other end of the communication system, he could hear Lafia's voice, but instead of talking to him, Lafia was just crying. Suru tried to contain himself. He asked Lafia what the problem was, but she began crying even more. Not sure of the most effective action to take in that situation, Suru took a deep breath and asked Lafia to do the same.

Lafia took a deep breath and told Suru that she had the results of her breast biopsy. She had been diagnosed with breast cancer. The news took Suru by storm, and his heart started pounding. At first, Suru was shocked and felt lost. After a moment of silence, he came to his senses. He told his wife he was sorry to hear that. In the seconds that followed, he felt horrible; it felt as if an elephant had stepped on Suru's heart. His heart did not give up, but the rhythm of his heart mutated into a cycle of accelerated push-ups. Trapped inside his thoracic cage like a piston inside an engine, his heart was pounding up and down.

Suru began thinking about what a terrible husband he was at that critical moment. His wife would need him to be strong per some social decorum or standards. He pulled himself together and took another deep breath. Suru went ahead and told Lafia she would get through that condition safely. He reassured his wife that she could count on him all the way through.

By the time their conversation ended, Suru realized that their life had been changed forever. Everything was on the verge of going south. He knew cancer was a horrifying, deadly monster, but he never thought it would hit him so closely and so early. Their children were only four, three, and two years old.

Suru was petrified. He felt depression and anxiety for weeks, but he had to push himself to keep on going. What do you do when your life is turning upside down? What you do when everything you value is collapsing or is on the verge of collapsing? What do you do in the face of existential contradictions?

Suru did not have any perfect answers. The questions triggered another meaningful question in his mind. "What is happiness?" he asked himself. It was not his first time asking that question. As a child, Suru had asked his mother that same existential question, and Iya had done her best to help him understand happiness. Over and over again, Iya would keep on challenging Suru to face his existential contradictions.

Suru grew to understand that facing existential contradictions is de facto a sine qua non condition for being happy. In the face of daily existential contradictions, you either actively face reality with optimism or you passively collapse under the weight of pessimism. Optimism radiates highly positive energy that enables you to pull yourself together and rebuild a happy life. Pessimism emits highly negative thinking that disables and paralyzes you.

In the face of his wife's condition and mindful of his mother's lessons, Suru got to a point where he learned what to do and how to rediscover the peace of mind and heart. He purposefully decided to resort to the tool of self-examination. Through the process of self-examination, Suru learned to live in a positive energy field for the sake of life and happiness. He had always valued life and happiness.

Thanks to his mother's advice, Suru repeated the process to face existential contradictions. At that moment of Lafia's diagnosis and throughout her treatment, his mother's philosophy about happiness inspired Suru with positive thoughts, feelings, attitudes, words, and actions. The diagnosis was one of many existential contradictions in Suru's life.

Earlier in the year of Lafia's diagnosis, Suru had lost a good friend in a brutal car accident. That friend was named Meki. Meki had been fatally run over by his own car. His sudden death was traumatic and extremely difficult to cope with, especially considering the circumstances.

Many more existential contradictions occurred in Suru's life, but Iya led him to understand the dynamics of existential contractions and how to face them for the sake of happiness. The present volume will not say much more about Lafia's condition and treatment. A future volume will say more about Lafia. The pages of this book are largely inspired by and rooted in what Suru learned from his mother on facing existential contradictions through self-examination.

The first time Suru told his mother that he was interested in getting an academic degree in conflict resolution and peace studies, Iya gave her son the main idea for this book. She said Suru should always remember to take care of his own conflicts first and then he would be able to help resolve other conflicts in his social environment. Iya explained that Suru should be mindful and focus on making peace first inside his heart and mind, and he would then be able to spread it to his surroundings and the entire world.

Iya's words struck Suru, and he found them powerful and meaningful. They remained inscribed in Suru's heart and mind forever. His mother's thought was etched on his heart and mind. Unaware of all the implications of what his mother meant, Suru took an immediate and solemn vow to do just that. He promised his mother not to disappoint her in that regard. He promised to fulfill her wish. He did not know all the ramifications of his promise, but he knew he would work very hard to keep it to honor his mother.

Suru's reflections on his mother's thought triggered a self-examination on his part. During the process of self-examination,

Suru got an invaluable revelation. He discovered that his mother had spent her entire life trying to teach him to do what she implied. Iya had been training Suru to take care of his own conflicts before he pretended to help other people with their conflicts. Iya had been coaching her son to build and value peace within his heart and mind. Patiently and diligently, she had been alerting Suru on the potential of self-examination for peace or happiness. This book presents Suru's discovery.

I have been happily teaching and practicing conflict resolution and peacemaking for some years now. Based on my experience, observations, and self-evaluations, I can sincerely testify that Iya's thought remains relevant in Suru's life, in conflict transformation, and in peacemaking. This book vividly provides a critical account of Suru's self-examinations and observations of his social environment. His mother's thought resonated beyond the scope of his existence. It was inscribed in his mind like a permanent mark. It set him up to begin to observe the dynamics of self-conflicts within and around him.

Suru carefully started examining the dynamics of existential contradictions. He revisited the dynamics of self-conflicts from his childhood and teenage life. A year after his memorable promise to Iya, Suru was admitted into a graduate program in conflict and peace studies. He began to engage enthusiastically with the study of conflict transformation in theory and practice. It did not take him long to begin to understand what his mother's advice meant and to assess its value.

Iya's insightful thought empowered Suru's mind to start tracking and thinking about his contradictions. He revisited his past self-conflicts and found lots of them. He became aware that human existence encompasses a daily process of conflict and conflict transformation. Once you transform a conflict, another one emerges. Suru noticed how his unresolved self-conflicts affected his interactions with others and triggered conflicts in his social environment. More importantly, Suru observed how his mother inspired and challenged him to transform and trade his self-conflicts for peace of heart and mind. Subsequently, he began to pay attention to how others in his social environment (especially his wife, children, other relatives, and friends) inspired him to transcend his self-conflicts. The following pages traced back Suru's self-conflicts from childhood to adult life. They take him back to explore the meaningful self-conflicts he experienced. They put him at the crossroads of contradictions of daily life. This book is one of Suru's self-evaluation. It is an examination of his life in terms of self-conflicts and peace. It is a review of his inner-self in relation with his social environment, but the book concurrently reflects his observations and analyses of dynamics of other people's self-conflicts.

Suru was born to a humble upbringing and was raised in a poor family and country. Nineb was an ill-governed and poor country. Suru grew up under a military and authoritarian single-party rule. The autocratic regime denied its people the basic rights of freedom some take for granted. Suru's father, Baba, was a truck driver. His mother was a stay-at-home mother with a small business.

Growing up in humble conditions exposed Suru to a series of contradictions. He sometimes ate cooked beans with dead weevils in it. How could you possibly understand this? You certainly could not imagine people eating beans infested with families of pests. At times, the only dry beans Suru's parents could get from the market were infested with weevils. They would remove the weevils they could see, sort out the beans, clean them, and rinse them.

When the beans were ready to cook, they did not see any other weevils, but as you cooked the beans, the hidden weevils would start running for their lives. Suru's father was fond of cooking beans and would do his best to remove the weevils he was able to see. Once the beans were cooked and served, Suru would still see isolated weevils on his plate as he tried to enjoy his meal. He would try to take them out, but that process never allowed him to enjoy eating his beans. In some cases, he ended up dumping his beans in the trash. If you were in his shoes, you would certainly be dumping that plate of beans. Who would want to eat food containing dead weevils?

Suru also remembers growing up in a house that sometimes hosted families of mice in addition to his family members. Mice were certainly not welcome under the roof of Suru's house, but they managed to sneak in anyway. You might wonder whether they were at least good tenants! No, they were not. They would get married and multiply in his parents' house without their agreement and without paying any rent. Mice ate his family's food for free, and they comfortably raised their families in the same environment Suru and his family lived in.

Suru's parents were aware of the risks of disease, and Baba would set traps to catch and deter the mice. Iya adopted a couple of cats to fight the mice, but it hardly deterred those relentless rodents from invading the family's space. In the morning, as soon as Suru's family vacated the house for their daily activities, the rodents would take advantage of a human absence to wander around the house. They would eat and play happily.

In the evening, as soon as the rats heard any noise, they would disappear in their hideout before the family showed up. Suru and his family did not know the small attic was a comfortable place for life until they realized how comfortable and safe the rodents felt there. Their attic was also a refuge and hospice for the mice. At times, Baba would joke that hosting and feeding the mice was like performing a random act of kindness. He implied that his family was being generous to the mice by allowing them to live in the house. Iya was never pleased to hear that joke. She would challenge Suru's father to be reasonable.

Cockroaches would visit the bathroom and the sacred space of Iya's kitchen. Those nasty pests were having fun in violating such private spaces. They were very aggressive in the process and would get away with offending Suru and his family.

Sometimes, Suru and his family were at the mercy of the rain in their own house. More than once, the rain found its way through the roof. The roof was leaking, and Suru's parents lacked the means to repair it in a timely manner. Unfortunately, the rain does not have the patience to wait for the poor to fix their roofs before it comes and surprises them. It falls on you without your consent. Nonetheless, its arrival was usually welcomed by Suru's neighboring farmers and their plants. The family would eventually join the farmers to celebrate the arrival of the rain. They all needed the crops to survive. Suru's parents would tolerate rain in their house, but they would not tolerate drought and famine. His parents failed to fix their roof on time, but they would never fail to provide their children with food. At times, the food might not be enough or the best, but they never failed to provide it.

At an early age, Suru learned to choose between helping his mother cook dinner and playing with his friends. He would help his mother cook and wash dishes while his friends were doing their homework. After helping his mother in the kitchen, he had to decide to do his homework, aware that his classmates, next door, were done with their homework and were watching TV. Suru has no regrets about that time with his mother; he traces his cooking skills back to those moments.

Suru was also required to spend some weekends helping his father around the house instead of enjoying playing with his friends. He would help Baba sweep and mop the floor, clean the single toilet, or fix this and that around our house. Over and over again, Suru was faced with the dilemma of requesting the privileges of being the little one he believed he was and renouncing some prerogatives because of his family's conditions. At times, he felt he was denied the right to be a little one.

His parents would justify their resistance to some of his wishes by arguing they were doing it out of love for him. Baba and Iya rarely put the blame on their dire financial constraints. They believed they were training Suru to be ready to handle daily life. On several occasions, his parents made Suru work like an adult against his will. He had nobody else to complain to. The more complaints Baba and Iya recorded from Suru, the more arguments they sharpened to counter his complaints. They would convince him to make what they thought was the right choice.

In some instances, Suru managed to solve his puzzle without his parents' help, but in many cases, he would ask them for help, knowing beforehand what their position would be. It was not his parents' habit to bribe him with candy. Suru learned to celebrate Christmas with toys that were not his choice. Baba and Iya often bought his Christmas toys without inquiring about it or exploring his interests. Suru was raised in an open environment, but family rules and regulations were rigorous and tight.

Suru was blessed with good parents. Baba and Iya cherished the nobility of marriage. They believed in the vocation of having children and enjoyed having them. They were dedicated to the mission of raising their children together. In general, their human weaknesses did not keep them from embracing the sacrifices and challenges of such a noble and delicate mission. Suru's parents were always there for their children regardless of their contradictions. Their limited financial means did not stop them from being attentive to their children's needs. Their shortcomings did not prevent them from keeping their hearts and minds open to the family's needs. Suru was brought up to learn about life by drinking from the source of wisdom in his parents' hearts and minds. This allowed him to grow, develop, and change in heart and mind under their protection and guidance.

The first time Suru met Iya, she introduced herself as his mother. Iya's physical appearance was natural, elegant, clean, and attractive. God made her tall, thin, and charming. Her dark, curly hair was appealing. A friend once described her as a nearly perfect incarnation of the adjective *beautiful*. That friend was right. Iya was an encapsulation of beauty.

Baba could not resist falling in love with Iya. She was forty-one years older than Suru, but every time Suru saw his mother, he still felt unconditionally attracted to her. Initially, Suru thought it was only due to Iya's physical beauty, but as time went on and Suru grew closer to his mother, he understood that her physical charm was a reflection of the magnificence of her golden heart, spirit, and mind.

Eventually, Suru realized his attraction to his mother was mainly due to the compassion of Iya's heart, her immeasurable love for humankind, the wonders of Iya's spirit, and the wisdom of her mind. For some reason, the universe or nature graciously put Iya on Suru's way to nurture him and give him strength, hope, consolation, and support.

Suru was not sure how it was planned, but Iya kindly agreed to be by Suru's side as a mother. She turned out to be his friend, his role model, his mentor, his advisor, his coach, and his teacher. Iya guided Suru and provided him with the pillars of life. She patiently coached her son on how to transform and transcend his contradictions for the peace of heart and mind. Suru would slowly learn from Iya how to lean on existential pillars of happiness.

Suru started learning from his mother when he was an egg in Iya's womb. After his birth, he learned from Iya's wisdom every day. His mother's lessons sustained his existence through gestation, birth, childhood, adolescence, and adulthood. Suru quickly became aware of this as a child. He learned to resort to Iya's advice about the ups and downs of existence, especially when the waters of his life become unstable and difficult to navigate. Patiently, Iya would paddle the canoe of Suru's existence into stable waters and into the path of happiness.

"What is happiness?" Suru asked when Iya formally exposed him to the concept at the age of seven. His question was triggered by all the birthday wishes. His father, siblings, relatives, and friends wished him happy birthday in slogans and songs at his birthday party. As Suru unpacked his cards and gifts, he also noticed it was written on everything in black, blue, purple, red, and white inks. Reading such wishes made Suru think deeply. He was curious as to what the happy wishes meant. He wanted to understand why everybody used the same adjective over and over again. The adjective *happy* was certainly a part of Suru's limited vocabulary. However, he became aware that he was not fully sure of what it meant. Suru was eager to learn all about it. He decided to ask his mother for understanding and clarification. "What is happiness? How does one get it?"

Iya paused, touched Suru gently on his shoulders, and told him that a tentative answer to such a question was worth a series of lessons. Iya bent her head forward to consult with her watch and check the time. It was nine o'clock. She smiled and said, "It is bedtime now, son. We will talk about this tomorrow."

When Iya woke Suru up at eight o'clock, Suru told her he was tired. He wanted to spend some more time in bed because it was Saturday morning. It was a tradition in Suru's family to stay in bed on Saturday morning and wake up at around eight thirty. Suru's father tried to explain the rationale behind that tradition. It was the best way to recover from the fatigue accumulated over the week, but Iya diligently reminded Suru things were different that morning. That

Saturday was special because they planned to be at the movie theater at nine o'clock to watch a new movie. That movie would be part of Suru's birthday treat.

Suru did not get ready right away. He spent fifteen minutes stretching his tiny body in his bed instead of getting ready for breakfast. Iya did not insist because she did not want to hurt Suru's feelings. It was not her habit to force him to break family traditions. By the time Suru woke up, Iya and everybody else had already eaten breakfast. They were all waiting patiently for Suru in the family room.

Once Suru finally showed up in his pajamas for his traditional good morning ceremony, Iya took him to the bathroom. She helped him brush his teeth, gave him a quick shower, and helped him get dressed. Soon after, Iya set up Suru's breakfast. He ate in a rush, and they jumped into a taxi that Baba helped recruit. Suru sat in the back next to Iya and his sister, Femi. His father sat next to the driver.

The movie theater was fifteen minutes away, and the movie was scheduled to start at nine. Suru asked the driver to speed up. He thought speeding would allow them to make it on time, but his father responded that the driver was doing a good job by going slowly. Baba did not want the police to stop them or give the driver a ticket for speeding. Iya added that speeding would not make anybody happy if they got into an accident.

Baba stressed that it would be disastrous if all four of them were in a car accident. The morning beach traffic made their drive even slower. By the time they reached their destination, the movie had started. Suru was not happy, and he rushed into the waiting line. The movie theater was packed. They sat down randomly in the last row since the best seats were all taken. Their time inside the theater went so fast.

On their way home, Iya asked what Suru thought of the movie.

He was not happy because he missed the beginning of the movie.

Suru said that watching the start of a movie would condition you to appreciate it.

His mother challenged his response. Using what her son later understood as a Socratic approach from philosophy classes, Iya asked Suru to think about why he was not happy. A series of thoughts crossed Suru's mind, but none of them stood up as a good reason for why he was not happy. He shared with Iya the one he felt was most relevant. He told Iya it was because he was late, but Iya pushed for more by asking why he was late. Suru thought the answer was obvious and wondered why his mother was putting him on the spot, but he did not want to disappoint Iya with his silence and said it was because he woke up late. Suru confessed to his mother that he should have listened to her and followed her when she woke him up.

Iya said that punctuality was a key contributing variable to happiness.

Suru understood his mother was trying to answer his initial question about happiness. He looked up, stared Iya in the eyes, and said, "What is the secret of happiness?"

Iya smiled, put her right hand on Suru's right shoulder, and said, "Son, that question is certainly a good one, but it's not the right one in this case."

"What do you mean?" Suru asked.

Iya said, "Happiness does not have any secret at all. A secret is something that is purposefully hidden, something that is known to somebody or to a group of people, but it is intentionally hidden to others. In my experience, happiness does not have anything to hide because it is open and accessible to all human beings. Nevertheless, it is up to human beings to be open to happiness. Instead of secrets, happiness has pillars that are visible and accessible to everyone who is open to and willing to see them, touch them and embrace them. The pillars of happiness are pillars of peace."

Suru listened to such meaningful words flowing out of his mother's sweet mouth. They resonated in his ears like a waterfall and appeased his heart like a stream. However, they would not convince his mind. Suru was amazed at Iya's approach to happiness, but his mind could not grasp the depth of his mother's thoughts. Iya's original perspective on happiness felt like thunder and lightning in Suru's mind. It was electrified and electrocuted. He struggled to understand the depth of Iya's thoughts. "What should be the right question then, Mother?"

Iya said, "What are the pillars of happiness?"

Suru begged his mother to tell him more about the pillars of happiness.

Iya smiled again and exclaimed, "Son, be reassured that I will provide you with pillars of peace!" From that point on, Iya started sharing her understanding and experience of happiness with Suru.

According to Iya, human happiness is a satisfactory state of being that translates into some peace of heart and mind. Happiness is a state of peace of mind and heart that makes you enjoy and appreciate who you are, how you feel, what you have, what you do, where you are, and others around you. Peace of mind and heart is more or less the sustained absence of troubles, worries, or fears. Whenever we are worried, upset, or afraid, we do not have peace of mind and heart. To be happy, we have to learn to counter whatever does not give us peace of heart and mind in order to acquire what grants us such peace.

We have to learn to transform or move from our zones of turbulence into spaces of peace. The peace of heart and mind is reflected in a healthy body and mind. As a result, the pathway to happiness combines caring for the mind and caring for the body. Such a pathway is built upon a number of significant and highly correlated variables that include listening, meditation, contemplation, consolation in decision and action, punctuality, planning, serenity in decision-making, taking initiatives, being responsible, being reliable, knowing your rights, fulfilling your duties, working hard, learning from your successes and failures, developing a good sense of humor and optimism, smiling and laughing by choice, being passionate, eating and drinking healthily, getting enough sleep, doing physical activities, being humble, being grateful, developing the quality of discretion, developing the sense of detachment, being obedient, loving, being generous, being honest, being fair, being faithful, being respectful, finding the right time to make a request in order to maximize the chances of getting what you want, showing remorse, apologizing for wrongdoing, forgiving, and respecting the rules of law and order. Happiness is not necessarily related to material gratification or assets. You can be financially or materially successful without being happy. Many wealthy people are not happy. You will also encounter poor people who are happy. Financial and material success could certainly contribute to happiness to some degree, but they are not sufficient factors or determinants of happiness per daily existential situations. Happiness echoes the peace of heart and mind you experience in the midst of existential contradictions, regardless of your financial conditions.

Per Iya's experience, the central principle of happiness resides inside of each human. You measure your peace of mind and heart by checking how you feel. If whatever you are doing does not make you feel good, you have to stop doing it and change your course of action or strategy. If you do not feel comfortable wherever you are, you have to move from there and find a location where you feel comfortable.

At first, Suru objected to Iya's criteria for measuring happiness. He thought such criteria were egoistic. They did not seem to care about the happiness of others. They also seemed to neglect the notion of self-sacrifice, but Iya would genuinely refute Suru's objections. At the core of one's happiness is other people's happiness and vice versa, per Iya's clarification.

Iya pushed Suru to think about it. "If you are not happy, chances are high that your social environment will be affected. You will not make them happy if you are not happy. Happiness is contagious. So is unhappiness to some extent. Happiness certainly integrates the notion and practice of sacrifice. However, sacrifice should not overshadow or overcome happiness. Moments of sacrifice put a bitter taste in the delicious soup of happiness. Their effects should not last forever. Moments of sacrifice should be brief. If moments of sacrifice outlast your peace of mind and heart, you are not happy. Happiness makes your peace of mind and heart outpace and outlast your moments of sacrifice."

Suru never fully understood what Iya meant by such measures of happiness until his years of spiritual training with the Jesuits. Nevertheless, from his mother's definition of happiness, Suru did understand what a happy birthday wish means. Whenever people wish you a happy birthday, they want you to celebrate or enjoy your birthday with some peace of heart and mind. They want you to use the opportunity to reconnect with your inner self, the source of your being. They want you to transcend all inner contradictions and reunite yourself for happiness.

CHAPTER 3

Pulled Away from Inattention to Attention: Listening

As Iya kept on with her instructions, the taxi driver stopped his car by their house.

Baba exclaimed, "We have reached home ad extremum!"

Iya said, "Home, how sweet! Nowhere can truly feel like it!"

Baba went inside the house with Suru's sister, Femi.

Suru stood outside with Iya for a few more minutes.

"It is lunchtime. We have to stop here for now," Iya said.

Reluctantly, Suru followed his mother inside the house.

In the dining room, Baba had set up lunch for the family.

"That was quick, Father," Suru said.

Iya added, "Your father has the right skills."

Baba smiled and responded, "I appreciate the compliments." He had two cups of Moroccan couscous, salad, and salmon ready for all of them in less than twenty-five minutes.

Suru said, "Why so quickly, Father?"

Baba smiled and said, "Because I am hungry, your sister is also hungry, and I think your mother is hungry as well. What about you?"

"I am equally hungry!" Suru replied.

His mother stepped in and said, "Let us enjoy the food then. It is getting late."

They all sat down at the table for lunch.

Suru ate his salad and couscous quickly. He wanted to finish before everybody. In doing so, he had a hidden agenda. His ultimate goal was to set up two chairs in the family room so he could continue listening to Iya's instructions on happiness.

Iya said, "My son, congratulations on finishing your meal! Now take your time to drink some water and enjoy some fruit before we all go for a nap."

Suru said, "Can we continue talking about happiness after lunch? It seems like it is too late for a nap."

Iya looked at Suru and said, "Son, we will certainly continue our unfinished business on happiness—but after a nap. Naptime is around the corner; your body needs a nap to digest and refresh for our instructions."

Baba nodded and said, "By the way, it is never late to take a nap on a weekend."

Suru's one-hour nap felt like ten hours of waiting. In his mind, it was as if the nap was lasting forever. Suru was impatient for it to be over. *This nap is taking too long.* He spent most of his time thinking about Iya's words on happiness. He could not wait to resume their session.

Suru started jumping up and down on his bed to disturb and wake up everybody. It was his habit to use such a strategy to get whatever he wanted from his mother. He was successful in getting this one. He heard familiar footsteps walking toward his door.

Iya knocked at his door and announced, "It is time to wake up, son!"

Suru jumped out of his bed.

"Why are you so excited?" Iya asked.

"I am eager to listen to you again!" Suru replied.

Iya said, "What do you mean by listening to me? What is listening by the way?"

Suru was speechless. His mother's question took him back to a scene in Iya's store a few days earlier. He could call it a spectacle on a Friday evening between his mother and one of her customers. A customer by the name of Ade stopped by in tears. Iya immediately had Ade sit down. That customer felt welcomed and stopped crying. Ade went on to tell Iya her story. She was a young widow. Her late husband, Kola, was addicted to alcohol. Kola was drunk when he was killed in a hit-and-run accident. The poor widow was having hard time raising her disabled son. Ade had no moral or material support from family members.

Kola's family blamed Ade for his death. Ade's own family had never accepted her marriage to Kola. Ade seemed to care about everyone in her family, but nobody cared about her. Nobody was interested in listening to her story. She went on with telling her story to Iya for nearly an hour. Suru's mother carefully and respectfully listened to Ade's story.

Suru could see, feel, and tell his mother's heart was beating with compassion as she listened to her customer. After Ade stopped talking, Iya gave her a loving hug and said, "Please, trust you have in me a friend you can count on to listen to you. Know that you are always welcome here in my house for help."

Ade smiled and told Iya that she felt better.

After Ade's departure, Iya whispered, "Son, sometimes, people just need someone to listen to them. They want nothing else but your attention. Listening to people has the potential to heal them."

Suru was unable to provide an answer to his mother's question about the meaning of listening. Embarrassed, Suru would eventually confess to Iya that he did not know how to define listening. And he really meant it. It was not clear what listening implied. He bent down and thought for a while. A series of thoughts and scenes kept flooding his mind and swelling his heart.

Growing up, he enjoyed talking more than listening. Suru had hard time listening to others. He was competing to talk with his siblings and friends. He did not care much about his parents explaining how people should take turns talking. Suru would scream to be heard if he had to in a discussion circle. *Talkative* is not strong enough to describe his penchant for relentless talking. His father got upset more than once with that. Baba told him to stop talking and listen. Sometimes, he would look at Baba and keep talking.

Baba went on to say that Suru had a crisis of listening. The more he talked, the happier Suru became. At some point, Baba shared his concerns with Suru's mother.

Iya convinced Suru to self-examine how he really felt about inexorable talking.

Suru realized he was too agitated.

Iya trained him to breathe in and out and calm down and how to control the pace of his words. She also alerted him to observe how his siblings, friends, and classmates felt whenever he ran the talking show alone.

It did not take Suru long to notice most of them were angry and frustrated. His mother's conclusion was straightforward, and Suru thought he got the message: not allowing others to speak their minds would ultimately not make anyone happy.

Iya asked Suru to listen to others, allow them to talk, and remain calm when they talked.

Suru seized the opportunity of a dinner to do so with his siblings. He also did the same thing on the playground with his friends and classmates. He noticed they were all excited to talk; it felt good to talk without Suru interrupting. He updated his mother about how he felt.

Iya's conclusion was clear. Allowing others to say what they need to say would eventually make everyone happy.

Suru thought about Iya's question about the meaning of listening. As his thoughts about listening jumped up and down in his mind, they did not convince him about what listening meant. He straightened up and said, "Mother! Can you please tell me what listening is?"

Iya gently took Suru by his right hand and said, "Do not worry, son! One of our lessons on happiness is all about listening."

Suru was glad to hear that. He felt good and started jumping up and down.

His mother looked at him and said, "Take a deep breath and calm down!"

Suru obeyed and did so.

Iya and Suru went into the family room and sat down comfortably.

Iya turned on the radio. It was time for the news. It was not what Suru was expecting his mother to do. He could not believe it. "Mother, I want to listen to you and not to the radio."

Iya smiled and said, "Let us just listen to what is in the news for a while."

Suru asked, "Should I consider your words as an order here, Mother?"

Iya smiled and replied, "If you think so, that might help."

Suru followed Iya's injunction and listened to the radio. The news was about the importance of vaccines.

A few minutes later, Iya turned off the radio and said, "Who did you just listen to?"

"I just listened to the broadcaster," he said.

Iya said, "What did you just listen to?"

Suru responded, "I just listened to the news about the vaccinations." He purposefully made his answers short to allow his mother enough time to start her lecture on listening.

Iya said, "Son, why did you listen to the journalist and the news he had?"

Suru became uncomfortable and said, "I listened to all that because you asked me to listen."

Iya smiled and said, "Son, I know you can certainly give a better answer to my question."

Suru paused to think, felt some empowerment, and said, "I listened to the newscaster because I wanted to learn from him about the importance of vaccination."

Iya enthusiastically put her thumbs up for Suru and added, "Well done!" Suru thought the satisfaction his mother expressed would put an end to her series of questions for him.

Instead, Iya said, "How did you listen to the journalist and his news?"

Suru thought of boycotting his mother's question; instead, he observed a moment of silence in protest.

Iya put her right hand on Suru's left shoulder and whispered, "I know you can do it, son!" The pace of her words reflected her affection and love for her son.

As Suru thought about what his mother said, he felt empowered. Iya's words provided Suru with some incentive to answer the question. "Mother, I made a conscious effort to hear the newsperson and paid attention to what he was saying."

Iya stood up, clapped for Suru, and said, "Son, I knew you could do it, and you did it so well. I am so proud of you."

Suru thought his mother would sit down after praising him for his good answer, but Iya remained standing. She showed Suru four fingers to indicate of who, what, why, and how. "My son, when thinking of or talking about listening, remember to always answer those four questions. Listening revolves around them. They represent its four pillars."

Suru begged his mother to say more about the four questions.

Iya cleared her throat, grabbed a cup of water, and started addressing all four questions.

She unveiled what listening meant. Suru thought it was time for his mother to lecture him. It did not take long before he realized he was wrong to think so. Instead of a lecture, they had a cordial discussion with questions and answers.

Iya challenged Suru to learn about the pillars of happiness. She took Suru back to his school on Friday and said, "Who did you listen to at school yesterday?"

Suru thought the question was an easy and obvious one. "I listened to my teacher," he responded.

Iya said, "Son, did you listen only to your teacher? What about your classmates? Didn't you listen to them?" Iya's hands were making inquisitive and magisterial gestures. The curiosity and depth of her look warned Suru that his mother was on alert. He had also listened to his classmates answering the teacher's questions and asking questions. He tried to imagine only listening to his teacher all day long. It would be impossible and boring.

Before Suru could give Iya the correct answer, she said, "Son, you certainly listened to your teacher—but also to your classmates. Who should you listen to, son?" Without allowing Suru time to provide an answer, Iya said, "You should listen to all people in your social environment." Iya urged Suru to listen to all human beings in his social environment regardless of age, gender, race, ethnicity, social class, or status. Suru should listen to them all—old or young, tall or short, big or small, male or female, black or white, and poor or rich. "You can learn from all human beings. Listening to your social environment paves your way to happiness."

Suru said, "Should I listen to myself sometimes?"

Iya smiled and said, "That question is relevant. I am glad you are asking such a worthy question, son!" She drank some more water. "Yes, son! You should always listen to yourself. Listen to yourself when you talk. More importantly, listen to your conscience in all situations you find or put yourself in."

Suru said, "Mother, can you tell me what you mean by conscience?"

Iya took a deep breath and said, "Your conscience is your innate sense or knowledge of right and wrong. Do you understand what I mean by innate sense?"

Suru responded, "You just read my mind. I was about to ask you the same question. I have no clue what it means."

Iya said, "Your innate sense acts like a voice inside you that urges you to do the right thing."

To be sure that Suru understood his mother's clarification, he asked, "How do I compare my conscience to God?"

Iya smiled and responded, "My son, you are dragging me onto the paths of theology, which I am not very good at. We should keep that question for the parish priest if you do not mind. Conscience is like a divine voice. God communicates to you through your conscience and through people. That is a reason why it is of utmost importance to listen to your conscience—but also all people. Your conscience is the voice of truth within you. The people are the voices around you. In doing so, you ultimately listen to God."

Suru jumped up and went to the restroom.

"Do you need a long break?" Iya asked.

"No, just a short one! I will be right back," Suru said.

On his way to the bathroom, Suru felt the voice of truth within him. When he listened to the voice of truth, he felt good and peaceful in his mind and heart. He got it. To be happy, you need to always listen to the voice of your conscience and follow—it no matter what. Your conscience is your truth teller, your best coach, and your guide.

On his way back from the bathroom, the image of Iya's four fingers crossed Suru's mind. They still had three questions to go through for the lesson on listening. It was four thirty, and Suru knew dinner was at six. Iya would need to get dinner ready. Suru decided to accelerate the process as if he were fully in control of it.

Iya said, "Are you fine, son? Is everything all right?"

Suru responded, "I am just fine. I am just enjoying this moment! What do we listen to, Mother?"

She said, "There should not be any rush, son! We will get it done because the rest of the questions are easy to answer."

Suru found Iya's statement very hard to believe, and he repeated his question.

Iya smiled and said, "Son, what did you listen to when you listened to your teacher and classmates on Friday?"

Aware of Iya's traditional strategies of instruction, Suru quickly responded, "I listened to my teacher's lesson on the seasons. I also listened to my classmates' answers, comments, and questions on the seasons."

Iya said, "Son, listen to what others have to say because all human beings have something to contribute to social discourses and interactions. You should listen to other people, whether you agree with them or disagree with them and whether what they are saying is good or bad or right or wrong. Doing so will not hurt you. On the contrary, it will allow you to get to know them in their differences—and you will learn from them all."

Suru felt Iya was trying to address the third question. "Mother, why should I listen to all they say?"

Iya stretched her hands and said, "Son, you should always listen to all they say because by listening to all you learn about things that are good and bad, right and wrong. You learn from good and endorse it, but you also learn from bad and refute it. By listening to what everyone has to say, you learn about society—and you learn from people's successes and their failures. Knowing the highs and lows of other people's life stories ultimately provides pillars for your own life." Iya stood up and stretched.

Suru said, "But how should I listen?"

Iya sat down and whispered, "Listening is a selective decision you consciously make to pay attention to what you hear in your social environment. Hearing is not necessarily listening. You can hear and not listen. Listening is a social art that human beings learn and cultivate. Hearing is a natural sense we are born with. Listening is voluntary. It requires a conscious effort to hear what is being said in your immediate and non-immediate environment."

Suru kept on listening to his mother carefully. By the time Iya paused, her message became clear to Suru. Listening is certainly an earnest decision you make to commit your utmost attention to yourself and others. It allows you to pay attention to who they are and what they have to say. Listening requires much attention to agree or disagree with what or who you listen to. If you agree with what you listen, you may endorse it or implement it. If you disagree with it, you may reject it. Hearing does not requires much attention. Listening implies some receptive attitude toward what or who you listen to. Hearing does not implies the same level of receptive attitude. Listening is vital for effective communication. Listening intrinsically requires patience. Patience implies waiting for a silent moment by giving the other party the benefit of the doubt as you allow the expression or manifestation of that other party. You could transcend existential contradictions by listening to yourself and others. Self-examination allows you to listen to yourself and others.

As soon as Iya paused, Baba emerged unexpectedly from the backyard and said, "Sweetie, do you need any help from me to get dinner ready?"

Iya looked up in the direction of the inspirational wooden clock in their family room. It was five thirty-five. "I will take care of it. Darling, it is my turn to do it!" Suru's mother and his father were taking turns cooking, and it was Iya's turn to cook dinner on that Saturday.

Nonetheless, Baba insisted, "Are you sure you do not need any help from me? I can take care of it in case you need to spend some more time providing your good instructions on listening!"

Before Baba's sentence even ended, Iya grabbed him by his shoulders with a smile and asked, "How do you know we have been talking about listening, dear?"

Suru's father said, "The mouse is often quiet in its corner, but it gets the smell of every food in the house. I could hear your entire conversation from the backyard. As I was listening to you, I thought I needed such great lessons on listening. I stopped all I was supposed to be doing, and I listened to your instructions. I found them meaningful and helpful."

Iya unexpectedly leaned forward with some tears of joy in her eyes and kissed her man on his lips, saying, "My king, I thank you for being always gracious."

Baba gently placed his left hand under his wife's head and used his right hand to lift and caress her chin. He looked Iya straight in the eyes and vibrantly said, "My queen, how beautiful your eyes are with such shining tears of love falling upon your cheeks like a rain of diamond jewelry!"

Iya swiftly closed her eyes. In a flawless move, she leaned her head forward and rested her left cheek like a golden treasure on Baba's large chest. It all happened before Suru's innocent eyes.

Suru could tell his parents unexpectedly became weak with passion. Both Iya and Baba were almost lost in love. There was a beautiful moment of solemn silence. It was so lovely for Suru to watch. He felt highly honored to witness the scene. Suru felt great admiration for his parents' unconditional love for each other.

Like two sounds in a faultless symphony, Iya and Baba went into the kitchen to get dinner ready. Suru quietly watched them with pride and emotion and thought about his own contribution to getting dinner ready. His father was cooking spaghetti, and his mother was getting the spaghetti sauce ready. Suru found his sister in her bedroom and said, "Let us set the table for dinner!"

Femi put her books away and ran down to the dining room with Suru. She set the silverware after Suru placed the plates. It was not something they would usually do unless their parents asked them to help do so, but—inspired by Iya and Baba—Suru decided to take the initiative. He wanted to make a good surprise for his mother and father.

Suru and Femi decided to do everything silently. Their strategy was to make no big noise with the silverware. They were so absorbed by what they were doing that the dining room was as silent as a monastery.

Baba was stirring the spaghetti and did not notice what his children were doing.

Suru whispered, "They will be surprised to see that we set the table without letting them know."

Femi responded, "They surely will be. Let us surprise them like this every once in a while."

Baba said, "Where are the children?"

As soon as Suru and Femi heard their father's voice, they hid in a corner behind the small door that offered access to the dining room.

Iya said, "They have been busy setting the table for dinner."

Baba said, "What do you mean?"

Suru and Femi came out of their hideaway, and Suru said, "How do you know what we have been doing, Mother?"

With her loving eyes fixed on Suru, Iya smiled and said, "I listened to you when you spoke to your sister. I have been watching both of you. You cannot escape my ears and eyes in this house."

Suru was amazed that his mother had provided him with such a significant example of what it meant to listen to your social environment. He thanked Iya for powerfully exemplifying what she just preached to him. "Good job listening, Mother!"

Baba gave Suru and Femi big paternal hugs and said, "I am very proud of you, my children. Thank you for helping! This means a lot to your mother and me! This situation confirms that I do need some lessons on listening!"

At first, Suru thought his father was joking, but it turned out that Baba was not joking.

At the dinner table, the family listened to one another as they enjoyed the food.

Baba indicated that the spaghetti sauce tasted healthy.

Femi said, "It is also delicious."

Suru said, "Thumbs-up for Mother! Well done!"

Everybody at the table gave Iya a standing ovation to congratulate her on cooking a tasty and healthy pasta sauce.

Looking at her husband, Iya said, "The spaghetti sauce would not do it without some very well-cooked spaghetti. Thumbs-up for your father for being such a good chef!"

Femi and Suru quickly gave their father a round of applause.

As usual, Baba appreciated the praise. He turned to Iya and said, "My queen, I would also appreciate if you could invite me to attend your lessons and instructions in the future."

Iya said, "My love, you are certainly invited to attend all instructions as a guest of honor—as long as your schedule allows it!"

Femi's eyes opened wide.

Everybody at the dining table could tell she needed an update.

Iya and Suru fully understood what Baba meant, and Suru did not hesitate to update his sister. It only took a few minutes.

Femi said, "I would certainly not mind if your majesty, the teacher, would allow me to also join her class for future lessons." Femi was good at imitating the royal languages she was reading in classical books.

Iya smiled and said, "Darling, you are certainly welcome to join us anytime you are able to take a break from your books!"

Femi enjoyed reading. Her books were her best companions; she spent a substantial amount of time reading.

Iya and Suru were very excited. Suru was thrilled that his mother had graciously opened her lessons to other members of their lovely family. He thought it was a promising idea to have his father and his sister join the learning process. Suru cherished the thought of forming a supportive community of learners with members of his family, and he said, "That is a good plan!"

Iya said, "What is a plan? What is planning?"

Suru was not sure what to answer and kept quiet. He had heard his parents use the word more than once in the past. Suru and Femi had also used the word. Suru's teachers were using it quite often at school. The word *plan* was also part of his friends' daily vocabulary, but Suru could not tell Iya exactly what planning meant. He was hoping that his father would come to his rescue with some comments, but Baba did not say a word. Suru turned to Baba and Femi and said, "Please help. Say something! Any thoughts about plan and planning?"

Femi said, "I have no idea what a plan is!"

Baba said, "With all your heavy reading, darling, you should be able to help us here!"

Femi offered no argument to her father's arguments. Ironically, she did not even bother to resort to her dictionary for help. She did not show a happy face either. She did not seem happy with her father's joke.

Suru thought Baba was right, and he felt like laughing at Femi, but he knew Femi would not take it well—and he needed help himself on the same account.

Baba was about to open his mouth to help, but Iya told him to allow Suru to think about it for a while.

After a few seconds, Suru said, "I am not sure what a plan means!"

Iya smiled and said, "That is a fair answer, son!"

Suru thought his mother would go straight ahead and tell him what a plan meant, but Iya did not. Suru said, "What should I understand by a plan? Mother, can you tell me please?"

Iya smiled and said, "My son, you just set the topic for our next lesson. We will work on it tomorrow."

Baba looked at the big clock on the wall above Femi's head. It was seven thirty. "Let us clean up and put the dishes away. It is time to move to the family room for some family time before we go to bed."

Iya and Femi stood up and took the dishes and silverware away.

Baba put away the leftover food and water, but Suru remained in his chair, wondering why they could not have their family time in the dining room. Suru forgot that Baba usually preferred spending his family time in the black couch in the family room. According to Suru's father, the dining room chairs were not so comfortable. Baba had reminded Suru more than once that the dining room was designed only for eating and not for playing or meeting.

What a poor seven-year-old Suru was! Suru's seven-year-old memory was packed with other files of more importance. He did not care much about the difference between a dining room and a family room. Following his father's lengthy explanations, Suru even took some time to double-check with his mother.

Iya bestowed on her son the same thoughts Baba lavished on Suru, adding that it was mainly so by social conventions or decorum. Some friends also told Suru that they spent their family time with their parents in their family room and not in the dining room. Everything Suru knew about the difference between a dining room and a family room crossed his mind as he remained in his chair. He had enough arguments to convince himself to get up and join everyone in the family room, yet he remained stubbornly seated in the dining room. *Why don't we have our family time here? Why can't we use the dining room as a family room? What are social conventions? Why should we care so much about them?*

Suru thought the notion of decorum and social conventions could be another great lesson from Iya. *Maybe that is another question for our lessons! This may well be part of planning for a new lesson on social conventions!*

Baba called upon him to help wipe the dining room table and join everybody in the family room.

Suru stood up and did what he was told to do. He wiped the table and joined everyone in the family room. He was still mindful of his thoughts on the dining room and family room.

In the family room, Suru sat on an empty couch that was more comfortable than the chair in the dining room. His food was traveling more easily in his digestive system. *Maybe my father was right.*

After a few minutes, he started falling asleep. He was yawning and ended up missing the substance of their family time.

When Iya and Baba took hold of his hands to go to his bedroom, Suru stretched his tiny body and muttered, "I now understand there is a difference between the dining room and the family room. The family room is designed to be more restful and comfy for the body."

Baba and Iya smiled.

Their silent smile resonated in Suru's mind as a powerful message that the most effective learning may be the one you get from experience. After making sure Suru had his pajamas on, Baba positioned him on his bed. Iya pulled the sheet up to Suru's neck. They covered Suru with loving kisses and wishes for a good night.

Iya whispered, "I hope you remember our plan for tomorrow."

Suru was not quite sure what she meant. He guessed his mother was talking about their lesson on planning, but he did not want to inquire about that because he was so sleepy.

Iya turned off the light in Suru's room, left the room, and closed the door.

Suru noticed that the light was still on in Femi's room next door. She was waiting for good night wishes and her daily bedtime reading with Iya. Femi would not go to sleep until Iya read some good stories to her. Femi was very consistent with bedtime reading. Suru was not as consistent. Depending on his mood, he was fine with skipping bedtime reading occasionally. Suru was still contemplating the light reflection when the god of sleep took him away in his refreshing arms. Suru was not sure when Femi's light went off, but it certainly went off at some point on that Saturday night. Femi would not trade her sleep time for anything—not even for reading.

CHAPTER 4

From a Disorganized to an Organized Existence: Planning

After a good night of sleep, Suru woke up refreshed on Sunday morning. He was physically and mentally ready for Sunday school, and he was eager for his mother's lecture on planning. At breakfast, Suru reminded Iya of her promise to instruct him on planning.

Baba and Femi also followed suit by beseeching Iya to keep her promise, but Iya reminded all of them that they ought to attend the Sunday service first.

Suru and Femi got ready with the intention of attending their traditional ten o'clock service at their Methodist church, but Iya and Baba met the children in the family room with an unexpected announcement.

Iya said, "As planned, we are going to the beach today after attending church."

Baba nodded. "Your mother is right! That is the plan!" He excused himself to go get ready for the trip.

Suru did not hide his surprise.

Iya said, "Son, you should not be surprised. Your father and I arranged this with you a month ago. We fully made you aware of it, and you were excited about it."

Suru said, "I apologize, Mother. We made such an arrangement, but I forgot it was scheduled for today. Why didn't you remind me last night?"

Iya said, "I am sorry! I tried to do so, but you were too tired and sleepy last night, and I did not want to further disturb your sleep. It can happen that we forget our plans." She told Suru and Femi to hurry up and be on time for the Sunday service.

During the service, Suru was physically present, but mentally absent. He adopted his traditional posture for spiritual focus. He bent his head over and kept his eyes closed. He spent most of the time thinking about his personal struggles over planning.

Growing up, Suru did not enjoy planning. Actually, he barely knew what it meant to plan. He was disorganized in his thoughts and actions. He enjoyed living in the moment. He did not care about the future or what came next. He did not even care much about the present. Nevertheless, he was keen to seize the present opportunity.

Suru did not like deadlines. He would wait until the last minute to study for his tests or exams. He would do his homework at the last minute. He would even hide his homework, school activities, and updates from his parents until the last minute. Suru would visit friends or relatives without notice. He enjoyed surprises. He did not hate making plans, but he did not think it was necessary or useful.

Suru's parents were not impressed with his lack of excitement about planning. Baba and Iya were not happy with their son on that account—despite Suru's young age. Baba and Iya thought his lack of planning was the source of some of his problems. Suru got some poor scores on tests and exams due to his lack of planning. He was often late to school when Iya was not able to take him there. He was also behind in some school activities.

Suru was never happy to score poorly on academic tests or exams. He felt irritated whenever his academic performance was poor. He was not happy when he was late for classroom activities.

When Suru complained about his poor academic performance, his mother told him to do his homework preemptively, timely, and daily. Over and over again, Iya beseeched her son to wake up early to get to school on time, but Suru would often not take his mother's advice seriously. When he received a poor report card, Suru was miserable. He was too ashamed to show Iya his report card. He hid it in his bedroom, but Iya found it. After reviewing it, she told him that she was very disappointed. Iya was not satisfied with Suru's academic performance.

Suru understood his mother's feelings. Femi also brought her report card home that day. Her face was filled with smiles. She was happy to show Iya her outstanding report card. Iya handed Suru the report card, and he read it reluctantly. He was ashamed.

Iya took the opportunity to praise Femi in Suru's presence. Iya purposefully emphasized how good Femi was at planning everything beforehand. Femi would do her homework on time or ahead of time. She would anticipate her school activities and plan for them preemptively and proactively. She would go to school ready and on time every day. Suru's mother said so many other good things about his sister in his presence. She was right.

The eye-opening experience led Suru to self-examination and triggered a turning point in his habits. Suru started doing his homework preemptively, daily, and timely. Whenever, Iya woke him up in the morning to get ready for school, he got up, got ready, and got to school on time. Suru began to anticipate school activities and studied for his tests and exams. He felt happy to be on time in class every day, and so did his teachers. He got a better understanding of class materials. He made more friends. His next report card was outstanding. His teachers were all impressed and happy with his performance. Suru was proud and happy to show his parents his report card.

Iya and Baba did not hide their satisfaction. They were very happy and proud of their son. The lesson was nearly clear to Suru. Planning would make you and others happy.

Suru was thinking so much about his struggles that he did not know when the Sunday service ended. He kept his head bent forward and his eyes closed.

Iya touched him on his left shoulder, and Suru opened his eyes to realize the Sunday service had ended.

They went home and quickly got lunch. After lunch, they headed by foot to the sandy KAJ beach in the Republic of Nineb. The beach was less than an hour away from their house.

On their way, Iya said, "What does a plan stand for, son? Do you have a definition for it now?"

Suru immediately recalled the scenario about making an arrangement to go to the beach, and he responded, "Yes, Mother. I do have a definition now. A plan is any arrangement made for doing or making something in the future!"

Iya said, "That is well done, son! A plan is a project, something one designs beforehand, a purpose you have in mind, or anything you set your mind to do immediately or in the near future."

They were all listening carefully.

Iya said, "A teacher in research methods class once assigned two groups of her undergraduate students to go to a shopping mall to conduct research on why people buy what they buy. A group of students followed their teacher's injunction and went straight to the mall after class to complete the assignment. Another group of students decided to take their time to first write a series of surveys and interview questions targeting a specific population and sample customers in a specific shopping mall. They carefully designed their research with structured closed-ended questions for survey and open-ended questions for interviews and data collection. In what they called their research proposal, the second group of students explained the purpose of their research and its rationale. The following day, they submitted their proposal to their teacher for feedback during her office hours. The teacher eagerly looked at it and gave them some constructive feedback for improving their research design. They decided to use their research proposal to go collect their data for the assignment.

"A week later, both groups were due to present the results of their assignment. The first group came in front of the class. All members of the group were grumpy and had a series of complaints. They found the assignment was too difficult. They did not know what questions to ask, how to ask them, and who to select for interviewing. They could not even agree on which shopping mall to select. They did not know why the teacher was asking them to complete such an assignment. In their opinion, the assignment had no connection to the course. As a result, they came up with no substantial written results. They all put the blame on their teacher.

"Following their presentation, the second group of students came to the podium with smiles on their faces. They looked confident and relaxed. They clearly presented their research questions, their interview questions, their survey questionnaire, the population, a sample of their research, the ethical concerns about the data collection, their techniques for data analysis, the findings of their research, and the limitations of their research as explained in the course syllabus and lectures, and as articulated in their research proposal. They did so to the applause of the entire class. The teacher congratulated them and asked the members of the group how they managed to do so well.

"A group member raised her voice and said, 'We had a research proposal and a clear plan for action as you explained in the lectures.' The other members agreed.

"The teacher turned to the first group and asked, 'Why did you encounter all the problems you indicated?'

"They said, 'We did not have a written proposal; we did not have any plan for action.'

"A member of the group added, 'We thought we could just do it without planning; it looked so easy firsthand.'

"The teacher concluded, 'I am glad you all learned your lesson. Regardless of how smart you are or what you think, you ought to always plan your research before conducting it.'"

Iya explained what is planning, its advantages, and its implications to Suru. "Planning is about using one's imagination to anticipate and formulate activities, tasks, or goals before implementing or achieving them. Whatever activities, tasks, or goals your imagination anticipates and formulates must translate into a design or a project, which is also called a plan. A plan calls for actions and actualization to materialize into a tangible reality that fulfills the initial dream or ambition of imagination. Life is all about and around planning. To be happy, we ought to always remember then and now for the future. Planning allows you to empty or free your mind by dumping out all you have to do. Planning makes you record all you have to do on another support besides your memory. It records them on paper or on an electronic support. Doing so lowers your stress level and ultimately grants you some peace of mind and heart. Consistent planning reduces your stress by allowing you to remember now and then for the future. In that process, planning tends to make you not worry to some extent. It has the potential to exhume worries and distasteful surprises from life. It makes life relaxed and happy to some degree."

Baba asked if Suru and Femi understood everything their mother meant.

Suru's answer to his father's question was a very quick no. Suru wanted Iya's explanations to be more practical. "Why do we forget our plans sometimes? Why did I forget our plan to go the beach?"

Femi said, "How do we make sure we do not forget our plans?"

Iya smiled and took a deep breath. "That is interesting, children! Your questions are very relevant! Our memory forgets certain things to be able to remember others; due to its limited storage ability, our memory every once in a while releases or gets rid of old items to make room for new items. Human plans can mentally evaporate when our memory cleans up to make room for new items. To maximize our chances of remembering our plans, we should write them down on a daily planner."

Baba smiled when Iya came up with the notion of a planner.

Femi also looked content, but things were not so clear to Suru. He was tempted to ask a question about human memory. Human memory seemed mysterious in the way it operated. He thought our memories would have enough room to save old items somewhere or somehow. He was eager to hear more about the advantages of a planner.

Suru asked Iya to tell him more about the benefits of having a daily planner.

She said, "A planner is a mini calendar in the form of a booklet. It is designed with dated pages, with space for listing your daily activities ahead of time. A daily planner allows you to schedule your tasks and appointments in advance and to anticipate how you spend time and pace your activities. A planner helps you remember your plans, and it contributes to reducing the level of stress in your life. When planning, write down whatever thoughts come to your mind right away. In doing so, you liberate your mind and feel relaxed." Iya stopped her speculation on planning at the sound of the ocean. Her family reached their destination: a popular sandy beach.

They all jumped happily into the water.

Baba urged caution.

Iya reminded Suru he was not good at swimming.

After only a few minutes, Suru quickly got out of the sea, and everybody followed suit. The family sat under a shady coconut tree. Suru could see his father's chest going up and down. Baba explained he was inhaling and exhaling the marine air. Baba would often do it for fun—even at home.

Suru asked Baba whether there were other reasons why he did so.

Iya explained that the marine air was very healthy for the body and mind.

Suru's father smiled and said she read his mind and gave Suru the right answer. Baba had no further comments to add.

Suru decided to imitate his father by inhaling the marine air. He did not regret doing so. It felt so good. After a few minutes of breathing, Suru felt relaxed and happy. He smiled and giggled as he reported his sentiment to his mother.

Iya explained to Suru that elation was the ultimate goal of their visit to the beach. Everyone needed to feel relaxed and happy. Iya beseeched Suru to keep on doing what he was doing with his father. Suru's mother stepped away with Femi.

Suru enjoyed the occasion for some time, but it did not last. An enormous fishing boat pulled up on the beach with a successful catch. A fisherman was counting the fish inside the boat. Two others were washing the nets.

Baba drew near the fishermen to congratulate them on their catch.

Suru admired how the fishermen were happily devoted to cleaning their nets.

Baba and Suru decided to join a group of people playing beach volleyball. Suru's father often played or watched volleyball. Suru also enjoyed playing and watching volleyball. They laughed and giggled as the ball went up and down and the players collided. They were having fun until when one player accidently got hit in the eye by another player. The victim collapsed, and the other players stopped playing to attend to the victim.

The game eventually resumed after a long break, but the victim quit. Suru quit too because he did not want to be the next victim. He watched from the sideline.

Baba resumed playing with the group, and Suru could tell Baba was having one of his best days. Baba knew how to have fun, and he knew how to work hard. Suru's father worked hard to take care of his family. As Suru kept watching the happy players, he soon started getting impatient. The game would not end, and it was taking longer than he thought.

Suru made up his mind to join his mother and his sister. Baba followed his son instantly.

Iya and Femi were watching the movements of the waves. They were so focused that they did not even know Baba and Suru were standing right behind them.

Suru's feet were close to his mother's back. His father told him to move them back to avoid his knees touching her. In the process of moving his legs back, Suru's knees touched Iya.

Iya screamed and turned around, and Femi jumped up.

Baba and Suru immediately apologized for scaring them.

Iya explained how beautiful it was to watch the waves. "You watch them dance to their own music, you feel their emotions, you sense their happiness, and you feel relaxed and happy in the process."

Iya sat back and encouraged her son to sit down next to her and contemplate the waves for a moment. Suru obeyed, and it was a wonderful exercise. The waves were beautiful and majestic. Their performance was outstanding and entertaining. In the process, Suru felt sleepy.

Femi clapped to wake him up and distracted everybody else.

Baba asked his daughter why she was clapping.

Femi said she intended to wake Suru up.

Iya said, "No, she was clapping for the waves."

Everybody laughed.

Iya said, "I mean it. Don't they deserve some cheers for their outstanding performance in entertaining us?"

Suru agreed with his mother.

They all laughed again and cheered for the waves. The scene was magical and relaxing.

They were some distance away when Suru saw a small crab crawling by. He decided to chase and catch it for fun. The crab was fast and unwilling to play, but Suru managed to catch it. He was having fun playing with its eyes, legs, and pincers. He was unaware the decapod was not having fun. Probably frustrated with that game, the crab pinched Suru's thumb with its pincers. He screamed and threw the animal away. It was such a painful bite.

Suru's screaming alerted Iya and Baba, and they came to his rescue. Iya looked at the wound on her son's finger with compassion and dressed it carefully. The look on her face echoed all the warnings she had given Suru about playing with crabs. She had warned Suru that playing with crabs was a risky game, but Suru never listened. At that very moment Suru became mindful of Iya's lesson on listening. He wished he had listened to his mother. He saw the incident as a golden opportunity to stop playing with crabs. It was not fun at all.

The family watched the crab running away. The little sea creature seemed happy to recover its freedom. Who would not be happy in such circumstances? I would certainly be happy to recover my freedom after a period of captivity. The little beast ran away excitedly to find refuge first in a hole and later in the ocean.

Suru learned his lesson the hard way. You do not force anything or anybody into a game they do not want to play. In the end, they might reward you with a slap in the face or a glass of a bitter and toxic potion. It was a meaningful lesson.

The pain from the crab bite was memorable. Suru did not sustain many injuries. He could count how many times he had sustained an injury of that intensity. The pain took him back to two other accidents. The first accident occurred with a swing set. Growing up, Suru enjoyed swinging. His family had a swing set in their backyard. It hung from ropes attached to a branch of the quinine tree. His parents thought that branch was strong.

One day, Suru was having fun swinging backward and forward. Unexpectedly, the branch broke. Suru fell on gravel and concrete. He did not knock his head against anything, but he sustained some injuries on his legs. He felt the pain and cried out.

Baba heard Suru's scream, grabbed his son, and took care of his wounds.

Suru reflected on what had happened. *In existence, things can quickly switch at any moment in directions you are not expecting. We can plan and try to predict the next second of our existence, but we can never fully control it or account for everything.*

The second accident was with his father's bicycle. As a child, Suru learned to ride a bicycle on his father's nice green bicycle. Baba was very protective of that bicycle. He did not tolerate anyone touching that bicycle, but every once in a while, Suru would defy his father's order. Suru would get the bicycle out and learn to how to ride it with the help of a few friends in the neighborhood. Every time he tried, the experience would go well and safely.

Finally came that day of bad luck. Suru was riding the bicycle by their house and fell down. Fortunately, there were no cars, motorcycles, or other bicycles running by at that time. It was a bad fall. Suru went down abruptly on his right knee. The right pedal scorched his knee. Suru screamed and cried out for help, but nobody showed up.

Most of the neighbors were absent or busy.

Iya was not able to hear her son from the kitchen.

Suru managed to get up and dragged the bicycle home.

As soon as Iya saw Suru crying, she stopped making lunch and took care of him. She was not pleased with Suru's behavior, but she took care of his wounds and addressed his needs. Iya felt bad for Suru. The bicycle did not sustain any damage, but Suru was in tears. He knew he was in trouble for defying his father's order.

Baba was not happy with the news. He was unhappy with Suru's behavior. He scolded his son and took away his toys for more than a week. Suru did not mind his father hiding his toys. He was expecting a worse punishment for his stupid behavior. Perhaps Iya asked Baba to forgive Suru. She often did so to get her son out of trouble. Baba probably felt sorry for Suru.

A few years later, Baba was riding his bicycle to work. He was having a nice ride on a breezy morning. For the most part, his ride went through peaceful traffic. When he got close to his workplace, an enormous commercial truck was coming in the opposite direction. It began to zigzag, and Baba had no time to escape.

He feared for his life and contemplated death. Right before the big truck struck him, Baba felt a glamorous light on his face. In a fraction of second, it turned into a solar eclipse. He felt lethargic, but he did not pass out. The whole scene slipped by like a shooting star.

Baba woke up behind bushes. He was unharmed, but the news about his bicycle was not so good. The bicycle was completely destroyed. Nobody understood how Baba was projected so far away. It was a miracle. At the scene of the accident, all the vehicles stopped. Bystanders searched under the truck, but no body was found.

Baba waved his hand from behind the bushes.

Everyone, including the truck driver, rushed over to him.

Kini, one of Baba's relatives, happened to be among the crowd of spectators. The accident forced him to stop. He recognized the bicycle and Suru's father. Baba also spotted Kini in the crowd, smiled, and gave thanks to God for saving his life. There was not a scratch on Baba's skin, and there were no broken bones or damages to his vital organs. His shirt and trousers were not torn. It was unbelievable. It was a miracle. It was a mystery.

Nobody, not even Baba himself, could explain how he was projected into the bush. Some bystanders started giving credit to Baba's magic. Suru's father explained that he was not a magician. He was wearing a rosary and invited everyone to join him in giving credit to God for sparing his life.

That morning, before leaving home, Baba prayed to entrust his life and day to the divine protection. Baba would spend long periods in prayer every morning before going to work. He was right in giving God credit for sparing his life on that day of misfortune. His family later joined him in thanksgiving.

Unless you witnessed the facts, you would think the whole story was a hoax, but it was real. It all happened to Suru's father as narrated here.

***

Suru believes in miracles. He believes in mysteries as much as he believes in science. There are things in existence you cannot or may not fully understand. Science cannot explain everything in existence here and now, but this does not mean science will not eventually be able to explain them in the future.

There were times in human history where people could not understand the earth was rotating around the sun; they thought it was the other way around. Today, we take it for granted that our planet spins around the sun. Moreover, there was a time in our history when human beings could hardly anticipate Facebook, Google, and Twitter. YouTube hosts tons of videos, and we take social media for granted.

Human history has also recorded periods when there were no vaccines or medications to counter HIV, hepatitis B, or hepatitis C. Science has made discoveries to counter many diseases and infections. We now have vaccines. We also have good news for HIV and hepatitis patients. Mysteries represent a highly fecund ground for science. The existence of mysteries provides a springboard for scientific curiosity and discovery. Paranormal phenomena can be reality because reality is very complex. Reality is far beyond what our eyes can see and what our reason can immediately grasp. Human reason ought to be humble and patient. Reason ought to believe.

***

As if the incident with the crab was not enough, Suru had another incident a few minutes later on the beach. He decided to focus on flying his kite. As a child, Suru enjoyed flying kites. He was doing it for fun. Flying kites was fun and one of his cheapest games. Suru's parents did not have to buy him anything to make a kite. Suru learned how to design and make a kite with cheap materials. He used empty plastic bags and other useless items. The only item Suru would buy was the thread. It was cheap, and his small savings was enough to purchase one from a nearby retail store. A kite was easy to assemble. Suru enjoyed putting a kite together, and he often made them.

As his kites flied high in the sky, so did his mind. Suru's mind would often fly very high with his kites. It felt as if his mind were on a vacation whenever he piloted a kite. Every time Suru went to the beach, he would fly his kite. He would not go to the beach without a kite.

After his painful interaction with the crab, the wound on his thumb did not deter him from flying his kite. He briefly thought his hand might not be able to operate the kite, but his right hand was operational. That was enough to fly his kite. It all started well. Suru watched his kite flying high. It was a wonderful moment, but Suru's mind was flying high with his kite.

Suru kept walking backward without checking what was behind him. He did not realize there was a small cactus behind him. He accidently stepped on it and screamed loudly. He released his kite instantaneously. Suru thought something was very wrong with him that day. It was as if he was cursed.

Suru felt like he was set up to keep falling in traps. It was a bad day for him.

Iya and Baba did not take long to remove the cactus from their son's foot.

Suru decided to be quiet and stick around. He did not want to continue to be a victim of the endless traps. He had learned another existential lesson about safety. Safety requires remaining focused and cautious. We should be focused without neglecting to be careful. Being focused should not prevent you from being careful. Your focus should not serve as a scapegoat to justify a lack of caution. To a large extent, your safety relies on the cohabitation of focus and caution in your conduct. We have the potential to remain focused and careful at the same time. Such potential is easily displayed in safe driving. Safe drivers are focused on the road and careful with traffic.

On their way home, Suru got close to his mother. As they walked side by side, Suru asked that Iya continue their discussion on planning.

Iya asked Suru to remind her where they stopped.

Suru indicated that his mother was talking about what a planner was.

Iya said, "Well done, my son! A planner could help you always remember then and now for the future. With a planner, planning becomes easy and practical. In practice, planning requires thinking ahead about the details of your activities and actions. For instance, before you go to the beach, you think of it ahead of time and schedule it. That is planning. Before going to do grocery shopping, you think ahead of time about what you need to buy and can afford. Ideally, you make a list of the items you need. Doing so will help you avoid exceeding your budget or wasting money. Doing so will help you buy what you really need. You should learn to stick to your plans except in cases of extreme emergency or life-threatening situations. Be flexible as long as flexibility does not shoulder stress for your life. Stressful situations trigger conflict with the self and with others. Stress makes ego conflict with the self and with the alter ego. A self that is stressed out can get sick, anxious, depressed, irritated, angry, and violent. Be open to making changes to your plans if such changes do not jeopardize your peace of mind and heart and others' peace. It is in our interest to plan everything. Daily life experience teaches you that planning is likely to bring you more peace of heart and mind. Take pride in planning your life in the present and the future. Planning allows you to take control of your present and your future. Life should be about planning before doing."

That was quite a lesson from Iya. It was a lot for Suru to think about. Once they got home, Suru spent the evening thinking about his mother's thoughts on planning. Her thoughts eventually opened Suru's eyes to critical questions about his identity and his future. That night, Suru had his first epiphany about his future vocation.

Inspired and resolved by Iya's lesson on planning, Suru made up his mind to plan his future and his existence. As the years passed, the most urgent thing for Suru was understanding what he was called to become. He wanted to become a teacher and peacemaker. He was not sure why. He knew he was full of admiration for his mother's disposition and strategies. He saw Iya as a great teacher and peacemaker. Suru enjoyed how his mother was teaching him peacemaking.

Suru's mother was inspiring him, but he started feeling like he was made to become a teacher and peacemaker. Everything would start falling in place to help Suru achieve his vocation. Providence was sending positive energies to drive Suru in the right directions and prepare him for the service of teaching peacemaking. Providence organized everything on Suru's behalf and for his sake. The training was a long process under his mother's supervision and under the divine leadership.

Suru grew up and developed in body and spirit.

Iya slowly guided him to push his way up to his vocation. She guided his steps into the path of happiness by providing Suru with pillars of life as the years passed.

CHAPTER 5

Eating and Drinking Healthy or Tasty

Upon returning home from the beach, Iya denied herself a well-deserved break. Following the long walk, they all sat in the living room to rest before dinner. Iya went straight to the kitchen to get dinner ready. It was about four o'clock, and they were all hungry.

Baba suggested that they order dinner from a restaurant because it was getting late, but Iya objected sharply. She had years of cooking experience. Iya's objection did not surprise any of them. No matter the circumstances, Suru's mother would prefer to cook fresh food than order from a restaurant. Her rationale was simple but meaningful. "Anyone who cooks knows exactly what is in the food they cook, but you are not so sure what is in the food you order from a restaurant. What goes in your food is what goes in your body. When you know what goes in your food, you also know what goes in your body—and you have peace of heart and mind. Homemade food is usually healthier than restaurant-made food. Restaurant-made food might be tasty, but it is not necessarily healthy for the body. In addition, homemade food is cheaper than restaurant-made. Homemade food allows everyone to stay healthy and save money. For those reasons, homemade food is better."

Suru's mother would always go for homemade food. She would often challenge her husband to stop both spending his money on eating outside and running the risk of getting sick at the same time.

Baba took Iya's challenge seriously. He was mindful of what his wife meant. He knew Iya was right, yet he would escape every once in a while to eat in a restaurant. It was mainly due his work schedule and location. The few times Suru snuck out with his father to eat in a restaurant, the food tasted good. Suru appreciated it. Baba and his son agreed on that.

Iya was never happy with that when she became aware of it. She would kindly remind Baba and Suru that the amount of salt was what made the food from the restaurant taste the way it tasted, and too much salt intake was not good for their health.

Suru's father often felt the impact on his health. When he ate in a restaurant, his blood pressure would go up. His heart would beat fast. The food in the restaurant was high in sodium. The food from Iya's kitchen was much lower in sodium. She was stingy with how much salt she put in their food.

In his adult life, Suru got caught in the trap of eating breakfasts that were loaded with salt and sugar. Following his salty and sugary breakfast, Suru's days were miserable to say the least. He felt heavy, lazy, tired, and constipated. By ten thirty, he would start feeling sleepy at work. His abdomen was growing, and he was feeling frequent pains in his chest. Suru panicked and went to check his heart. The medical exams revealed everything was normal. He did not have high cholesterol or high blood pressure.

Suru decided to surrender to a series of self-examinations over his eating habits. He remained mindful of Iya's tips on barely eating salt and sugar throughout the process. His breakfast was the only food in his diet with too much salt and sugar. Lunch and dinner were low in salt and very healthy. His tiredness and chest pains would start about four hours after breakfast.

Suru's self-examinations led him to a clear conclusion. His salty and sweet breakfast was the source of his health problems. He decided to change his breakfast habits. He started eating a breakfast that was full of fiber with barely sugar and salt. His body felt the change, and his health responded immediately. He started feeling light and lively. His constipation problems dissipated. His abdominal six-pack slowly returned. The pains vanished from his chest. Suru was quite awake and felt energy throughout the morning. The quality of his life improved drastically. His days were happier. Suru knew that too much sugar or salt was not good for him. Too much salt or sugar is certainly not good for you either, dear reader!

As they waited for dinner, Baba entertained his family with funny stories. He was very good at telling jokes and funny stories. His stories always made them laugh and giggle. Suru's father would make them laugh regardless of their mood, but that evening, Suru was paying less attention to Baba's stories. Instead, Suru's attention was directed toward his mother's moves in the kitchen.

As Iya checked around her kitchen, Suru watched her with admiration. Suru thought his mother was looking for the right-sized pots and pans to boil rice and beans.

Iya opened the kitchen cupboard, and Suru saw a series of containers of spices. Suru wondered why there were so many spices in the cupboard. He had no idea about the importance of the spices in the cupboard. He only knew they were all for cooking. Suru enjoyed cooking and learned from his mother at an early age.

Suru also enjoyed eating, and he often thought that anyone who enjoyed eating should also learn how to cook. You are better off knowing how to cook what you love eating. Chances are you will often get what you enjoy eating.

Suru stood by his mother, and Iya put her hand on her son's shoulder and explained that she was missing so many ingredients for dinner. It was too late to get fresh vegetables from the local market. Iya would go to the market to buy the ingredients she needed.

Suru offered to go with his mother to keep her company, and Iya welcomed her son's offer. She was fully aware of how hungry everyone was. She warmed up some leftover food and served it for dinner. It was some rice and collard greens with bitter leaves and smoked fish.

Suru was not very excited about eating that for dinner. He expressed his discontent to his mother as they sat down to eat. Suru grew up eating a lot of collard greens, spinach, and other leaves. Besides, he ate okra quite a lot.

Iya would cook all those green vegetables several times a week. They had leaves for almost every meal: in the morning, at noon, and in the evening. Suru's mother would either steam them as a soup with spices and fish or fry them. The food from Iya's kitchen tasted delicious, but it was not so delicious when it was Baba's turn to cook. Suru's father would just boil it all without much seasoning.

Suru got tired of eating such green leaves every day, and he voiced his feelings about it to his mother.

Iya made a note of her son's complaint, but she promised Suru that she would address his complaint on their way to the market. Suru ate dinner reluctantly that evening. He was hungry and had no other option.

After dinner, Iya and Suru walked to the market. The market was located in a rural area, in the vicinity of a bushy zone, about twenty-five minutes away from their house. Suru and his mother had to walk past some cassava, corn, and sugarcane fields. Suru watched the farmers harvesting corn. They removed the husks and bagged the kernels. Suru marveled at how much corn one seed could produce. One being hosts the potential to become many. That observation seems relevant to every living being.

Suru and Iya encountered a black plastic bag that kept jumping up and down much. He had never seen anything like it before. It was unusual and scary. He ran away and told Iya to run for her life, but she did not move. Instead, Iya shook her head in disbelief. Iya could not believe Suru was so scared of a tiny plastic bag. She told her son to keep calm.

Suru found his mother's reaction strange and cautioned her to be careful.

Iya told him she was not always careful.

Suru thought about it. His mother was right. Later, Suru's philosophy classes would allow him to understand this even better. Human beings can neither be always nor perfectly careful. They would fail to be careful at times because they forget. Forgetting is vital to human existence. We ought to forget certain things to be able to remember others. If we do not forget, we cannot remember. We ought to forget in order to be mentally sane. If we do not forget, we get sick and lose our minds.

Suru's mother got closer and closer to the jumping bag. She reached out to a long dry baton on the ground and lifted the bag.

To Suru's surprise, their neighbor's black cat was under the bag.

Iya looked at Suru again, and he stopped trembling.

His mother laughed at him, and Suru thought Iya was right to laugh at him. Suru was ashamed that a small cat could scare the hell out of him. He asked his mother how she knew it was a cat under the plastic bag.

Iya explained how the cat was fond of snatching plastic bags and playing with them. The cat would get inside the bags and risk suffocation. It would get scared and start hopping up and down.

Suru listened to Iya in disbelief. He thought only a crazy cat could act in such a way. He managed to move past that thought, and they resumed their walk toward the market.

Their neighbor emerged from the woods with her dog. Fati looked like she was running away from danger. She looked worried and out of breath. Suru was ready to run away, but his mother held his hand tight.

Iya asked Fati if she needed help. Before Iya could finish asking, Fati explained that she was deep inside the woods. She overheard Suru's alert to run for her life. She thought she was in danger and started running. She realized her cat was putting on a show and slowed down. Fati witnessed part of Iya's intervention with her cat. She paused for a moment to express her gratitude and show her appreciation of Iya's act of kindness.

She told Suru and his mother a story about the rivalries between her cat and dog. The cat was often jealous of the dog and vice versa. She often had to address rivalries between the two animals. That evening, she decided to walk her dog. Her cat decided to follow them for some reason. As they walked past the woods, the cat and dog started fighting.

In an attempt to stop the fighting, she decided to isolate the dog in the woods for a few minutes. She wanted to use the opportunity to allow the dog to take care of some basic physiological needs. Fati was not afraid to leave the cat alone. The cat knew its way around and was not running any risk of harm. Fati's house was around the corner. The neighborhood had a reputation for being friendly and safe.

Fati was attending to the needs of her dog when the cat found its way into a plastic bag. Suru's neighborhood had no gun violence, shootings, or stabbings. There was not much stealing either, but it was not the most salubrious neighborhood to live in. It was dirty. People urinated in every corner. Loose pigs wandered around and ate human excrement. Dogs competed with the pigs to snatch feces as soon as they became available on the ground. Most of the dogs were not getting enough leftovers from their masters' tables. As a result, they would break their chains and rush out to eat human feces to survive. It was not uncommon to spot underprivileged children and adults trying to hide behind bushes to move their bowels. There were no laws or policies regulating or prohibiting such nasty behaviors. If there were any of such laws or policies, poverty did not foster their enforcement or implementation.

In general, Suru's neighborhood had tremendous issues with waste management. With no reliable system of garbage collection, garbage bags were thrown around or dumped in corners. People would put trashes in public areas. There were no trash cans. Littering was not a crime; it was not fined. No one was fined or punished for such behaviors.

Neighbors would neglect or ignore most health initiatives and campaigns. The pigs were later slaughtered for pork chops or ribs—much to the taste and enjoyment of the impoverished local people. What existential contradictions! Suru and his parents felt consoled to live in a neighborhood with low crime rates. You cannot get everything in existence. In life, you get certain things and not others.

Suru and Iya were speechless as they listened to Fati's story. Iya felt bad for Fati and her stubborn cat. She indicated to Fati that pets always need our help, just like children. Iya stared at Suru with a smile. Iya's eyes and Suru's crossed, and he understood what she meant. Iya implied that Suru was as stubborn as that crazy cat. Suru admitted he was stubborn, but he could only hope he was not crazy.

Fati walked with Iya and Suru in the direction of the marketplace.

Her house was on their way to the market. Once they reached her house, she rushed her cat and dog home to her husband and walked with Suru and Iya to the market. Suru thought Fati intended to purchase a few items from the market, but it turned out she wanted to keep Iya company. It felt like it was Fati's way of showing Iya gratitude for saving her cat.

Fati updated Suru's mother on everything happening in the neighborhood. Apparently, she had a lot to update Iya on. Fati just kept talking. Every once in a while, Iya would get a chance to respond to Fati.

Suru did not have any opportunity to breathe a word. And he was not so happy because he had a lot of questions for Iya and Fati.

Iya noticed her son was not happy but did not interrupt Fati until they got close to the market. Iya slowed down, looked up in the sky, and invited Fati and Suru to do the same thing.

They all stopped and looked up at the sky. Iya did not say anything else for a few minutes. Four eagles were flying high and having fun in the sky. Iya calmly stopped for a while and watched the four eagles in amazement.

Suru was surprised by his mother's attitude. He thought Iya was in a hurry to get to the market and get back before sunset. She was taking time to watch birds.

Iya assured Suru that she experienced peace of mind and heart every time she watched the eagles. Watching the eagles was therapeutic.

Fati agreed with Iya.

Suru had no idea what his mother was talking about, but he refrained from asking Iya about it. Suru was trying to save time. He could not wait to reach the market.

Iya had the same attitude when she watched a rainbow. Iya's mind and heart were flattered by the harmony of the majestic mosaic of colors.

Suru had no time to waste in asking his mother about her admiration of the eagles.

Iya, Fati, and Suru walked through the thickest part of the forest. The market was on the other side of the forest.

Suru's eyes fell in love with the dancing leaves on top of the happy trees. The leaves were dancing to the rhythm of a refreshing breeze. Suru wondered how such leaves could be so green and healthy when nobody watered them.

Fati smiled and admired what she called Suru's curiosity. She indicated that God was the gardener who was taking care of them day and night. God watered the trees with seasonal rains and massaged them with delicate touches of life-bearing breezes.

Suru's mother welcomed and appreciated Fati's input. She said, "Nature takes care of all things in the same way it takes care of human beings."

Suru did not understand what his mother meant, but his classes in ecology, biology, psychology, geography, zoology, ethnography, anthropology, philosophy, and theology would allow him to understand the message later on. Nature, indeed, takes care of everything that is part of it and everything that nature is part of. Science and all academic disciplines largely contribute to explaining that hypothesis.

As they kept walking, Suru's ears became fond of the symphony of singing birds. He felt as if flocks of birds were orchestrating a harmonious choir for their entertainment. Suru thought the scene was so timely. He was nearly dancing to the music. It felt good and peaceful. Suru looked at his mother's eyes and knew they were on the same page.

Iya almost felt the same way. They experienced nearly the same emotions while listening to the birds.

Suru asked whether the birds attended a music academy.

His mother shook her head.

Suru asked how they became so good at singing.

Iya explained that the birds were only following their natural instinct.

Suru wondered what his mother meant.

Iya depicted an instinct as an aptitude.

Suru was not satisfied with his mother's answer and asked her to tell him what she meant.

Iya looked at her son and whispered that he would learn more about instinct in his classes in philosophy.

Suru did learn a lot more about instinct as a powerful innate disposition to behave in a certain way. Nature generously empowered all living beings with instinct.

At the market, Iya, Fati, and Suru saw a big boy bullying a little girl. A few bystanders watched in silence.

A few boys were supportive of the big boy and were laughing at the girl.

The girl was crying, but her tears did not deter her bully. Instead, the bullying cycle escalated to more offensive words.

Suru's mother stepped in and commanded respect. Iya was beloved.

Suru was impressed by the silence his mother's arrival brought to the setting. It looked as if everybody on the scene knew who she was. Iya called out the boy by his name, asking him to stop bullying her. The boy's name was Lola. Suru wondered how Iya knew Lola by name. Lola politely followed Iya's order and calmed down.

Suru's mother asked the two parties what the issue was and invited both parties to listen to each other. The girl's name was Bintou. She was carrying bananas, mangoes, avocados, and papayas on a large tray. Bintou was walking around and trying to sell the fruit. As she was walking around in the market, one of her papayas fell from the tray. Lola offered to help Bintou pick up the papaya, but Bintou refused Lola's offer. Lola got frustrated and assumed Bintou had refused his offer to help because she thought his hands were dirty. Out of frustration, Lola became verbally aggressive toward Bintou with all types of nasty insults.

Bintou never mentioned Lola's hands being dirty.

After Iya clarified the issues with both parties, Lola ended up understanding the motivation behind Bintou's attitude. Bintou did not want Lola to touch the papaya for other reasons that had not much to do with dirty hands. Bintou's parents had told her to avoid too many hands touching the papayas. Apparently, the papayas were too ripe. Too much touching was not good for them. It would make them too soft, and customers might not want to buy them. Bintou was merely following her parents' advice.

Lola concluded there was nothing wrong with following parents' advice. He knew Bintou was doing the right thing in obeying her parents. Lola immediately turned toward Bintou and told her he was sorry.

Iya, Suru, Fati, and other witnesses felt satisfied with Lola's apology. Bintou sad face became shiny and happy. She leaned forward to express her appreciation and gratitude to Suru's mother for her intervention. Lola respectfully thanked Iya for intervening.

Iya asked Lola how his mother was doing. Suru was not expecting that because he was not aware that Iya knew Lola's mother. Lola indicated that his mother's condition was improving. Iya made sure she sent her thoughts and prayers to Lola's mother.

Lola was in the market to sell tomatoes, onions, fresh garlic and ginger, oranges, watermelons, and pineapples on behalf of his mother. He pointed in the direction of the counter where his fruits were as an invitation to take a look at his produce.

Iya knew Lola and his parents well, and Lola knew Iya very well. Lola's mother, Yemi, was one of Iya's customers. Under normal circumstances, Lola would be in the market with Yemi. Unfortunately, Yemi was sick with typhoid and was recovering slowly. Iya knew Lola was obedient to his parents.

Suru, Iya, and Fati looked at Lola's produce in the large bamboo baskets. Iya bought tomatoes, fresh garlic, ginger, onions, and oranges. Iya also bought some papayas and avocado from Bintou.

Fati took a leaf from Iya's book by purchasing some mangoes and bananas from Bintou and some pineapple and watermelon from Lola. Iya and Fati acted so beautifully.

Bintou and Lola smiled and were visibly overjoyed.

The people who witnessed the scene were amazed at Iya's intervention. The news of her intervention quickly spread around the neighborhood.

As they moved away, Fati kept wondering how such a respectful boy could be bullying. She was shocked to witness the contradictions and could not believe it.

Iya leaned toward her and whispered that the condition of Lola's mother was certainly a factor in to his aggressive behavior. His mother's illness could potentially make him vulnerable.

Fati agreed that Lola was going through a lot with his mother's sickness. The tough time at home was spilling over into his social environment. In that process, innocent people like Bintou became Lola's victims.

Suru noticed a group of boys playing catch and throw with a black and white ball. Another group of children was playing hide-and-seek. Hide-and-seek was one of Suru's favorite game. He wanted to play with them, but he was not ready to step away from his mother in the crowded marketplace.

Iya moved on to another counter to purchase freshly cut cassava leaves, bean leaves, bitter leaves, eggplant, and okra. In addition to the green leaves, there were baskets of green and yellow plantains, bunches of sugarcane, baskets of freshly harvested nuts, and buckets of cassavas and yams.

As Iya was paying for the produce, Suru noticed a farmer waving at them. He thought that farmer was trying to get their attention to come and check out some of his vegetables. The man was standing next to baskets of green breadfruits and potatoes, but before Suru could let Iya know, Fati quickly walked over to the farmer. They happily gave each other big hugs. It turned out the farmer was Fati's cherished brother. His name was Tunde.

Suru and his mother joined Fati and Tunde as they talked and giggled.

Iya mentioned that Fati was lucky to have a farmer in her family.

Fati agreed that she was lucky to have a farmer—and a good one—and complimented Tunde on his devotion to farming.

Tunde appreciated Fati's compliments.

After she introduced Iya and Suru to Tunde, Fati updated him about her cat.

Tunde loved that cat dearly. In appreciation to Iya's act of kindness, he loaded a plastic bag with cucumber, carrots, green beans, red, yellow, and green peppers, and radishes and cabbages. He also put some potatoes, green breadfruits, and fresh corn in another bag. He handed the bag to Iya and gave the other bag to Suru. Tunde didn't ask for any money in return.

It felt like a miracle or a dream to Suru, but it was not a dream. It was reality.

Fati said she was not surprised. Her brother had acted in such a kind way on several occasions toward other friends in her presence. Tunde's harvest was, in general, abundant with blessings.

Suru and his mother thanked Tunde enthusiastically. As they were saying goodbye, they noticed eight people heading toward Tunde's counter.

The generous farmer welcome his new clients, and they bought a lot of vegetables from him. His counter was nearly empty after their purchases.

Tunde would later confess to Fati that Iya's stop by his counter brought him some luck. Business had not been booming that morning. He gave so many vegetables to Suru's mother in part because he did not want to carry it home after the market closed. Tunde's act of kindness toward Iya and Suru resulted in a blessing for them and for him.

The two bags of produce would increase the load they had to carry home. Considering the distance, Suru was not willing to carry such a heavy load.

Iya lifted up each bag and suggested the bags were not too heavy. The bags might not be too heavy for Iya, yet Suru felt they were outnumbered by the bags. They were only two people to carry five bags. Suru suggested that they transfer or put some products together in the same bag, but Iya did not want to mix certain vegetables for reasons that Suru did not find convincing.

Iya thought some of the vegetables would crush others in the same bag. Suru's mother did not want to promote the rule of the jungle inside the bags.

Suru knew it was easy for Iya to handle two or three bags over a long distance. His mother had done it more than once, but he was not ready to carry more than one bag. He was still wondering how they would handle all the bags when Fati offered to help carry one bag. The puzzle was solved. Iya grabbed three of the bags, Fati snatched the bag of vegetables, and Suru got the bag filled with potatoes, breadfruits, and fresh corn.

While Tunde was loading the bags, Suru had noticed some colorful baskets on his counter. The baskets were filled with cucumbers, carrots, and radishes. Other baskets were full of green beans, collard greens, purple cabbages and eggplant. Other baskets hosted green peppers yellow peppers, red peppers, and tomatoes. Suru saw white and brown mushrooms next to red beets and yellow squashes. He could not refrain from expressing his admiration of the colorful baskets.

Iya seized the occasion to lecture Suru with some existential lessons about eating colorful and healthy. Suru listened to his mother carefully and digested her words. "The human digestive system appreciates colorful food in the same manner your eyes admired the colorful baskets of vegetables. Nature provides the colors to make human existence enjoyable and healthy. The green, the red, the yellow, the orange, the purple, and the orange ought to be combined or blended for a healthy lifestyle. Like the rainbow, a colorful meal is attractive and creates harmony. A colorful breakfast, lunch, or dinner appeases the mind and the heart with healthy and lifesaving reflections of natural colors. Eating colorfully is vital to our health."

After his joyous and meaningful contemplation of the colorful vegetables, Suru felt some peace of heart and mind. He felt calm and ready to head home.

Iya, Fati, and Suru left the market happily at six thirty. Their hands were full. Suru's mother did not hide her satisfaction.

Suru saw a black snake crossing the path. It did not surprise any of them. Suru stopped unexpectedly and froze. He had never liked snakes. He was always scared of them. They allowed the ugly beast to escape from their sight before they proceeded.

Fati suggested trying to kill the snake. She explained that the snake would be dead if her husband were around. Daouda was fond of killing snakes. She thought snakes were not good for human environments.

Suru quickly agreed with her. He also sided with her on the urgency of killing snakes, but Iya disagreed with Fati and Suru sharply. Suru's mother suggested that snakes play some role in the balance of the environment. She advocated protecting them just like Fati's cat.

Iya's analogy took Fati's breath away and made her giggle.

Environmentalists would certainly be happy to hear Iya's point, but that did not impress her son. Suru expressed some reservations about his mother's opinion. He doubted Iya's point was relevant. It sounded completely irrelevant in his small head. Suru could not share his mother's viewpoint because he thought snakes were dangerous and aggressive beasts.

Iya replied that a snake's aggressive behavior toward a human being usually occurred as a response to a human attack or a human threat.

Suru challenged Iya to provide sufficient proof to illustrate or support her point.

Iya explained how a snake was like a receptacle of good and bad energy—just like every other part of the universe. She paused for a few seconds before putting forward a very moving analogy. She explained that an ordinary kitchen knife was destined for cooking. It would cut an onion and get dinner ready. Criminal records might reveal that some knives had become weapons of destruction in crazy hands, under despicably unreasonable circumstances, including instances of mental dysfunction or disabilities.

Fati said, "God forbid it!

That heartbreaking analogy triggered Suru's mind to start grasping how a snake was a double-edged beast. One edge could venomously bite you and threaten your life; the other edge would sharply cut the grass to somehow benefit the environment.

Fati concurred that knives from a dining table could also do disservices under crazy circumstances.

Iya said, "God forbid it!"

Suru knew his mother did not want her son's innocent mind to ingest such negative analogies.

Iya smiled and reminded her son of a famous adventure Baba had with a black snake in their backyard.

Suru's father was lying down under a shady eucalyptus tree after a long day of hard work. Presumably mistaking Baba for a piece of wood, a snake climbed on top of him. As soon as Suru's father noticed the strange body crossing over him, he got scared. He managed to hold his breath and stop moving.

The snake passed through quickly and went on its way.

Baba caught his breath, pursued the serpent, and tried to kill it.

The clever beast found a way to escape and slipped into the bush.

Suru's father failed to kill the snake that day, but he would end up killing it eventually.

Iya was stunned and disappointed to hear that her dear husband ultimately killed the snake. She thought the snake deserved to be rewarded. She did not hesitate to confront Baba and express her frustration. She criticized her husband's act and cried out loudly at the contradiction inherent to Baba's act. The snake did not kill Suru's father, but he killed the snake. The snake was kind to him, but he failed to be kind to the snake.

Baba could not even show any gratitude to the snake. He explained that he did not share his wife's approach to snakes around a house. He respectfully apologized to Iya. He knew how to apologize so well.

Iya graciously accepted Baba's apology and moved on.

After thoughtful self-examination, Suru's father would come back to Iya a few days later with remorse. Baba was distraught. He felt disturbed about killing the snake. He felt ashamed and sad for killing a snake that had spared his life. He acknowledged being wrong in sentencing the snake to death. He admitted poor judgement and resolved to never kill snakes again. He vowed to no longer kill any snakes. He would find ways to send them away without doing any harm.

Not long after Iya, Fati, and Suru moved past the snake, Suru noticed a squirrel under a small palm tree on the wayside. The little creature was relaxed and comfortable. At first, Suru thought the animal was praying. It was a typical position for a squirrel. As soon as the animal saw Suru, it scurried into a palm grove. The squirrel ran for its life, and Suru understood. The little rodent did not want to get caught and transformed into "bush meat." The tremendously bushy neighborhood was not a favorite place for squirrels. They were often trapped and slaughtered for human consumption. The squirrel population drastically receded in the neighborhood. Most of them escaped, and the small number of squirrels that chose to remain in the neighborhood were vigilant. Suru was impressed with the little creature's quick decision. He marveled at its speed. Suru hoped it would not become the prey of the black snake.

Iya, Fati, and Suru saw a group of children playing soccer and decided to watch for a few minutes. Though it was late, Iya allowed her son to watch for a few minutes. They had to walk home fast. Suru's mother still intended to cook before bedtime.

As they walked past her house, Fati invited them in for a drink. Fati and her husband, Mouni, warmly welcomed Iya and Suru into their home. Fati updated her husband about the cat. Mouni exploded in gratitude and looked around their house for a present for Suru.

Fati started getting ready to serve dinner to Iya and Suru.

Suru could smell the food, and it made Suru's mouth water. Suru was disappointed when his mother declined Fati's invitation to stay for dinner. Iya said they should not worry about serving them dinner.

Suru understood that Iya needed to get home to cook supper for her family, but he was also hoping to taste the neighbor's food.

Suru's mother explained that the only thing she needed from Fati and Mouni was friendship. "Friendship requires spending time together, finding time to talk together, and being present for one another in times of joy and times of hardship." Suru's mother concluded that she already had all of that from Fati and Mouni.

Fati and Mouni acknowledged Iya's act of kindness, and Suru's mother gently lifted her son's left hand. Suru stood up and reluctantly followed Iya out. They left and starting rushing toward their house.

The sky was getting dark. Nighttime approached, but Iya did not seem worried about darkness. Instead, she reassured Suru that they could count on the moonlight and the stars to enlighten their path.

At home, Baba and Femi were playing dice. Suru's father enjoyed playing dice and was very good at it. Suru's sister was also a good dice player, but Suru was not good at it. As soon as Baba and Femi saw Iya and Suru, they welcomed them home and stopped their game to help put the vegetables away in the kitchen. Baba was impressed by how much his wife came back with.

Iya and Suru told them about Tunde, and Suru's father and sister were thankful to heaven. They offered to help with cooking, but Iya did not want the small kitchen to be crowded. She needed enough space to move fast and capitalize on the small time she had to cook. It was getting late. Baba and Femi went back to dice, and Suru helped his mom in the kitchen. By the time they finished cooking, it was eight thirty. They had a very late supper that day.

***

That short trip to the market taught Suru some meaningful existential lessons. The most important lesson was about eating healthy. What you sow in your stomach is what your body harvests. You eat to give your body life. Do not kill your body while feeding it. Your food is your health. Eating healthy is a good job, a very rewarding one for your wellbeing. Parallel to ingesting healthy aliments, we should take time to enjoy our food by granting enough time to our taste buds to distinguish among bitter, salty, sour, and sweet. We should make sure we savor the flavor of everything we consume by enjoying its taste, smell, and texture.

We should not rush while eating. Rushing your food does not allow you to enjoy its taste. It stresses out your digestive system and ultimately affects your health. We should not be trapped by taste alone. Some tastes can slowly intoxicate and kill the body. Suru's eating habits revealed that too much of certain tastes is not healthy for his body. The less salt and sugar he consumes, the better he feels.

Suru reached that level of healthy eating habits by carefully listening to the language of his body. Before achieving that milestone, he spent years without listening to the language of his body. His body kept on warning him about the risks of salt and sugar. The warning signs included headaches, chest pains, and other forms of malaise, but Suru did not get his body's messages. He did not understand its language and did not heed its warnings.

Suru ignored the alerts for a long time because he was sold to taste and absorbed by flavor. A self-examination would eventually make Suru become aware of how his salt and sugar intake was ominous to his well-being. His self-examination enlightens Suru to learn the language of his body and heed its warnings. He learned to understand the language of his body and made a U-turn that redeemed his eating habits. If you listen to its voice, you will hear your body telling you what food or drink is good for your health.

The voice of your body chiefly sounds in how you digest what you ingest. It makes sure what you send in your stomach will come out easily. If you ingest a stone, you can be guaranteed it will create a malaise in your system and come out painfully. Some aliments are more likely to easily come out than others. You should try to identify what works for you and stick to it. In Suru's case, his digestive system easily handles and sends out water, romaine salad, wheat bran, cooked beans, baked fish, collard greens, kale, papaya, and watermelon.

The voice of your body is also echoed in how deep and restful your sleep is. In Suru's case, milk, tomatoes, romaine salad, spinach, collard greens, kale, and others help. Figure out what is good for you. The voice of your body resonates in the quality of your mood. Some foods put you in a better mood than others. In Suru's case, chocolate, milk, and tomatoes work well for him. This might be different for different individuals. Once again, you should work on finding out where you stand.

With that approach to eating, Suru was able to take care of his constipation and insomnia. As he listened to his body, Suru slowly understood the needs of his body for his health. He understands that water is his best drink. Water is the healthiest drink Suru has ever tasted. The more he drinks, the better he feels. Water hydrates and makes Suru's body happy. Every time he drinks it, it rehydrates his body and refreshes it.

Suru's mother also figured out that too much of certain types of bread was not good for her digestive system. Iya would easily get constipated after eating it. She had other concerns about eating too much of it and gaining weight. She once wrapped up some of her concerns in a meaningful joke. She joked that once the bread was in her stomach, it would make her body rise up like yeast.

Suru's mother was gifted with an extraordinarily slender physical appearance. She wanted to remain slim. She was never fond of adding any extra weight. She would do everything in her power to maintain her skinny shape. Nothing could deter her from paying attention to her waistline. Iya did not mind people wondering whether she was on a food strike. Friends in her neighborhood often joked that she was feeding everyone in her family except herself.

People would indeed wonder whether Iya was deprived of food until they saw her eating. Suru's mother could eat. She had a good appetite, but she also had a strong metabolism with an elegant body. Baba often took pride in saying his wife's body was one of the best shapes ever designed. He would occasionally joke that Suru's metabolism resembled Iya's. Suru's appetite was usually voracious. Suru could eat and eat without much of it showing up on his body, but Iya's metabolism was not the only factor contributing to her good shape.

Suru's mother was very fit. She knew how to take care of her body with physical activities. She would walk long distances every day. She had no scientific proof or supporting evidence about eating too much bread. It was a joke based on her experience, but it was a meaningful one. Every time it is needed, we should be ready to lay down taste for health in order to save our lives. We can renounce taste to embrace health.

The second most important lesson from that trip was about friendship. What ultimately defines a good friendship is how much time you spend together. Friendship is in your devoted presence when your friends need you most. It is not so much in the materials you give them but in your loving presence beside them. Your presence strengthens your friendship and your relationship. The presence of your spouse can prevent divorce and preserve your marriage. Suru has seen marriages dissolve due to a lack of presence. This could happen when you are always present for your job but not for your spouse. Do not be more present for a career than for your love ones. Friendship ultimately boils down to presence.

The third important lesson from that trip was about kindness in bystanders' interventions. Nobody, not even pets, should be left on their own in times of distress or suffering. It is always good to intervene to help those who need assistance. Any act of kindness you perform will sooner or later come back to you in the form of a reward. Inspired by goodwill, neighbors can watch over one another—even in the absence of a formal neighborhood watch system.

The fourth lesson was about the human potential to be good. We all have the potential to be good and do good things. Even bullies have that potential. Society just needs to help them flourish. They need a lot of help, including the bystanders in bullying cycles.

Another existential lesson is about the importance of taking time to contemplate and enjoy nature or the environment we are part of. The nature is beautiful. It deserves to be contemplated. Contemplating eagles or birds has the potential to reward your heart and mind with peace.

In that process, we also need to be mindful of the natural assets of our own bodies. The human body is beautiful and precious by its nature. It is healthy for our hearts and minds to admire our bodies and take care of them.

Another meaningful lesson was about the power of apology. When we feel sorry and express it to the people we offend, using the words "I am sorry," we empower those people for happiness. We free them from the captivity of tribulations, sorrow, and sadness. We subsequently grant liberty to ourselves. An apology does not diminish your human status or social prestige. It boosts it. It makes you a great human being.

Last but not least is the lesson about the fulfillment you experience in saying thank you! Saying thank you is an empowering signal of blessing to you and your social environment. It generates a type of energy that makes you and your environment feel good and happy. We should always be thankful to be happy.

CHAPTER 6

Pulled between Indecision and Decision: From Fear to Courage

Suru treasured the trip to the market and agreed to take another trip with his mother a week later.

It was Iya's habit to go shopping at the market every weekend. She decided to take Suru to a larger market called Kotnad. The market was located on the shore of a lake in a town center. The market was less than thirty minutes driving distance from Iya's house, depending on the traffic. Suru and his mother had the option to go in a taxi, but they also had the option of walking or crossing the lake in a boat. Some fishermen were using their small boats to taxi passengers to the market. The taxi boats were more lucrative than catching and selling fish.

The market was on the other side of the lake, and Iya and her son decided to go by boat. Suru was excited for his first boat ride. The boat trip was quite strange and unique. The boat was far out in the lake when a storm hit. The boat was tossed about by the waves and the wind. Many of the passengers were terrified, including Suru. Suru's legs and hands began to shiver.

Iya grabbed Suru's left hand, but she did not breathe a word to him.

He screamed with fear.

Iya whispered, "Courage—do not be afraid. We will be fine!"

Iya's words did not make him calm down, but the wind died down and the waves became still again. It was as if Iya's words had sent an order to the wind and the waves to be quiet. And they obeyed her injunction. Not long afterward, the boat successfully crossed the lake and landed safely by the market. The passengers were thankful to God. Suru could breathe again.

As Iya and her son were shopping, Suru tried to find out why the wind stopped after her words. Iya said, "We should never panic in front of a danger. In dangerous times, we should keep calm and have faith." She took her son back to her instructions about planning and decision-making.

Iya's instructions on planning empowered Suru to take control of his life. Suru would understand his existence was in his hands—and so was his future. It was up to him to plan his future. Under his mother's guidance, he started learning how to make conscientious decisions. Suru began to risk the path of decision-making with success. His thoughtful and careful decisions allowed Suru to experience an existence filled with freedom and happiness.

His conscientious decision-making processes resulted in a series of consecutive conscientious decisions over the years. One of the first decisions Suru conscientiously made was immediately upon his return from the Kotnad market. It was the decision to kill a fly. For the reader, this story might look like a joke. Its conceptualization might seem exaggerated, but it is not kidding. The author means what he writes here.

Upon returning from the market, Suru was dying of hunger. Iya quickly fixed some leftovers for lunch. She made sure everyone had a little bit of what was left in the pot. She put some yam porridge, collard greens, and grilled mackerel on Suru's plate. Suru was the last person to get his food, and the pot was empty after his mother served his food. He was savoring his meal, but a nasty fly began to hover around the dining room. Suru knew flies could carry and transmit diseases, but he never liked killing them. He had no idea why he lacked the courage to kill flies. The few times he felt the pressure and tried to kill a fly, he was never successful in hitting his target. The fly would manage to drift away and escape. It turned out he never conscientiously decided to kill a fly. Suru was never fully committed to killing a fly. Deep down in his conscience, he never wanted to kill a fly. If he really wanted to kill a fly, he would succeed in doing so.

Decision represents an active desire for success. Decision would call for a commitment to succeed, but things went differently. He made a conscientious decision to kill the fly wandering and buzzing around. Suru mentally justified his decision through a quick internalization process. The fly was bothering him. He was running the risk of getting his food contaminated. The presence of the fly was not good for his health. That internalization process made Suru aware of the costs and benefits of his decision. He felt good about the process. He resorted to the means he needed to succeed in implementing his decision.

He took a deep breath in order to get focused and identified the location of the fly. He cautiously stepped away to get a fly killer from the door. After Suru stood up, the fly landed on an empty chair not far from where he was eating. Suru thought the fly was in an ideal position to be killed. He went ahead and smashed the fly, but he did not cover his plate. After Suru hit it, the fly got confused and ended up dead inside his plate—on top of the food he was devouring. Suru was shocked and disappointed.

Iya felt sorry for her son.

Suru's father joked that the fly took its revenge on his son.

Suru was not pleased with Baba's joke. He had to dump his food in the trash can. A win for him came with a loss. He felt he won in successfully smashing the fly, but he paid the price of losing his food. Existence often puts self in zero-sum situations where wins sometimes result in equal losses for self.

Suru's experience was less traumatic than zero-sum situations countless of people experience daily around the globe. Large numbers of refugees around the world try daily to ignominiously risk their lives, hoping for a better existence. Many of them try to escape suffering or persecution from countries they experience as hell. Unfortunately, hundreds of them perish in that process—drowned and even buried in oceans as they try to reach the countries of their hopes. Those who manage to successfully cross the oceans and survive the journey end up trapped within other types of ostensible persecutions in their host countries. They easily become targets and victims of discrimination, xenophobia, and inhumane treatments and injustices. Some families of refugees even get separated, with children (including infants and toddlers) gruesomely taken away from their mothers or fathers by border patrol agents for unknown destinations. In comparison with the risks and treatments refugees experience daily, losing a plate of food for a dead fly was bearable. With nothing left to eat, Suru had to wait until his mother cooked dinner. It was a painful decision, but Suru was very satisfied that he was able to exterminate the fly. Plus, from the successful implementation of that decision, Suru learned to cover his plate in the presence of any fly hovering around before trying to eliminate it.

Three years after his mother's meaningful instructions on planning, and motivated by Iya's insights on planning, Suru started making some major existential decisions. He was ten years old, but he felt free and determined to give a clear orientation to his life. One of the first major decisions Suru made was to leave the Methodist Church for the Catholic Church.

For several years, Suru's parents revered God under the banners of the Methodist Church. In general, Iya and Baba did a good job of exposing their children to Methodist traditions. Suru was good at attending Sunday services with his young sisters. His older brother and sisters were not so good at attending church, but the family was pleased with the Methodist faith.

As time passed, Suru's parents bought a new house and relocated. The new house was located relatively far from a Methodist temple. Suru and his sisters still managed to attend Sunday services in the closest Methodist temple for a few years after they relocated. However, Suru got tired of the long walk to church at some point. In the same time period, he noticed a Catholic chapel just a few blocks from their new house. Suru considered attending the Catholic church, but he was concerned with how Iya and Baba would react to such a move. Suru was afraid of what his parents and others would think and say about it and reluctantly continued to attend the Methodist church. He was no longer happy to do so, yet he did it to please his mother, his father, and other members of their Methodist congregation.

Suru did not understand why he had to go that far every Sunday to worship God. He did not understand it and did not like it. Yet, he felt unable to decide what to do due to fear. Suru was conditioned, trapped, and chained by potential or anticipated reactions from his parents or others in their congregation. He was like a slave of his social and structural environment. Suru started feeling frustrated. Every Sunday, he had to take the long walk to attend church. He became grumpy during Sunday services. He felt anxiety, instability, and disharmony inside his heart and mind. He experienced some sleepless nights thinking about it. Suru began to ask himself existential questions about God. Why would God want an unhappy worshiper? Did God really want him to go that far every Sunday to worship?

Eventually, Suru would remember his mother's lesson on listening. His conscience called him out not to be afraid to listen to the only voice of truth within him. Suru earnestly complied and listened. He was able to find answers to his questions. God wanted him to worship happily. He could worship God from wherever he was, including from the most secret temples of his heart and mind. Such answers reconciled Suru to himself. He felt stability and harmony from within.

Once he got the answers, a decision followed immediately. It became obvious to Suru that he needed to break the chains of his mental or psychological slavery. He thought it would never be easy to break the chains, but all slaves need to break them to be free. If being free would hurt his parents' feelings of religious belonging, Suru was ready to do so. He was aware that his departure from the Methodist Church could set an occasion for gossips in the narrow world of their congregation and within local circles, but he no longer cared about such intimidating group conversations.

Suru decided to start attending Mass in the nearby Catholic chapel. His younger sisters decided to join him in his decision. Once his decision was made, Suru was unaware of the unknown, yet he was filled with joy. He felt peace of heart and mind. After making his decision, Suru shared it with Iya and Baba. He was not sure about his parents' reaction, but he trusted his decision and liked it. Iya and Baba were supportive! Suru was glad and proud of his parents for their support. Iya did not hesitate to seize that opportunity to engage Suru in what she called "freedom of decision."

Suru made his decision on a Friday evening. He informed his parents that night. On Saturday, at daybreak, his mother stood by Suru's bedside and grabbed him. "Do not worry, my son! I just want us to take the occasion of this beautiful sunrise to discuss the freedom of decision." Suru's mother knew how to skillfully exploit the impact of the weather on the body and mind to reach her goal. It was a lovely Saturday morning with a stunning daylight.

Suru took a deep breath, sat down on his bed, stretched his arms, and asked, "What do you mean by freedom of decision, Mother!"

Iya responded, "I am glad you ask, son! You just exemplified it last night with your decision." She sat down next to her son and walked him through what she meant. Iya went far beyond her son's expectations.

Suru watched and listened carefully.

Iya said, "We all have the freedom of decision. Freedom enables us to enjoy limitless time and space in being, in moving, and in doing. Without freedom, we may not be happy. Freedom of decision means the free will that allows us to actively select where we want to go, who we want to be, what we want to do, and how we want to proceed with going, being, and doing. Freedom of decision reflects some inherent human power that enables us to choose what to think and how, what to say and how, who to be and how, where to go and how, what to do and how. It does not have any restriction as long as it does not hurt life and others. It should always respect and promote life across time and space.

"Whenever a human subject uses it constructively, it results in creating peace of heart and mind. For all constructive actions or states of being, it generates synergy with subjective innate emotions. It is not always easy to decide. Making a decision can be difficult due to human resistances, social decorum and pressures, or the fear of the unknown. Yet we ought to dare to decide in order to achieve happiness.

"Some friends are not happy because they cannot decide to give up who they appeared to be, where they were, or what they had. They could not move on to who they should be, where they should be, and what they should have. They were actually miserable because they were afraid to decide. Our freedom of decision represents a pillar of our happiness. To some degree, happiness depends on people's ability to decide where to go, who to be, and what to say or do. To be happy, we ought to constructively exercise our freedom of decision. We are free to decide where we want to be or go, who want to be or become, what we want to do, and how we want to proceed. I decided to get married and am was happy with it. I also decided to have you and am happy with that.

"The courage to decide conscientiously contributes to some level of happiness. When you manifest the courage to make sound decisions and stick to them, you bring some peaceful energy your way. You get peace of mind and heart over most conscientious decisions. We should not resist to deciding, mindful of how tough it can be at times.

"However, you should not let people or circumstances dictate your decisions to you. We should not allow people to decide for us without us. Do not let circumstances force you to decide with a rush. You should not decide under extreme emotions of joy, anger, or fear. Be mindful to decide at the right time for you and after serene inner deliberations. You do not decide because you are pushed by others to do so. Sometimes, people or circumstances may assist or contribute to your decision-making to some degree. They can illuminate you in the process. Nevertheless, they should not take control of the process and outcome of decision-making. You should have control over the process and outcome of your decisions. As much as you can, exercise your decision-making ability when you are at your best, in all serenity."

Most decisions Iya made under extreme emotions were poor decisions. She ended up regretting them. On the other hand, Suru's mother enjoyed all the decisions she made when she was at her very best. Your personal experience would certainly teach you. Existential experiences are often good teachers.

A good friend kept complaining to Iya about a boss who was giving her a hard time at work. Ola was angry and frustrated with her supervisor. She told Iya about her plan to quit because of that manager. Ola admitted to Iya that she loved her job—except for the treatment of her manager.

Iya told Ola not to let her manager's behavior dictate the decision to quit. Reluctantly, Ola followed Iya's advice and decided to keep her job. A year later, her manager quit—and Ola was made manager. Ola's happiness in her job increased. She came back to Iya and confessed that the decision to keep her job was one of the best decisions she ever made.

Another friend was caught in a similar situation. Adu shared his plans to quit his job because of the poor treatments of his supervisor. Iya encouraged him not to let that supervisor's behavior dictate the decision to leave his job. Adu did not listen to Iya's advice. He quit his job anyway. A few months after starting his new job, Adu stopped by and told Iya that his decision to leave was a poor decision. His former supervisor left the job about three months after he quit. Adu felt his current supervisor was worse than the previous one. He explored other options, but none of them was better than his initial one. Adu was not happy where he landed and started looking into the possibility of going back to his former employer. He reapplied for a new position in his initial workplace, but he was not recruited.

"Son, you just made the first big step by selecting where you want to be. Remember that you still have a long way to go. You still have to decide who you want to become, what you want to do, and how you want to proceed. Have compassion for yourself and others in the process of making and implementing your decisions. Regardless of the decision you make, you ought to be ready to accept and assume the consequences. Your decision can result in good or bad outcomes for you and others. Take the time to think before you decide. Once you decide, you are responsible for your decision and its outcomes. When a decision translates into good outcomes, you celebrate and record it as a success story to capitalize on. However, when a decision turns ugly, you humbly learn from your mistakes and adjust for a better move in the future. In cases of poor decisions, show compassion for yourself and for the victims of your poor decisions. Your compassion would trigger sentiments of repentance and the willingness to repair any damage done to yourself and others and to improve."

Suru kept his eyes and ears open as he listened to his mother. He did not want to miss a single word. Iya's words helped Suru understand that he had made the first big step in a long journey toward his future, his vocation. Suru felt confirmed in his decision and his new direction. He spent the rest of the day happily, except when a wasp stung him that evening.

Suru was removing dust from the entrance to his parents' house and noticed a wasp buzzing around in a top corner of the door. The wasp was fixing its nest, and Suru wanted to see what was inside the nest. He used the broom to break the nest, and the larvae fell down. The wasp was not happy, and Suru could understand why.

The wasp had worked hard to build that nest. How would you feel if someone destroyed a house you worked hard for? How would feel if that person nearly killed your children in that destructive process? You would be frustrated. Anyone would experience frustration in such a situation. The wasp felt that level of frustration.

Furious, the wasp stung him on his hand—the very hand Suru used to destroy its nest. It was painful. Suru ran away from the site, screamed, and alerted Iya.

Baba came out and managed to kill the wasp.

Suru's mother took care of the sting, but Suru's Saturday ended on a bad note. While Iya was taking care of Suru's hand, lightning flashed across the sky. The thunder began to flex its muscles. The thunderstorm smashed and pounded the sky. The resounding echo made the clouds shatter into raindrops. The passage of a refreshing shower allowed Suru a good night's sleep. Suru tends to enjoy his sleep when it rains.

On Sunday morning, Suru woke up in a good mood and attended his first Mass in the small Catholic chapel in his neighborhood. It was quite a positive experience. Suru enjoyed the songs, the creed, the cult, the symbols, and the liturgy. As a newcomer, he was a little bit lost in the ritual, yet he felt very welcome within the vibrant congregation. The members were all enthusiastic.

Suru and his sisters were introduced to other kids, and Suru met some of the young altar boys. He expressed his admiration for how they helped the priest during the service. He was able to connect with some of them after Sunday school. By the time Suru headed home, it was clear that he had to go through years of initiation to the Catholic faith. He needed to learn the creed, study the Catholic doctrine and traditions, and know the meaning of the symbols. Suru would ultimately need to be baptized in the Catholic faith. As soon as he came home, Suru told his mother about his intention to complete his inscription for catechism or religious instruction.

Iya reminded him that it was his decision.

Suru spent months checking the costs and benefits of embarking on a journey to attending catechism. It was obvious it would take time. He was concerned about whether he would be able to combine the load of his religious instruction with his regular schoolwork. Baba would not appreciate if Suru fell behind at school due to catechism. Suru was also aware that attending catechism was his only way to remain in the Catholic Church. It was his great desire to remain in the Catholic Church.

Suru felt good about attending his new church every Sunday and making new friends within the congregation. He knew his parents wanted him to do whatever good things would make him feel happy. Suru's cost-and-benefit analysis convinced him to attend catechism.

A few months later, he completed his inscription for catechism. His initiation process into the Catholic faith was launched. Upon Suru's inscription, Iya told her son she was very proud of him. His mother's compliments were encouraging; they empowered Suru to commit himself seriously to Catholicism. A mother's compliments are meaningful to her child. Suru appreciated Iya's compliments and promised not to disappoint his mother on his new journey. And he did not disappoint.

Suru embraced catechism classes with extreme devotion. Per his teachers' evaluations, he was performing very well on all religious tests and exams. His scores presented strong evidence of excellence in performance. He was able to successfully balance catechism and his regular academic load.

Suru's religious instruction enlightened and supported his schoolwork and other extracurricular activities. His years of religious instructions went by very fast. They prepared him to receive the precious sacraments. Suru was eager to open the doors of his heart and mind.

After a few years, he graciously welcomed all the precious sacraments of his faith. He first obtained the sacraments of baptism and Holy Communion. Suru consumed his Lord and Savior. He felt he did not deserve such a privilege, but God mercifully and gracefully came inside Suru for his peace of heart and mind. Suru graciously welcomed the divine presence. The divine presence tasted good to Suru and made him feel good. He felt good indeed. Suru was forever grateful. How magnificent is your love, Lord! Suru received the sacrament of confirmation in the Holy Spirit. He opened up his whole being to the Holy Spirit to take possession of his body and mind. And it settled inside of him just like in a temple. Suru felt good with his decision to attend catechism. He felt gratified mentally and emotionally.

His decision to attend catechism was one of the best decisions Suru ever made. He will never regret it. It boosted his relationship with God. He got a clearer understanding of God as his Creator and Savior. He was exposed to the nature and face of God. God is present in the tabernacle of his heart and mind. God is in him and you, and everyone, and everywhere. All creatures live by God.

Suru has experienced the divine love and compassion for the poor, for the vulnerable, and for all humankind. He has witnessed God's sense of humility and service. He reveres the divine incarnation. He venerates the divine death and resurrection. The presence of the Holy Spirit inspires Suru daily. He believes God will resurrect the dead in a life that will never end. Suru's religious instructions initiated him into a faith tradition that he continues to enjoy.

Iya and Baba eventually joined Suru and his sisters in Catholicism to the glory of God.

CHAPTER 7

From Inquietude to Quietude: Contemplative Meditation for Peace of Mind and Heart

Suru's attendance of catechism helped reinforce and formalize his good habits of morning prayers. His mother certainly knew that. Before Suru's conversion to Catholicism, Baba would wake up his entire family early in the morning to pray with him. Baba would pray for his family's health and protection, for the sick, for the dead, for travelers, and for the entire world. Baba would start praying alone. Midway, he would stop and wake his children up to join him. The children would spend some time with him praying in their own words, but they could not sustain his rhythm and style of prayer. Baba would spend hours on his knees in prayer.

Iya agreed with Suru that Baba was too devoted to praying. Suru and his sisters prayed together next to their father. Suru would lead the prayer in his own words. His words were often not well organized and formalized. He would use all words he thought of as they came. It was not fun.

After Suru started attending catechism, he bought a book of prayer with formally written morning and evening prayers. It contained a formula of morning prayers designed for every day of the week, including Saturday and Sunday. That book made Suru's morning prayers easy and almost enjoyable. It would be wrong to presume that Suru knew how to pray. His morning prayers were filled with words. He was caught up in routine recitations of written formulas.

The routines made Suru behave as if his heart and mind had no room for any silent prayer. Though his morning prayers became easier with his daily recitations, Suru did not enjoy them. He often did not feel enthusiastic or excited about his morning prayers. He was not spontaneous at the thought of praying.

Every morning, when Baba woke him up to pray, Suru reluctantly pulled his legs into the prayer room. This happened over and over again. Left on his own, Suru would not be going there every morning. He felt like saying no to his father sometimes, but he would obey Baba's order for prayer simply to please him.

In the prayer room, Suru would speed up the process of recitation so that the prayer could end as soon as possible. At times, he was tired of the routines of recitation. Some mornings, he felt prayer was too hard; it required too many words and was too much work; it was time-consuming and too demanding; it was boring.

Suru was not happy with his prayers. He was not exactly sure why he felt unhappy with his prayers, but he knew he was tired of saying tons of words and reciting the nicely crafted formulas. Every time he boycotted his daily recitations, he felt good. Suru's boycotts of prayer occurred when his father traveled. Whenever Baba was away, Suru's prayer was not filled with words. He would not even use the book of prayer. Instead, his morning prayer was silent. He would fall on his knees and spend some silent time in the prayer room. He would stay there quiet and passive before the holy images. He would just be there. He would do nothing more than that.

Suru put no pressure on his mind or thoughts. He was simply present and relaxed. In the process, Suru would even fall asleep. He would usually spend twenty-five or thirty minutes and leave the prayer room with feelings of inner peace, positive energy, and ready for a new day. Suru was not sure how to explain it. He thought he was being just lazy, spending time catching up with his sleep in the prayer room. That could be the case! His father would have interpreted it the same way, and he would not be happy with it.

Suru never told Baba this, but Suru increasingly sensed that his silent prayer made him feel good. He thought it helped him connect with the source of peace. He also got the opportunity to observe his mother's prayer whenever his father happened to be away on a trip. Again and again, Suru observed how Iya's prayer was also mute. Iya would just kneel down quietly before the divine presence. Unlike Baba, Iya would keep quiet—with her mouth and eyes closed. Suru could have asked his mother about the contrast in praying styles between her and Baba, but it never occurred to him. At times, Suru thought his mother was just boycotting the morning prayers. He felt happy to have Iya on his team, but he was only an innocent child.

On a Sunday morning, Suru decided to implement Iya's lesson on listening at church. He listened to the parish priest carefully. Three words from the priest's sermon caught Suru's attention: *contemplation, action,* and *meditation*. Baba thought the priest did a good job of explaining all three words in his homily.

For some reason, it never took much time for Suru's father to be satisfied with pastoral addresses. The son was unlike his father on that account. On that Sunday morning, Suru dedicated all his attention to the priest's discourse from its beginning to its end, but he had no clue what the good man of God meant by the three words in his oration.

Under his breath, Baba would jokingly tell Suru that his mind was too young to understand the preaching of the charismatic parish priest. And that would be right. At home, Suru wondered what the three words meant. His attention to the sermon was not enough to help him grasp the meaning of the words.

Suru needed Iya's help to understand *contemplation, meditation,* and *action*. Her reaction to his inquiry was immediate. Iya smiled and took Suru by hand. They went to the quietest corner in their house. Iya called it the meditation corner. Suru understood they needed to be in a quiet place for this lesson, but he did not fully understand his mother's whole intention.

Iya grabbed a box of matches and lit a candle. She told Suru that the lighted candle symbolized the divine presence. She sat down on a mat on the floor. Suru was not very familiar with that sitting position, but it reminded him of Buddha's sitting position that he saw in pictures and movies.

Iya asked him to sit down on the floor in the same position. Suru tried hard. It was difficult achieving it on his own, but he made it with Iya's assistance. Suru was looking at Iya to see what would come next. His mother said nothing to him and made no move. Her eyes were closed. Iya remained silent.

About five minutes later, Suru wondered if his mother was doing fine. She responded positively by nodding. Suru decided to also close his eyes in imitation. To his surprise, he remained in that position for a long time.

Iya was not surprised. When Suru opened his eyes, Iya smiled and asked how he felt. He felt good, calm, and relaxed.

They moved to two chairs, and Iya lectured Suru on the meaning of contemplation, action, and meditation in theory and in practice. She shared her own experiences with specific accounts. He listened to her with admiration. She explained how contemplative meditation pacifies and triggers positive feelings, thinking, and actions in human life. From the time Suru was a baby growing in her belly, Iya started her days in contemplative meditation. She was doing so by using all her senses.

***

Iya spends the first hour of her day in contemplative meditation. With her eyes closed and in silence, she imagines herself before the divine presence and contemplates the creation in its magnificence. With her imagination, she observes the earth and all its marvels. She contemplates the hills and mountains in their height, the latitudes of valleys, the attractiveness of waterfalls, the deepness of oceans, the mobility of rivers, and the stillness of lakes. She contemplates the grittiness of sand and the massiveness of rocks, the greenness of grasses and trees, the colors of flowers, the ingenuity of bees and the impressiveness of butterflies. She admires the symphony of buzzing insects, the enchantment of eagles flying high in the blue sky, the cleverness of the snake, and the trickeries of the fox. She marvels at the slowness of the turtle and the quickness of a shooting star, the usefulness of the air and the coolness of water. She observes the diversity of climates, the cycle of the seasons, the solemnity of the blue sky, and the somberness of clouds.

She is delighted with the splendor of the rainbow, the glare of the stars, the whiteness of the snow, the exuberance of the day, the darkness of the night, the brightness of the sun, and the glow of the moonlight. She is mindful of and amazed by the allure and coordination of her legs and the motion of her hands. She listens to the music of waves, the sound of the wind, the noise of rain, the melody of a voice, the symphony of a laugh, the pace of her heartbeat, and the rhythm of breath. She appreciates the harmony of a smile and the mystery of sleep.

Iya feels the changes in the weather, the strength of the thunderstorm, and the intensity of lightning. She ponders the magnitude of cyclones and earthquakes, the speed of the wind, and the sensitivity of moods and feelings. She considers the pace of time, the immensity of space, the population of the earth, the activities of the brain and memory, the impact of the digestive system, the worth of kidneys, the redness and richness of blood, the multitude and fullness of hair, and the enigma of conception and gestation. She savors the flavor of food, the beauty of the human body, and the importance of the senses: the ability to see, smell, touch, taste, and feel. She muses on the aptitude to think, understand, and remember, the mystery of life and death, the irresistibility and symbiosis of love, and the goodness and power of the Creator of the universe.

Per Iya's experience, contemplation lets you watch, inspect, and admire the grandeur of your natural, geographical, and social environment. It provides you with the opportunity to observe and feel the majesty of the creation and the Creator. You contemplate your external and internal environments. Your internal environment encompasses the gift of your life, your existence, your talents, your skills, your relationships, your interactions, and your activities. You celebrate or rejoice for the miracle of your existence, your dispositions, your qualities, and your skills, but you also acknowledge and confess your weaknesses and shortcomings. You venerate the Creator of heaven and earth. You observe and appreciate the creation for imitation. Your observation of the creation constructively affects your daily creative actions.

Suru's mother was usually animated by the desire to perform good actions and activities. She was eager to do good things after her contemplations. Iya was working hard to contribute to creating a good environment in the image of creation.

Meditation allows you to ponder the contemplated creation and reflect upon your actions. Meditation assists you in examining your daily existence and activities. In silence and with your eyes closed, you put yourself in the presence of the Creator of the universe, admire creation, and ask metaphysical questions about human existence and your life. You become aware of the Creator's image in you. You move on to evaluate how your actions follow suit. You assess how your actions reflect the beauty of creation.

Contemplative meditation provides a symbiosis of contemplation and meditation. It makes you feel, experience, and enjoy the mysterious beauty of the universe and the power of God in and around you. It creatively boosts your sense of wonder. Contemplation enlightens your actions, and meditation analyzes and weighs them. You spend time watching and admiring the Creator throughout creation. You listen to them. You present your joy and pain to them. In that process, you learn how to behave and relate to your environment constructively. Such experience empowers you for creatively positive actions. Such learning impacts your daily activities; it tends to feed your interactions with your social and physical environment. Contemplative meditation puts you in a peace garden. You feel God and good; you taste and see the magnificence of nature and creation and the majesty of the divine.

As little Suru was growing inside of her, Iya patiently contemplated her baby's shining face. Suru's little feet were kicking his mother from within. She projected how Suru would come into existence. Iya was meditating on who her son would be, who he would become, what he would do in life, and how he would serve and contribute to creating his social environment.

Iya's contemplative meditation on her baby's moves provided her with leisure and happiness. She savored and loved the feeling more than the best menu on the planet. While pregnant with Suru, Iya started giggling in the kitchen. Baba wondered why. She told her husband it had to do with how nice Suru's moves were within.

On another occasion, as Iya was washing dishes, Suru's older sister, Awa, caught a smile on Iya's face and asked about it. Iya told Awa how Suru's kicking triggered the smile. Another day, while doing laundry, Iya caught herself laughing loudly. Surprised, she wondered if everything was fine with herself, simply to realize that her baby boy was just making some enjoyable moves inside. On a regular checkup at the doctor's office, Iya's gynecologist, Sena, caught her smiling in the waiting room. Sena smiled in return, and Iya responded that she was just contemplating her baby's movements with enjoyment. Contemplative meditation helped Iya handle the stresses of pregnancy with humor and hope.

When it was finally time for labor and delivery, Iya relied on contemplative meditation in the midst of her pain. As her pain became intense during labor and delivery, so did her contemplative meditation. Suru could only wonder how. In the middle of her pain, Iya focused on the little angel coming out of her womb. Suru's mother observed and admired the loveliness of that innocent being she had cocreated. Her mind was on the causes of her pain. She acknowledged that she had to endure the pain in order to give life. Her heart was anticipating the joy that followed delivery.

That exercise gave Iya hope, which helped her transcend the pain. After pushing her baby out safely, Iya screamed loudly. The midwife, Aye, was worried. Aye quickly took the newborn away for cleaning and came back to attend to the mother.

With tears in her eyes, Iya groaned and looked at Aye.

Aye gave her a paper towel to wipe her eyes.

Iya recovered her smile and told Aye that she was happy to cocreate such a beautiful human being.

Aye responded jokingly that Iya should wait until she saw how handsome her baby was, but Iya said that she had already seen the baby.

Aye asked when and how she did it. The newborn was quickly taken away for cleaning before the mother could open her eyes.

Iya told Aye how she had contemplated her baby's face and body ever since the implantation and throughout the days of gestation.

Aye could hardly believe that and took it as joke, but Baba told Aye that his wife actually meant what she said. Iya's serious mood made Aye reconsider. After bringing the newborn back to his mother, following the routine toilet, Aye handed the little angel to Iya. Iya held her baby for some time, tightly against her warm chest, and she smiled. She handed baby Suru to his father.

Baba covered his newborn son with his warm arms.

Aye sat down by Iya's bedside to chat.

Iya shared the transformative potentials of contemplative meditation. Aye listened and cried with emotion and admiration. She could not stop expressing her appreciation for listening to Iya. Suru's mother teasingly told Aye to try it out; the best form of gratitude in that situation would require that Aye consider embracing a daily practice of meditation. In the same breath, Aye promised to embark on such a journey. From that moment, Iya and Aye became good friends.

Six months later, Aye explained to Iya that she was thankful for her lucky stars. Her encounter with Iya transformed Aye's life for good. She went on to share her life stories. In the process, Aye indicated how doctors diagnosed her ten-year-old daughter, Lati, with ADHD. Aye depicted how Lati's behaviors had been driving her family crazy. She stressed how medications would calm Lati down for a moment and how she got wild whenever she failed to take her medications. Aye introduced her daughter to contemplative meditation and noticed major changes in her behaviors. About three months after Lati started practicing meditation consistently, she was transformed and completely calmed down. Lati was focused, she paid more attention to her mother and teachers, and she slept restfully at night.

Throughout her son's childhood, Iya would lean on contemplative meditation to raise Suru up. At home, while she was very involved in different domestic activities, Iya was also contemplative and meditative. Suru could remember some stories in that regard.

On a Saturday morning, Iya was busy cleaning the house with Baba. Suru kept walking behind his mother with his dirty shoes. He was staining the carpet and the tiles.

Iya kept advising her son to join Femi in the playroom with his toys.

Baba also warned Suru over and over again to stop walking on the freshly mopped hardwood floor in the family room.

Suru would not listen to his parents. He kept spreading the dirt because he thought it was funny. Suru was having fun sliding with his shoes in the soapy water on the titles in the kitchen, but he fell down and broke his fingernails and lost his front teeth. Suru cried tearfully because it was so painful. It was such a terrible fall.

Iya immediately stopped her cleaning duties to spend time with her son. She used her nursing skills to care for Suru. She disinfected his wounds and put some dressings on them. She gave Suru some aspirin for the pain.

Baba also helped in that process.

Afterward, Iya and Baba went back to cleaning, but Suru did not learn his lesson. His fall did not deter him from causing trouble. As Iya was busy cleaning the bathroom, Suru went to visit his mother. His intention was not bad. He intended to help and repair the damage, but he came in with his dirty shoes because he was not ready to give them up.

Baba noticed new stains on the wet floor, expressed his frustration, and put Suru in time-out. Iya came along and observed the stains. The magnitude of the stains would require Suru's mother to clean them. Iya got mad and yelled at her son.

Baba extended Suru's period of time-out and took away all his toys for a week, but Iya turned to Baba in the midst of his anger and reminded her husband that he probably did similar things to his parents when he was Suru's age.

Baba said that Iya caused similar stress to her parents. Iya and Baba smiled and considered how patient their parents were. She imagined how patient God is with us daily. As a result, Baba reduced Suru's time-out period. In the midst of the stressful days, Iya meditated contemplatively on God's patience with all creatures.

Suru's mother resorted to contemplative meditation on many other occasions when her son was stubborn or pigheaded. On a weekend morning, Iya was making an omelet for breakfast. Suru offered to help, but his mother said she did not need his help. Suru went to the living room.

As soon as Iya stepped away, Suru quickly turned into a chef. He was having fun breaking the eggs without paying attention to where he was putting the contents. Everything went so fast. In less than a minute, Suru broke six eggs. Unfortunately, the kitchen floor was the receptacle of his mess.

As soon as his mother stepped out of the bathroom and noticed the mess, she could hardly believe her eyes. Iya screamed with anger.

Baba jumped in from his office; he could not believe it. Suru's father took away all his toys for the rest of the weekend and put his son in time-out again.

After taking a deep breath, Iya cleaned the mess and restarted her cooking from scratch. His mother's silence bothered Suru. From his time-out position, he asked Iya why she was not talking to him anymore.

Iya replied that Suru's behavior put a short embargo on her mouth and words.

Suru did not understand what his mother meant.

Iya added that she was in a contemplative meditation of God's infinite patience with human beings.

Suru understood Iya's frustration and appreciated her contemplative attitude.

On another occasion, Iya stopped by Suru's school with a taxi driver to pick up her son. Iya helped Suru buckle up his seat belt before taking her own seat in the back of the taxi, but she got distracted while talking to the driver and another passenger.

A few minutes later, the taxi reached a police checkpoint.

Iya was surprised when the policeman observed that Suru was not wearing his seat belt. The taxi driver was dismayed. Iya looked at Suru and gently swallowed her anger. It was on a Friday evening, and Iya was tired from a long week of hard work. However, her fatigue did not deter her from adjusting Suru's seat belt prior to the police checkpoint.

The taxi driver also double-checked, but he did not make a big deal of it. In some countries, drivers do not take the requirement of wearing seat belt seriously.

Suru managed to take advantage of his mother's distraction to unbuckle his seat belt.

The police officer asked the driver to pull his car to the side of the road and took his license away. A few minutes later, he told the driver to pay a fine before he could get his license back.

Distraught and trembling, the poor taxi driver stretched out his left hand with some money to the policeman. In return, the policeman gave him back his license and let them go. Nineb, like many other poor countries, was dealing with a severe corruption crisis in the public and private sectors. Even its police officers were corrupt.

Once the taxi got back on the road, Suru's mother gave the money back to the driver. He was happily surprised and thanked Iya for her gesture. Iya indicated that she and her son were responsible for what had happened.

After they got home, Suru expected his mother to put him on punishment, but she smiled, took a deep breath, and whispered, "God is certainly very patient with all his creatures. I am testing how long I can sustain being patient with you, son!"

Suru instantly understood that his mother's contemplative meditation had redeemed him once again. He was grateful to have learned his lesson. From then on, Suru would always put on his seat belt.

Later that day, Iya was making her son's bed just before bedtime. She was very tired after a busy day of housekeeping, and he decided to help her. Iya accepted Suru's offer to help. However, as soon as he put his hands on the sheet, some big stains appeared on it. Iya checked her son's hands, and they were full of oil from the spaghetti sauce.

Suru's mother asked why he did not wash his hands after dinner, and she wondered why he had decided to help with dirty hands.

Suru said, "I forgot."

Iya reminded her son to wash his hands before and after dinner. Suru was expecting his mother to punish him for being so negligent. Instead, she quietly put a clean sheet on the bed.

Suru asked his mother why he was not punished for staining the sheet.

She told him that it was a human thing to forget, but it was important to learn from his mistakes. Suru understood that he owed that gracious lesson to Iya's contemplative meditation.

On Saturday of that same weekend, Iya and Baba took Suru for his swimming lesson in a park. On their way to the park, they urged their son to follow the regulations and the guidance of the lifeguard. Iya alerted Suru about how dangerous the water in a swimming pool could be. She provided him with some statistics about drowning.

Neither Iya nor Baba were dressed for swimming. They went to the park and waited patiently for the lifeguard to show up. Iya and Baba were holding Suru's hands, but Baba headed to the restroom.

Suru pulled his hand away and jumped into the swimming pool.

Iya screamed for help and jumped into the water behind her son.

Baba turned back and followed them into the water. He grabbed Suru and pulled him up.

Iya and Baba were able to rescue Suru before he sustained any injuries. Suru was certainly aware of his parents' swimming skills, but he did not know how they managed to do so without any swimsuits. All he noticed was their wet clothes and hair. Before the lifeguard showed up, they headed home. They changed their mind about the swimming lesson. Iya thought it was not a good day to swim due to the incident.

Upon returning home, Suru expected to be put in a time-out, but his mother and father did not talk about it. He asked his mother why, and Iya explained that she felt responsible for what had happened. She did not hold her son's hand firmly enough.

Baba also indicated that he should not have left them. The parents took time to meditate on the behaviors that contributed to the accident.

Suru promised his parents that he would meditate on his own behaviors. Later on, he did meditate on the incident. Eventually, he learned to behave around water.

A month later, instead of doing his homework after school, Suru went to play with the neighbor's dog across the street. He did not like doing his schoolwork, but he adored playing all day and all night.

When it was time to play, Suru felt the joy of heaven. However, when it was time to do homework, he felt the heat of hell.

Iya was fully aware of her son's feelings about homework and playtime. Whenever Suru was doing homework, his mother would stick around or check his progress. Iya was not able to check on him that evening. He suspected that his mother was busy in the kitchen and took a chance to cross the road and play with the dog. It was not a smart move. The dog was not friendly that evening. Once it saw Suru, it started barking, which was unusual for that dog.

Suru thought they knew each other well. Suru reached out to calm the dog.

It jumped up angrily and tried to bite his finger. How could Suru know the dog was very hungry and looking for someone to eat? Suru screamed. He was scared.

Iya rushed out of the bathroom with a towel around her chest and waist and pulled Suru away.

The neighbor, Afa, showed up and pulled her dog away.

Suru's mother checked his fingers and noticed a small scratch on his thumb. Suru had his tetanus and other relevant vaccinations, but Afa reassured them that her dog had been vaccinated.

Suru had no clue what Afa meant, but his mother got the message.

Afa apologized and explained that the dog had not eaten all day. She had been away and did not anticipate that it would take all day. As Iya and Afa continued to talk about the dog, Suru interrupted his mother. He said Iya should not worry because the scratch was not bleeding.

Iya stopped the conversation and thanked Afa. Suru thought he would get in trouble that evening, but his mother put the blame on herself. Iya indicated that she should have checked on Suru while he was doing his homework. Suru learned another lesson.

There were circumstances where Suru's stubbornness made him like a ping-pong ball swinging between his mother and his father. On a Saturday afternoon, Iya was sweeping and mopping their living room and bedrooms. Baba was busy fixing something in front their house. Suru did not know exactly what his father was doing, but he was pleased to hang out where Baba was working. Suru wanted to watch and count the motorcycles and cars passing by. He ran after every motorcycle or car he saw.

Baba thought the game was dangerous. Suru was running the risk of being run over by a motorcycle or a car. His father did not want that to happen. Baba warned his son over and over to stop, but Suru would not listen. He did not pay any attention to his father's warnings.

Fed up with his behavior, Baba sent Suru back inside to help Iya sweep and mop the rooms. Suru rejoined his mother in the living room, but instead of helping her, he ended up giving Iya stress as well. Suru did not ask for any directions. He did not think it was important or necessary to check with his mother about whether she needed his help. Perhaps he thought it would be a waste of time to ask for directions.

He started pouring water on the floor where Iya had already swept and mopped. She would not tolerate such stupid behavior. Suru's mother got frustrated. The tone of her voice echoed the feelings expressed on her very sad face. Iya sent him back to help his father, without knowing why he was in the living room in the first place.

Suru wished his mother knew what made him join her in the living room, but she did not know a thing about it. He did not tell his mother anything about it.

Baba did not have any opportunity to update Iya about what had happened outside.

Suru followed his mother's order, and he went back to his father.

Baba was very busy and did not notice his son was back. To make his father aware that he was back, Suru made a loud sound like a motorcycle.

Baba looked around and seemed scared. He looked like a motorcycle was about to run him over. Suru started laughing. Suru's father was known for displaying braveness and defying situations of fear. He was tall, strong, and physically and mentally intimidating. It was difficult to scare him. Suru felt happy he was finally able to scare him. His feelings translated into his laughing at Baba, but his father did not find it funny.

Baba did not like his son's attitude and behavior. He told Suru to never scare him or anyone in that manner. He made it clear that scaring people could make someone have a heart attack. He said he almost passed out. Baba could hardly believe Suru defied his order and came back outside, but he did not ask his son why he was back. He probably guessed Suru was giving his mother stress.

Suru did not bother telling his father what had happened in the living room.

Baba went back to what he was doing. However, he sternly put a condition forward: his son should keep silent and not distract him.

Suru remained silent until he saw the next motorcycle. As soon as he saw it, he broke the cycle of silence and renewed his vow of sounding like a motorcycle.

Baba yelled at his son and sent Suru back inside to help Iya.

Upon Suru's return, his mother tried to understand what was going on. Suru felt like a ping-pong ball going forward and backward between two players. Iya understood the game, and she patiently welcomed her son back.

Iya's very meaningful lessons on contemplative meditation resonated throughout her son's childhood and affected his teenage years and adulthood. During Suru's crazy teenage years, his mother helped him see the image of God in his social environment and in all human beings. Iya trained her son to contemplate and meditate on the divine will in the face of his successes and failures.

Suru leaned on his mother's training to identify the handiwork of God in existential situations and to be thankful to the Creator of the universe. In middle school, Suru had a classmate who everyone kept complaining about. The classmate's name was Alu. Suru complained to Iya a couple of times about Alu, and Iya addressed the problem each time.

Alu was bullying everybody. As a result, nobody wanted to associate with him. Alu was not invited to birthday parties because of his personality. As Suru's birthday party got closer, Suru made a list of his guests and did not include Alu.

After checking the list, Iya asked her son if he would mind adding Alu to the list. Suru's answer was negative.

Iya suggested that he think of Alu as a good human being with bad behaviors.

Suru responded that he was excluding Alu precisely for his bad behaviors.

Iya insisted that all human beings have their qualities and weaknesses. "We all have our bad behaviors. Our identity goes far beyond our behaviors. Who we are should not be defined only by our bad behaviors. We should not only be judged or treated solely based on our bad behaviors. Alu has the potential for good behaviors."

Suru wondered why his mother was advocating for a devil she did not even know. He even wished below his breath that his mother would stop playing devil's advocate.

Iya said, "We ought to give the devil its due by giving everyone the benefit of the doubt or a least a chance. All bullies are products of their social environments. Bullying certainly has something to do with the socialization process. Society is partly responsible for bullying behavior. Excluding bullies from positive situations does not necessarily help society."

Suru got his mother's message about separating Alu from his bullying behavior. If bullies were integrated into constructive interactional dynamics, they may stop going to the devil—and their behaviors could change.

Suru reluctantly added Alu's name to the list of guests for his birthday party. When Alu got his invitation, he was caught by surprise. His mother was also surprised. Alu attended the party with his mother. Her name was Davo. Suru's friends and other classmates were all shocked to see Alu at the party.

Suru found creative ways to appease everyone with some explanations and incentives. Everybody accepted Alu and was nice to him. A good ambience reigned that evening. By the end of the party, most participants came to realize Alu was the best-behaved classmate at the party. Alu's behavior at the party took Suru's breath away. There was no bullying, and all the classmates were amazed at his behavior. It was unusual. Alu was known to bully people even when he was sick. Suru noticed Iya spent a long time talking to Alu's mother at that party.

That same night, after everybody left the party, Iya and Suru sat down to briefly evaluate the event. Suru thanked Iya for making him invite Alu and asked about her motives.

Iya said, "All human beings were created in the image of God. As such, we all have the potential to be good. Always contemplate God's image in all fellows. Alu's parents went through a bitter divorce when their son was only two. Alu's father, Oba, was abusive and ended up in jail. At the age of six, Alu ended up losing that father in a car accident. Davo, Alu's mother, had to live in a shelter after Oba's death. Davo had to struggle with three jobs to have ends meet."

Suru understood that Alu was a victim of socialization.

The following day, Alu and Davo stopped by Iya's house with a card: "Thank you for my first birthday party at the age of thirteen. God bless you!"

Suru was shocked, and he cried. From that day on, Suru and Alu became friends. Alu confessed to Suru that the invitation was a turning point in his life. It retrieved him from his isolated world, and it spared him from becoming a criminal in his adult life. He was grateful for that. Suru was his first friend. He trusted Suru, and he enjoyed the experience of trusting someone. Eventually, Alu gave up his bullying behavior and became a good man.

Iya told Suru to pay attention to people who are marginalized. Suru learned to contemplate God's image in the homeless next door and in prisoners. We all should find constructive ways to integrate those who are excluded from society for one reason or another. Society is not happy when some of its children are left out.

Suru leaned on Iya's assets in contemplative meditation through his years in college. As a college student, Suru once studied hard for a test that he ended up failing. He had to retake the course the following semester. Suru was irritated and frustrated. He spoke to his mother about his frustrations.

Iya encouraged Suru to contemplate the handiwork of God in successes and sometimes in failures. Suru explained that his rational mind could not afford to do in his philosophy classes. In philosophy, Suru learned that he was responsible for his own success and failure.

Iya agreed with Suru on that, but she quickly added that philosophical perspectives could not explain all existential experiences. "Philosophy could be shorthanded in some situations and ought to humbly give up to theology in such instances."

Suru did not fully understand what his mother meant, but he

decided to spend some time in contemplative meditation on his failure. It was hard, but Suru listened to Iya's advice and registered for the course. The course was taught by a different teacher—the best teacher Suru had in college. His name was Dr. Bayo. That teacher was highly regarded among the faculty members in his department and in the university at large. His excellence in teaching and the quality and scope of his research and scholarship were impressive. Suru learned more qualitatively and quantitatively in that class than when he first took the course. With Dr. Bayo, Suru enjoyed the course. That teacher had the reputation of being a tough grader, but Suru scored high on all his tests. Due to his high scores, Suru ended up getting a paid position as a research assistant in the department in his senior year. While he was retaking the course, Suru felt happy all semester long. He thought he was taking his best course in college with the best teacher ever. Eventually, Suru thanked Iya for convincing him to see how God intervenes in our successes as well as in our failures. Suru learned that God can transform our failures into great opportunities for learning and success.

Suru's mother proactively and efficiently stood her son in a good stead with contemplative meditation. Iya shaped Suru with contemplative meditation by sharing her own experiences. She carefully trained Suru to embrace the practice of contemplative meditation in his daily existence.

In his adult life, Suru was blessed with more formal and sophisticated training in contemplation and meditation. During his Jesuit training, Suru was exposed to and anointed with the process and potential of meditation. Suru's memorable Jesuit experience transformed his existence forever. He formally acquired the habit of a daily practice of contemplative meditation. Based upon his own experience and practice, Suru understood how contemplative meditation allows human beings to contemplate the life of a mentor. Ideally, such a mentor is spiritual leader. We contemplate their lives for inspiration and motivation.

As human beings, we need role models to inspire us and motivate us on good behaviors. Their lives tell us that it is possible for human beings to do good deeds. Every morning, you connect with your mentor in contemplative meditation. You contemplate in meditation someone you admire to inspire your actions. You contemplate how they react or would react to real-life situations. In the beginning of the process, you can read an extract from a book that tells the story of their life. You can also use their speech or words. As you read on them, you contemplate them and listen to them. As you contemplate them, you make the resolution to model your daily actions after them. You resolve to follow the good example they set through their life stories. You set to imitate them and spiritually ask for their help in doing so. It does not matter whether your mentor is still alive or has breathed their last breath. Suru contemplates daily in meditation the life of Jesus Christ, his mentor and Lord. Suru seeks Jesus's assistance to model his life after his.

Looking at his daily activities and interactions, Suru can certainly testify to some benefits of contemplative meditation. All days Suru is able to practice contemplative meditation go smoothly. Such days are highly productive, and Suru feels happy throughout. His interactions are constructive in the course of those days. A colleague once suggested that Suru would smile at everyone and everything, including trees. That colleague exaggerated.

Suru does get grumpy, but his social environment often tells him that he smiles a lot. Suru is not always mindful of it. Every once in a while, he catches himself smiling. Another colleague once asked Suru for the secret behind his smile. Suru knew that when he failed to practice contemplative meditation, his face was not so smiley.

His response to that colleague's inquiry was straightforward. Every morning when he practices contemplative meditation, it allows him to spend time in the divine presence of his best friend and coach. In silence, he would contemplate and meditate on God's goodness for allowing him a new day and the divine patience with him. In gratitude, Suru would present himself to the divine presence with his problems, his fears, or his stresses. In the process, Suru reviews the daily miracle God performs by miraculously healing people from diseases and protecting travelers on the road, in waterways, and in the air. Suru contemplates how the divine presence repairs his body from fatigue as he sleeps. He also presents to God his objectives and challenges for the new day. He asks for divine advice and guidance, and he calls for God's assistance in daily activities and interactions. He commits himself and all his day to God by trusting in the divine providence.

Contemplative meditation allows Suru to share his existential problems with his best friend and coach. The divine presence listens to Suru and enlightens him. Suru listens to and learns from the divine presence. The process is spiritual and therapeutic. It allows Suru to communicate with the divine presence in his life. It also allows him to release stress and negative energy. It allows him to embrace the positive divine energy by means of positive thinking in contemplating the goodness of God.

By the end of Suru's hour of contemplative meditation, he feels relaxed, ready, and excited for the new day. His personal experience teaches Suru that contemplative meditation beneficently affects his body and mind. Whenever he practices contemplative meditation, he notices its impacts on his appetite and metabolism. Suru eats and sleeps well after contemplative meditation.

Some friends tell Suru that he eats a lot, but it does not show up on his body. In response, he tells them that he exercises and meditates.

Contemplative meditation may have something to do with the appearance of the human body. Its practice also affects Suru's emotions and feelings. It helps him constructively counter moments of anxiety and depression. Contemplative meditation sanitizes Suru's body and mind by helping reduce or remove toxic wastes and negative energy or thoughts. Whenever he practices contemplative meditation, Suru feels calm and happier. It affects his interactions. When he practices contemplative meditation, Suru handles conflict more peacefully and transforms it into an opportunity for learning, change, and growth.

Suru once came home exhausted after a long, tough day at work. After he opened the garage door, his children ran to him with joy to welcome him home. After parking his car carefully, Suru took the time to hug his kids one by one with a smile—even though he was very tired.

A week later, Suru came home exhausted after a long, rough day at work. As usual, Suru's children innocently rushed with joy to welcome their father home, but this time, Suru put down the windows of his car and started yelling at the kids to get out of the driveway to allow him to park his car. After he parked the car, Suru shouted at the children, ordering them to avoid rushing into the garage when he comes home.

The innocent children cried bitterly; they were not happy with their father's behavior. They could barely understand why he yelled at them. Suru's three-year-old son later explained that he was scared when his father was shouting. Suru was grumpy and failed to hug them as he usually did.

That night, before bedtime, Suru's self-examination allowed him to understand he was wrong. He felt guilty. And that feeling of guilt haunted him all night long.

The next morning, as Suru was using his contemplative meditation to review his behavior from the night before, he thought about what made that day different. Suru could not identify all the factors that contributed to his behavior, but he was able to observe that he did not practice contemplative meditation on that devilish day.

In comparing with the two days mentioned above, Suru observed that he had the same quality and length of sleep, interacted with the same people at work, ate the same food, performed the same tasks, and had the same activities in the same environment. The weather was also the same. He even drove the same car. The only thing that was different was that Suru practiced contemplative meditation on the day he treated his children decently and hugged them. He failed to practice contemplative meditation on the day he yelled at them. Later on, Suru apologized to his children for yelling. Suru's personal experience allows him to attest that the practice of contemplative meditation creates peace and harmony in human existence.

Suru has friends who believe contemplative meditation helps them transcend anxiety and depression for serenity. A friend of his came back from a military deployment with a severe post-traumatic stress disorder. Ayi spent several years taking different medications prescribed by doctors to treat his condition. He did not get any tangible satisfactory outcomes for his health. He admitted that his stress level lowered drastically shortly after he started practicing contemplative meditation. Ayi even acknowledged how contemplative meditation made him feel relaxed and happy in comparison to the years he was on medications. Contemplative meditation has the potential to calm the body and mind.

Suru's mother spent time understanding the impact of contemplative meditation on the body and mind by relying on her culinary experiences and observations. Her cooking experiment with water is meaningful here. When you put fresh drinking water in a pot and let it sit still, it is calm and peaceful. Its freshness allows you to drink such water without running any risk of hurting your mouth or digestive system. As you put the pot on the stove for the fresh water to boil, the heat triggers the ebullition process. The water slowly loses its calmness. It gets agitated, troubled, and hot. If you try to drink the hot water, it will burn you and harm you. That harm may even be fatal.

If you were to keep the heat on over a long period of time and not turn it off, the water would eventually dry up and result in fire and further damages. That would be a stupid and criminal option. When you turn off the heat, the water slowly calms down and recovers it freshness after cooling off. You can drink it without hurting yourself.

In the same way, the social pressures and turbulences of our daily activities turn the heat up on us; they shake us and stress us out. We get agitated, troubled, and hot. They create fatigue in our bodies and confusion in our minds. We get angry, vulnerable, and irritable. Contemplative meditation makes us turn off the heat. It allows our bodies and minds to calm down and cool off. A few minutes of silent contemplative meditation allows us to cool down, relax, and rejuvenate happily. It provides some peace of heart and mind. According to Suru's mother, contemplative meditation lays a great foundation for happiness. It connects you to the peaceful source of happiness and gives you a key to unlock the door of happiness.

In observing his mother and by relying on his own practice of contemplative meditation, Suru experienced how meditation could empower meditators for peacemaking in their social environment. Whenever he meditated, he was able to better listen to others and patiently collaborate with them for problem-solving. Other meditators Suru surveyed confirmed that meditation predisposed them to listening and negotiation for conflict transformation. If meditation positively affects your body and mind with peace, it also has the potential to shower your social interactions with peace. The peace your heart and mind enjoy through meditation will likely spill over as you engage with other people or parties for your happiness and theirs. If we have peace within us, the odds are we will make peace with others. If we are truly happy, we will make others around us happy by all odds. Meditation helps build peace in us and out of us.

If contemplative meditation provides a key to happiness by helping for peacemaking with self and others, the reader could wonder what some of the other keys to happiness are. Suru's mother would certainly assert that contemplative meditation represents an angular pillar in the construction of a peaceful or happy life, but there are other significant pillars in the architecture of happiness. Iya's perspective on dreams is meaningful in that regard.

CHAPTER 8

Bridging the Gap between Dreams, Professional Reality, and Vocations

During Suru's initiation to the Catholic faith, Iya decided to check whether her son's attendance at catechism was affecting his academic performance at school. On a Friday evening, she asked him how his school day was.

Suru was excited to share Martin Luther King Jr.'s "I Have a Dream" speech. Suru was awestruck and amazed by the speech. He thought it was a meaningful, well-written, and eloquently communicated speech. Suru had to fully understand what a dream meant, but after reading King's words, he felt a strong awareness that there was a gap between dreams and reality.

Suru started asking himself existential questions about dreams and dreaming. He struggled with a series of dream-related questions over a period of time. Out of all the questions, one remained relevant and intrusive in Suru's mind. How could he bridge the gap between his dreams and reality? He kept ruminating on that question. Just like Martin Luther King, Suru thought he had great dreams, but he was not sure how to achieve them.

Martin Luther King was confident in his dream for a better American society, but Suru was not sure where and how Martin Luther King got his motivation to be so hopeful. Suru struggled with his main question for a relatively long period, but he was not able to solve its puzzle.

During Iya's academic check-up, Suru seized the golden opportunity that time offered him without any reservation. He asked his mother to tell him about her own dreams in an attempt to find a solution to his challenging question.

Iya seemed surprised by her son's interest in dreams. Suru did not know a lesson on dreaming was in the horizon on his mother's schedule for that week. He certainly would not mind adding such a lesson to her wish list. Instead of responding to Suru's request, Iya drew near, took her son to his bedroom, and wished him a night full of dreams. It was almost eight o'clock, Suru's bedtime. He understood immediately that it was too late to speculate on dreams.

The next morning, Iya asked if he had any dreams while sleeping. His answer was negative. After breakfast, they walked silently in the beautiful garden behind their house. A few minutes later, they sat down underneath a eucalyptus tree Baba had planted in the yard. It was the same eucalyptus tree Suru's father was lying under when the snake crossed over him. Iya asked her son what he thought of the tree. Suru had no idea about his mother's motives or expectations, but he described the well-groomed, well-rounded, and lovely tree.

Suru's mother explained that the tree was the outcome of a dream by his father. Her husband dreamed of having that tree in his backyard. Baba loved eucalyptus trees. When he first saw a eucalyptus tree in front of a neighbor's house, he loved its large branches, green leaves, and shade. Whenever he passed by the tree, he enjoyed its branches, the shade, and its fragrance. Standing by the tree made Baba feel good and happy. He bought a young tree for his own house, planted it, and carefully watered it. It grew into a well-groomed, big, and colorful tree.

Iya and Suru were interrupted by the music of birds in the eucalyptus tree. Suru looked up and saw two sparrows making a nest on the tree. They seemed so busy. Apparently, they had a lot to do and had no time to waste. Even Iya and her son's presence did not deter them from focusing on their duty. Suru and his mother were amused and enthused while watching the enthusiastic birds. The two sparrows looked very safe in the tree. Later on, Suru would understand their attitude. Birds only land or nest in trees that look safe and attractive. The trees in Baba's backyard hosted nests of a flock of sparrows. There were also trees with no nests on them. Suru's father was fond of feeding sparrows. Every weekend, he provided them with a plate of seeds. He would also refill a jar of water for their drinking and entertainment. Baba was so dedicated to them, and he requested that everyone respect the presence of the birds.

Iya and Suru could also tell the birds enjoyed Baba's presence. They were not afraid of him. They would rush to welcome him as soon as they saw him. Suru's father was beloved by the sparrows. In general, Baba was a lover of birds. He enjoyed their company. All birds were welcomed in his backyard except the owls. Baba's parents associated those flat-faced and hooked-beak night birds with witchcraft in part due to the nocturnal habits of the birds. As a result, owls were perceived as witches' nocturnal helpers.

Whenever Baba saw an owl in the backyard, he would attribute it to a witch's visit and try to kill it by any means. He once killed a lost owlet. Knowing the cultural setting Baba came from might give you a glimpse into his beliefs and attitudes vis-à-vis owls. When we become aware of where people come from, we may understand some of their attitudes or behaviors. How we view the world is in part rooted in our cultural environment. Our worldview owes a lot to the cultural ocean we swim in. Our philosophy of life is the product of our cultural cradles. Suru's father grew up with voodoo and people who believed in paranormal phenomena. Baba was involved with voodoo before his conversion to Christianity. Owls are perceived as witch birds in voodoo. In that perspective, Suru's father had an aversion to owls. He did not want to see them around. On the contrary, he was attracted to other birds such as sparrows.

Mindful of Baba's affection for sparrows, and to avoid distracting the two sparrows from fixing their nest, Iya and Suru decided to move to another corner of the backyard. It was a very spacious backyard with a variety of trees, including papaya trees, a guava tree, and an avocado tree.

As soon as Iya and her son stepped away, a lizard rushed from behind the trunk of the tree they were heading to. Suru suggested that the lizard probably either lived in the tree or had its hole underneath the tree.

Iya said that lizards, birds, and even squirrels seemed to be enjoying the trees in the backyard. The list was not limited to lizards and birds. It also included butterflies, dragonflies, mantes, spiders, and flying bats.

Three butterflies were hovering on top of the tulip tree. Not too far away, two more butterflies were inhaling the roses and sunflowers that decorated the fence. Two dragonflies were happily hunting for mosquitoes. Two spiders were weaving a web in the nearly hidden space between the fence and a rose tree.

A couple of meters away, a mantis was holding another insect hostage. The mantis seemed to be enjoying its prey with its spiny forelegs. Suru was amused while watching the mantis. Its gestures gave Suru the impression that the mantis was grateful to heaven for catching its prey. In another corner of the backyard, some brown bats had a nest in an acacia tree.

Some nights, the backyard was lit up by fireflies blinking in every corner. As Suru watched all the animals and insects in the beautiful backyard, he got the impression that they all fully embraced their natural environment and enjoyed its fullness. Of all living species, only one tends to resist or refute nature and push it to the side. Only human beings trade assets of their natural environment for artificial ones. We pay a high price for doing so. Our health and happiness suffer from our rebellion against nature. We are bound to live by the nature for happiness and peace.

If the squirrels were able to have their holes in the backyard, Suru thought foxes could also make theirs there. Suru shook his head in dismay, hoping there was no fox wandering in the backyard. Suru was as scared of foxes as he was of snakes. He was aware that some snakes visited the backyard sometimes in pursuit of mice and chicken eggs. His father killed serpents in the backyard more than once—even though Iya often prevented Baba from killing them.

Suru was not entertained by snakes or foxes. He would not mind sharing his living space with birds and butterflies, but he found it terrifying to share the space with snakes or foxes.

Iya indicated how the backyard and the house emerged from human dreams.

Suru asked his mother to define a dream.

Iya said that dreams were a set of human thoughts or sensations that human subjects worked on to become a reality.

Suru thought that definition was vague and asked Iya to illustrate it with her own dreams.

Iya started telling her son how he was a product of his parents' dreams.

Suru requested further clarifications.

Iya explained how she dreamed of having a baby boy just like

Suru. It started as a thought that crossed her mind, a product of her imagination. She shared it with her husband, and they launched the actualization of their mutual desire. This slowly translated into a pregnancy.

Iya had no doubt that she was pregnant with a baby boy. All through the gestation, she knew a boy was growing inside her. Before hearing her baby's gender from the gynecologist, Iya decided to start preparing to welcome a baby boy. She bought a series of blue T-shirts and blue toys. She also purchased a blue draping for the baby's crib.

Baba asked his wife to check with the gynecologist before spending money on blue clothing, but Iya claimed it was not necessary to check. She remained faithful to her dream. To Baba's surprise, the next visit to the doctor proved Iya was right. It was a boy. Iya was extremely happy.

Baba asked her to be cautious because doctors can make mistakes. He told Iya to wait until the arrival of the baby before celebrating. Iya insisted it was a boy. Before labor and delivery, she explained that only a baby boy could kick the way her baby was kicking. She thought baby girls would not bother mothers that much—at least based on her experience giving birth to girls.

A few hours later, Suru came out as a boy.

Iya owed that great achievement to the Creator of all things, but she also owed it to her dream. Suru's mother stressed how all good dreams could be achieved as long as the dreamers actively believe in the power and their dreams and their potential for realization. Suru was very impressed with his mother's conceptualization. He was eager to listen to more of Iya's dreams.

His mother took him back to the family room and asked him to look straight ahead. In front of Suru, there was a painted board with a word translated in several languages. It was the handiwork of his mother's friend. Fatou was a very talented artist who spoke a dozen languages.

Iya asked him how many languages he was able to speak or read.

Suru was only able to speak four languages more or less fluently. That was not many when compared to how many languages Fatou could speak, but Iya proudly acknowledged that her son's ability to speak multiple languages was an outcome of dreams. She wanted Suru to be multilingual, and she worked hard to expose him to several languages.

Iya's reaction surprised Suru; it was not her habit to seek credit for her achievements. He understood it was only fair to give his mother credits because she deserved it.

Iya confessed to her son that it was hard, but she never gave up on that dream. Suru was not always an easy child to teach. The result was gratifying: her adolescent son could speak multiple languages.

Suru felt an obligation to express his gratitude to his mother.

Iya quickly indicated that he should be grateful to the human ability to dream. She said, "Human beings dream, and nearly nothing can stop them from dreaming. Nevertheless, they ought to sort out their dreams and find creative ways to achieve their dreams. Constructive dreams and destructive dreams often visit our imaginations. We ought to let negative dreams go their way, and we must welcome positive dreams. To welcome our good dreams is to rely on our potential to carry them through. Self-determination and self-confidence eventually overcome all barriers and pave the way for means of realization."

Dreams call reality to life. Some people dreamed and invented the telephone, radio, and television. Others dreamed of inventing computers, the internet, Facebook, Google, YouTube, and Twitter. They also achieved their dreams. Barack Obama dreamed of becoming the president of the United States of America, and he made history.

The author of this book dreamed of writing it, and it happened.

Iya said, "Dreaming dynamically affects reality and sustains its being. Between dreams and reality is a bridge made of resolutions and actions. Positive dreams bring resolutions that materialize into concrete acts. A positive dream is a wake-up call for self-actualization. When you act resolutely on your dream, reality of happiness comes your way."

Iya asked her son another question about his dreams. She was curious about what Suru was dreaming of becoming in life.

Suru immediately responded that he wanted to become a peacemaker.

His mother smiled and asked him to work toward achieving that dream. She indicated that it would require hard work, daily commitment, and sacrifice.

Suru begged his mother to say more about what she meant.

Iya responded that achieving a dream would take the dreamer through different ways, hills, and valleys with moments of clarity and darkness. In the midst of highs and lows, the dreamer should not give up. Regardless of the circumstances, the dreamer should keep their head up and look at the horizon of achievement because humankind holds the potential for actualization.

Suru did not understand what Iya meant, but he saved his breath this time. He kept her golden advice in mind like a treasure.

When Suru became a teenager, he heard a divine calling to become a priest in the Roman Catholic Church. At that time, he thought the best way to achieve his dream of peacemaking was to become a diocesan priest. Suru wanted to do so in order to teach and preach peace and teach peacemaking. He was a well-behaved altar boy. At the age of fifteen, he decided to leave his parents and go join the minor seminary of Meji. Meji was a small village located between the twin cities of Hicon and Bomy in Nineb.

Iya and Baba did not oppose their son's decision. They welcomed it with respect and told Suru that he was always welcome home if he happened to change his mind.

Suru did not take such words seriously, but he would understand what they meant later on. So was launched Suru's training toward priesthood. In the first month at the seminary, Suru started wondering if he was in the right place to achieve his dream. He had the assistance of good spiritual advisors who guided him patiently and kept Suru going on his training path. In the process, he made some good progress physically, emotionally, academically, mentally, and spiritually. However, his doubts remained about whether he was in the right place and on the right path toward achieving his goal. His teachers, trainers, and spiritual guides were all satisfied with his progress and enthusiasm, but Suru was not happy inside. He felt and decided to leave the seminary after eleven years. It was a tough decision. He ran the risk of losing all the privileges and prerogatives he had as a good seminarian. He was faced with contradictions from colleagues, friends, teachers, and parishioners with whom his decision was not welcomed. He felt social pressures from all corners of his environment—except from Iya and Baba—but he felt some peace of mind after his decision to withdraw from the seminary.

Suru's mother welcomed her son's decision and reminded him of her initial warning about the challenges of achieving any dream. Immediately after Suru's decision to quit the seminary, Iya woke him up. Suru wondered what his mother's motives were. With a smile, Iya whispered that a path was closed, but his dream would leave on ever.

Suru enthusiastically agreed with his mother. In the same breath, he spoke to her about his decision to embark on a new path toward achieving his dream. He decided to join the Jesuits. The Jesuit order was founded by Saint Ignatius of Loyola. Suru initially thought his decision to quit the diocesan seminary had something to do with his lack of efficient spiritual methods to help build peace within himself. He thought the Jesuit spirituality would provide him with spiritual tools of discernment. Suru was full of respect and admiration for Jesuits, and he was in love with the Jesuit spirituality.

Iya and Baba welcomed their son's decision to become a Jesuit priest. In times of decisions, Suru's parents would often respectfully leave him to his own devices. Suru was excited to join the Jesuits.

He was admitted to a Jesuit novitiate in a different country called Nocam to start his initiation toward becoming a Jesuit priest in the Catholic Church. Suru's doubts emerged. He was thoroughly exposed to the spiritual techniques of examination of conscience, discernment of spirits, meditation, contemplation, and others presented in the *Spiritual Exercises of Saint Ignatius of Loyola*, a powerful spiritual classic. Spiritual strategies took Suru's breath away. He enjoyed the thirty-three-day retreat when he mingled with the exercises. They helped him develop skills in spiritual discernment, meditation, and contemplation.

At the end of the exercises, Suru formally decided to become a Jesuit, but he still had some hesitation about the right place for achieving his dream. With the spiritual exercises, it appeared that God wanted Suru on the path of teaching peace and peacemaking.

His decision to serve as a Jesuit was made official when he professed his religious vows some months later. In total, Suru spent two years of very well-ordered spiritual training in the Jesuit novitiate. Following the profession of his religious vows of chastity, poverty, and obedience, he went on to pursue his training to become a Jesuit priest. This journey took Suru to an institute of philosophy in another country called Decog.

The journey of Jesuit training would take Suru to many other countries, but three years after professing his religious vows, his doubts about becoming a priest and serving in a religious order grew even stronger. Suru thought religious celibacy might not be his calling. He felt he would be happy if he could get married and have children. Suru became more and more uncomfortable at the thought of spending his entire life in religious celibacy without a wife and children. It was not just a crisis; Suru's mind encountered relentless fears in that regard. He also felt trapped in the challenges of mystics and politics. Suru felt some malaise about the degree of politics occurring within religious communities. He became critical of some incoherence in the religious community and beyond. His eyes opened to the misery and weaknesses of the human condition—regardless of our intentions to serve God. He discovered his own weaknesses and naïveté. Suru developed some good habits over those years, but he also developed bad habits. As much as he did wonders for his spiritual methods, he went to the devil more than once. He lied to protect himself, to make gains, and to succeed. All such feelings and circumstances became scary and made Suru anxious. His times of desolation were longer than his moments of consolation.

Suru was not happy where he was. Thankfully, the Jesuit spiritual exercises granted him well-balanced tools for decision-making in such circumstances. Per the Jesuit devices of spiritual discernment, whenever your feelings of happiness about a decision, a location, or a project are stable and enduring, you have made the right decision, you are on the right track, and you belong where you are. You should stay there and enjoy yourself.

On the other hand, if your happiness is unstable or short-lived, if you feel between the devil and the deep sea, if you feel worried or troubled by a decision you have made, what you are doing, or the location you are in, you have made a wrong decision, are doing the wrong thing, and are in the wrong place. You should revise your decision, review your strategy, change your path, and move to a different location. You should turn your ship in a different direction.

Suru used his toolbox in that situation. By listening to his conscience and the movements of consolation and desolation crossing his spirit, mind, and body, he made a serene decision to leave the Jesuit order. It was not an easy decision due to all the risks and social pressures.

As Suru expected, his colleagues and friends were not happy with his decision. Some teachers and spiritual guides were disappointed. They did not understand his rationale for leaving. They could not believe he was not happy. Suru could not blame them because they were judging him on his appearance. They saw a good Jesuit with an upbeat spirit, a smiling face, and great potential for transforming society constructively under the Jesuit banner. Suru was well thought of in his community. His appearance put him in a good stead. Suru felt relieved and happy after making his decision. He ended his dream of becoming a Jesuit, but his pursuit of his ultimate dream, his vocation, continued. What was his vocation? That was the question Suru was eager to find an answer to. He would patiently expect the right answer. It would eventually come along.

Your vocation is what you feel happy doing. We are not in a vocation primarily for the money or the prestige, but because we love what we do. It would be good if all types of vocations and human service could be equally recognized and respected. Equal recognition and respect might imply churning social reassessments and adjustments for equal treatment and rewards across the spectrum.

Suru often wondered why some professions are highly rewarding financially and others are not. You need to forgive Suru's naivety here. He hopes you will forgive him if what he thinks here does not make any sense to you. Society is certainly good to humankind. Society is very supportive of human nature and existence.

Suru finds it hard at times to comprehend the rationale or justifications of some social traditions or the status quo. Some social standards challenge the notion of equal respect for all human beings. Suru may need some help to understand social structures and systems fairly. You can disagree with Suru on some of his perspectives. Medical, legal, and accounting are high-paying professions in Nineb.

People would justify their high salaries by telling Suru that medical doctors carry the burden of treating patients over long hours. Lawyers spend long hours preparing for and standing on trials. Accountants can get very stressed out while spending hours handling money. Suru highly regards medical doctors and values their dedication to human health. He also recognizes lawyers and appreciates their service to society. Suru respects our accountants for their much-needed services. He knows money can add stress. You can get extremely stressed out dealing with money daily. Suru endorses such hardworking professionals. It is fair that their hard work should result in high compensation.

But what about our teachers in elementary, middle, and high schools? Do they not carry the burden of spending long hours educating our children? They do. It would be hard to imagine anyone achieving their dreams of becoming a respected doctor, lawyer, or accountant without the relevant educational prerequisites in elementary, middle, and high schools. We owe a lot to our teachers.

Suru would advocate that even stay-at-home mothers should be financially rewarded for accepting all the stress it takes to raise the next generations of eminent doctors, lawyers, accountants, and leaders. Suru would thank his mother for taking all the stress from his childhood to allow him to be where he is now.

Suru was a wayward and capricious child. He was pigheaded and happy-go-lucky at times. If not for Iya's total dedication and willingness to raise him up, Suru would not be who he is today. Staying home to raise a child is a full-time job. Out of modesty, our brave mothers would certainly not request a salary for doing what they do. In most cases, they humbly and happily dedicate their lives to raising their children without asking for anything in return.

What if we could reward our stay-at-home mothers with high salaries? After all, they work so hard to bear us and raise us. Suru could not imagine how our mothers and teachers manage to do it all so patiently and kindly. He could not understand how those brave kindergarten teachers manage to successfully deal with the group dynamics of dozens of children assigned to their classrooms. God bless them!

Suru has a few little children and gets some taste of what it entails. You cannot imagine the group dynamic in his house during weekends unless you have children around. It can be challenging to supervise children. In the midst of the challenges and stress he often experiences in the deployment of his children's highly energetic interactions, Suru often feels his skills in conflict resolution are poor. He often needs to pile up loads of patience to handle them. In that process, Suru often mindfully gets his inspiration from the patience teachers exemplify in their classrooms. Teacher salaries remain extremely low in comparison to others. Society needs to find fair ways to reward teachers more lucratively and repair what Suru perceives as discriminations in professional salaries.

Discrimination in professional pay scales could lead people to select professional paths that do not suit them. Such people would wear professional suits that do not fit them; the size is either too small or too large for them. Many of us are driven into a given profession that is not our vocation. We embark on a profession simply because it would stand us in a good stead on one or another account. In general, we end up in professions that are not our calling due to social pressures mounting from prestige, peers, family, or financial advantages.

If we are happy while doing what we do, our happiness radiates constructively in serving others in our social environment, regardless of how lucrative our service is. Doctors are primarily in the field for quality in patients' care. They are not so much into the quantity of patients they see but the quality of care and the time they dedicate to each patient.

Suru is fortunate to know many good doctors who he admires and respects for their noble services. Do all health care providers perceive their services as a vocation? Only health care providers could sincerely and adequately answer that question from the bottom of their hearts. Suru can only hope there are no health care providers who are in the field primarily for the money. If there were, Suru would not want to be a patient of such providers. Suru can only hope there are no lawyers who are in the practice just for the money. If there were, Suru would certainly not want to be their client.

If we are in professions that are not our vocations, chances are high we will not be happy doing what we do. And if we are not happy in doing our jobs, we run the risk of doing harm to ourselves and to others. If we are not happy in our professions, it is in our best interest and in the best interest of our social environment to find our vocations.

If your profession is not your vocation, you should keep on searching until you uncover your vocation. Though your current professional reality may not be your vocation, it is not a waste of time. Suru's personal experience has taught him that everything we learn or do or go through in terms of profession or training prepares us for our vocation or calling within society. As a result, you should never boycott or neglect any job or training opportunity.

The general education students get from elementary school, middle school, high school, or college prepares them to unlock the door to a field of specialization or what they enjoy doing. In the same way, your profession can prepare and propel you to land on the ground of your vocation. No one would want to remain an elementary school student or a middle school student or a high school student or even a college student forever. You might feel uncomfortable at some point. In the same way, you might feel uncomfortable spending your entire life in a profession that is not your vocation.

You may want to be mindful to use the ground of your profession to dig for your vocation and move on at the right time. It is never too late to discover your vocation. When the time feels right, don't hesitate to switch your professional coat for happiness or peace. Do not be reluctant or averse to taking off your professional coat for your vocational suit.

Suru knows some great minds and hearts that did just that. They subsequently became happy in doing what they do. Suru thinks of a trained medical doctor, Ada, who practiced modern medicine for years. She certainly was successful in her practice, but she was not happy. Among the contradictions Ada encountered in her profession was the volume of patients she was required to see daily and the pace she was required to observe while seeing those patients. Adding to other nerve-racking factors in her life, the fast pace of her job resulted in a stressful lifestyle to the detriment of her own health.

After thinking about it carefully, Ada courageously quit that profession, which was obliterating her well-being. That move granted her time to uncover her vocation. Ada ended up finding her vocation in stimulating people's minds to help cure their bodies. She felt happy in her vocation.

Suru had a teacher, Oni, who was trained as a lawyer. She practiced law for decades, but she did not feel very happy in the process. Oni did not experience the legal path as her vocation. Her legal career opened her eyes to what would become her vocation: helping people deal with conflict by focusing on their interests. Oni found her vocation in teaching and practicing conflict analysis and resolution. She felt happy in that vocation.

Suru's good friend, Eka, was trained as a lawyer. She practiced law for several years, but she aspired to a vocation of teaching and practicing conflict resolution.

Afo initially graduated with degrees in business and mathematics, but he turned his back on a career in business or mathematics. Instead, he happily welcomed a successful career in music.

Another famous music star, Desi, initially graduated with a degree in geography. She ignored professional opportunities in geography and enjoyed a vocational path of singing. The list could be longer. Many people, including Suru, have found their vocations for peace of mind and heart.

CHAPTER 9

Troubles over Punctuality: Be on Time and Earn Peace of Mind and Heart

Suru's years of training in the minor seminary of Meji went by quickly. His first weeks were challenging. He got to meet good teachers and great friends. Most of his fellow seminarians were friendly and well-mannered. Most of the teachers were smart and caring, but Suru was fifteen, and it was his first time living far away from his dear family.

The fact that the seminary was located in a remote village added to his injury. He felt the distance harshly; it was difficult. At times, he felt isolated and lonely. Slowly, Suru learned to handle the distance and cope with his new environment. It was a very long learning process. However, the distance was not his main challenge. Suru's foremost problem had to do with punctuality. In the seminary, students were all required to be on time for all activities. They had to wake up every morning at the sound of a big bell. They would shower and show up for the first daily prayer and Mass. Students also had to be on time for classes.

While Suru was living at home with his parents, he had enough time on his hands for his daily routines. He usually had the ways and means for all activities, but in the seminary, he had to rush to do everything. He had to hurry to brush his teeth and take a shower before the first prayer and Mass in the morning. Seminarians had between fifteen to thirty minutes every morning for such routines. Suru was among those who thought the amount of time was too short. He was very slow in taking his shower. It would take him forever to get ready. As a result, he was often late to attending the matins and laud, morning prayer, or Mass.

Suru's fellows who were in charge of the matins and laud were required to write down the names of all seminarians who showed up late for the morning prayer. Suru's was often the first on the list, and he was often punished because of it. Suru detested washing and sanitizing the common bathrooms or sorting the corn and beans in the kitchen. Washing lavatories was not the most desirable job. Plus missing his nap never made Suru comfortable. With his parents, he had developed a habit of enjoying his nap in his bed. And he liked it.

Suru's nap time was sacred for him. It was hard to trade it for anything. He did not like purging a punishment during the time allocated to nap, but he had to obey the rules and regulations of the seminary or bear the consequences.

He resolved to work hard on being on time for the morning prayer and Mass. He would rush his shower to make it on time to the chapel. Sometimes he was successful, but other times, he was not so successful. During his shower, Suru enjoyed taking time to feel the water running along his small body. It was refreshing and good for his body and mind.

Baba trained him to take his time and enjoy the shower. He said, "The morning shower is a healthy way to start the day. You enjoy it by allowing fresh warm water enough time to massage your nerves, and you feel the touch. A slow shower should be the first treat every human being begins the day with. It is a nice, healthy way to take care of yourself. It is therapeutic and healthy for the body and mind."

Unfortunately, Baba's great advice did not seem to help the young seminarian. Suru was deeply disoriented and concerned. He decided to take the matter to his mother. Through a short letter, Suru made Iya aware of his issue and requested her advice.

A few weeks later, following lunch in the refectory, Suru was told he had a female visitor in the visitor's kiosk. It was a Sunday afternoon. On Sundays, seminarians were allowed to welcome visitors, but Suru was not expecting anyone. He rushed out of the cafeteria and headed to the kiosk. The kiosk was about four minutes away from the cafeteria. Suru's imagination was bubbling about his unexpected visitor. He was very curious but did not think it could be his mother. When Suru saw Iya as he got close to the kiosk, he could not believe it. It was a great surprise.

From a distance, she said, "Surprise!"

Suru thought it was his mother's response to his request for advice on punctuality. He happily gave her a big hug.

Iya's visit was in response to her son's request about punctuality. Suru was overly excited. The kiosk was crowded with visitors. Suru and Iya thought they needed to find a quiet place to talk confidentially. The green garden of the seminary crossed Suru's mind, but he did not give much consideration to it. It was a hot summer day, and Suru was not sure where to hide for an in-depth conversation with his mother. He invited Iya to follow him. They explored other options. It was difficult to find a secret hideout.

His mind shifted back to the green garden that took his breath away. He got caught up with the idea of sitting under the big mango tree in the center of the garden. Suru and Iya moved closer to the tree and admired its large branches and the shade it provided.

Iya was fond of the shape of the tree. She took some time to contemplate its gray branches and luxuriant green leaves. They were nicely dancing to the rhythm of the breeze. Suru's mother listened to the music of the birds. They seemed to be having an improvised concert to praise the famous tree they found refuge in. Iya could see some of their nests. The scene was beautiful.

Suru thought the mango tree would offer a refuge, and Iya thought it was the ideal location for them to talk. They found two bricks to sit on under the mango tree. Though the bricks were not the most comfortable seats for a long conversation, Iya and Suru spoke for hours. They felt relaxed and safe to talk privately without been disturbed by any curious ears or eyes.

Using her own life stories, Suru's mother spoke to her son, and he listened to her carefully. It was a golden opportunity to improve his lifestyle in the seminary. Suru wanted to show his mother that he took her advice so seriously that he decided to take notes on what she had to say. He was happy that Iya allowed him to do that.

Suru's mother had received her son's letter about his troubles with punctuality. She strategically stood Suru in a good stead to listen to her. She urged her son not to feel bad about his issues with punctuality. Iya pointed out that Suru was not the first to encounter such issues. He was not the only one, and he would not be the last person to deal with punctuality issues.

Punctuality constantly defies human nature. Human nature finds it a challenge to always be on time. We all experience difficulties with being on time at some point in our lives. By nature, we were born to be relaxed and enjoy time. We were not made to rush. We were made to follow the pace of nature, but society and social interactions impose time limits to be on time and rush in some cases. Eventually, society and life experiences train us to adjust and learn to be on time. Iya shared life stories to raise Suru's awareness of how punctuality would remain a consistent challenge that would require consistent attention.

Suru's mother was glad her son was faced with punctuality issues. They had come Suru's way in the past. They did not make him happy then. His mother knew they would come his way again. Being late for activities or events does not instill anyone with good feelings. Iya had no doubt about that. She mentioned the incident at the movie theater on his seventh birthday, which trapped her son in an unhappy feeling. Punctuality contributes to happiness.

Iya invited him to revisit and understand the meaning of that lesson. She encouraged him to seize every issue or problem as an opportunity for growth, change, or transformation. She invited him to observe his troubles over punctuality as an opportunity for growth and change.

"Being late for morning activities could not make you happy, but it could remind you that you had the option of not going late."

If Suru wanted to boost his chances for happiness in his new environment, he must find a way to be on time for his activities. Iya shifted the focus of their conversation to her own life story.

Suru listened to his mother patiently.

When Iya started dating Baba, they happily decided to meet every Saturday evening in an open marketplace to spend some quality time and watch the sunset together. The market was located a few kilometers from the house of Iya's parents. It was not too far from the house Baba's mother was living in. His mother's name was Koa. Iya was still living with her parents, but Baba was living about thirty kilometers away in the city where he worked.

Baba would visit Koa every Friday night, and he spent time with her until Sunday afternoon. Baba and Iya agreed that Saturday evening was the best time for them to meet and spend time together. They only had about forty-five minutes for that due to their schedules and other existential circumstances.

Baba would usually arrive late and tired on Friday evening. Upon arriving, he would eat Koa's special supper and go sleep. The next morning, Koa would update her son on all the events happening in the village and proudly take him around to greet the neighbors. By the time their tour ended, it was time for dinner.

Baba had to go early to bed on weekends to rest and release the fatigue from his busy workdays. Baba would never argue with Koa over that. He was a workaholic and was always busy. Before meeting Iya, Baba was killing himself with a heavy workload. He always had a lot of work to complete, but he had discipline. He planned his time and activities well. He liked to be on time or early. He was usually on time for most of his activities.

On the other hand, Iya was relaxed and laid back. Aware of her daughter's attraction to Baba, Ejo was willing to let her meet him every Saturday evening on two conditions. Iya would help Ejo cook dinner on Saturday evenings before leaving for her date. Iya also had to be home within two hours after dinner.

Iya agreed with her mother, but in the beginning, it was a challenge to be on time to her rendezvous with Baba, her hero. On the first Saturday, Iya was late. It took her forever to get ready after helping her mother in the kitchen. She was also late on the next Saturday. Every time Iya was late, she missed Baba. He would come on time, spend about thirty-five minutes waiting for her, and end up leaving unhappily.

Every time she happened to be late, Iya was frustrated and unhappy. She experienced how miserable one could feel being late to a rendezvous. She also put herself in Baba's position and anticipated how she would feel in such a situation.

Iya and Baba did not have a phone to communicate.

Iya spoke to Ejo about her frustrations. At first, Ejo laughed at her daughter. She told Iya to learn to hurry up instead of spending so much of her time in front of the mirror checking how her dress made her look.

On the third Saturday, Iya followed her mother's advice and managed to catch Baba on time. Iya felt great when she saw her man. She was very delighted to see her hero. He was sitting on a small chair by a tree. Baba was wearing a white shirt, black trousers, and black moccasins. He was fond of moccasins and bluchers.

Iya was wearing a fancy black and white skirt, a white blouse decorated with flowery designs, and a bodice. She wore colorful pearls around her neck and other beautiful jewelry around her right hand. Her left hand had some silver ornaments. Her shiny earrings were fake gold. Her curly hair was beautifully combed.

Iya believed in the power of the messages of our dresses and vestments. She was earnest and clean with her clothes. She said, "If you dress neatly and nicely, you show respect for your audience. You should also dress nicely to market yourself. Your dress could reflect the state of your heart and mind. A clean and decent dress reflects a warm heart and a clean, decent, organized mind. A dirty and indecent dress indicates dirtiness and disorganization to some degree. This has nothing to do with being poor or rich. You can certainly be rich and dirty or indecent. You could be poor and clean or decent. Ultimately, your dress symbolizes a channel of communication with others. It does not matter where you are going. You should always dress neatly. What you wear does not have to be expensive or extraordinary, but you need to be clean and decent."

On that romantic evening, Iya's goal was to be neat and charming for her hero. She dressed up to delight, impress, and conquer Baba. She walked up behind him.

Baba did not seem to be aware that Iya was coming, and she

decided to surprise him. She stopped and listened to him singing while he thought nobody was paying attention. She was not aware that he could sing so well. As she got close to him, she walked gently and discreetly on her toes until she reached his back. She covered his eyes with her frail hands, and he did not seem scared. She asked him to guess who it was.

He replied, "It could not be anybody other than my dear."

She smiled and responded that she did not know she was his dear.

He laughed and said she was his dear, his sunshine, and his everything. She felt the fragrance of love being poured in her heart. Iya felt anointed with love. The ointment made her feel good.

She threw herself down on her knees in front of him, and Baba could not hide his admiration. Iya's dress caught his eye. He feasted his eyes on it. His compliments on her dress were straightforward. She looked beautiful. She was dressed like a queen. Baba enjoyed seeing his beloved in her black and white skirt. He made eyes at Iya. He briefly contemplated Iya's face with a covetous smile and landed his hands on her smooth cheeks to feel them. Next, he touched her chin, which made Iya chuckle. She rested her left hand on his right shoulder and used her right hand to feel his rough chin. She had an eye for its roughness. She lifted up her head and massaged Baba's nose with her chin while he leaned forward. Iya made it difficult for Baba to resist her thirst for him. Without any self-control, she started licking her man's lips.

Baba gently buried his tongue inside her mouth. She sucked it, and it tasted sweet. She was about to bite it in order to hold it and savor it longer, but Baba quickly pulled out and said he needed to get her a chair from a store.

Iya replied that Baba's chair was large enough to host both of them; they did not need an additional chair.

Baba tried not to smile, but it did not take long before he nodded. They both saw eye to eye.

In a magical move, she sat astride his open legs. Without his permission, she sat down on his lap and laid her right cheek on Baba's chest. The smell of his skin was irresistible. Iya's right ear was listening to the rhythm of his heartbeat. His heart was beating like a drum. She told him she wanted to dance to the music of his heartbeat.

He was speechless and held her against his chest like a baby. She could tell he was enjoying the moment. She felt warm and happy in his arms. He felt the same way. They both giggled as she said how delighted she was in his arms. He replied that it was her idea. She said that was the whole idea and purpose. They were crazy with love. They were lost in love.

Baba looked at Iya and wondered what happened to her the previous two Saturdays.

Iya confessed her issues with punctuality, apologized, and expressed her frustrations with herself.

Baba also expressed his frustrations.

Iya was aware that you can make people feel miserable when you miss a rendezvous or come late. They both consoled each other and felt better. That evening, they spent a great time watching the sunset, the early moonlight, and the shiny stars in the sky. It was beautiful. Iya was sold. They felt so good and happy together. From that evening, she knew they belonged together.

As Suru listened to Iya, he caught himself daydreaming at some point. He silently wondered why his mother was assailing him with all such details of her relationship with his father. Suru did not understand what it had to do with the young seminarian who was only requesting some advice on punctuality.

Iya thought her story would raise Suru's awareness of the

challenge of punctuality and his potential to transcend it for happiness. "Whenever you are late, you probably miss a lot, including things that make you feel good."

On the way back to her parents' house, Iya devised a strategy for punctuality. That strategy would help her be on time for future dates for weeks and months leading to her wedding to Baba. Iya's strategy was to take her shower and get her dress ready before cooking dinner.

Baba confessed that he did not mind if her body and clothes smelled like food, and he meant it. He once jokingly whispered that the smell would be a reminder of how spicy her body was.

Iya felt flattered and returned the favor with her own compliments. She thought she was lucky to meet such a well-mannered and well-favored man. He was respectful, caring, and dedicated. Most importantly, he was funny. He was fun to be around. He knew how to make people laugh. He knew how to make people comfortable and happy. So far, Iya's astute strategy worked. It helped her be on time from then on. She understood her mother was right in advising her on good time management. Initially, Iya thought she was wasting time in the kitchen, but it turned out she was spending too much time showering and getting dressed in front of the mirror. Iya also learned that when she was late, she hurt herself and others.

As Suru continued to listen to his mother, she moved on to another meaningful story about punctuality. Suru's mother had a group of five business-related friends. They were all involved in the same type of business. They created a support group to network and socialize. They would meet monthly to discuss business, share their experiences or issues, and support one another. Members of the group were taking turns hosting the meeting. Hosting the meeting required some preparations, including cleaning and providing refreshment and dinner. The meeting would usually start at three o'clock in the afternoon and end at five o'clock.

All the members of the group were always punctual—except one. Enu was late for every meeting. Whenever it was her turn to host the meeting, the meeting would start late. Enu always had excuses. Her husband was not feeling well, she was not feeling well, she was not able to find the right items to cook dinner, or she did not have time to clean up her living room to set up for the meeting.

More than once, Enu would start setting up for the meeting only after the other members started showing up at three o'clock. They helped her clean and set up. The meeting would start late and end late. When the meeting ended late, it affected other activities.

Baba was not very happy when Iya came home late because dinner was delayed for the family. Some members of the group voiced their complaints about Enu. Obviously, none of the other members of the group were pleased with Enu's lack of punctuality. Iya was not happy with Enu's attitude about time management. Her time-management skills were very poor.

The group tried to bring other members' concerns and feelings to Enu's attention over and over again. That did not make any change. It did not help Enu get her act together. Iya spent a great amount of time talking to Enu in private without any success. Enu did not take into account any of Iya's suggestions. Enu lost all respect because she was never on time for meetings.

Other members of the group did not feel comfortable in her presence. Enu was uncomfortable whenever the group met. That affected the group meetings and transformed the dynamics of members' interactions. The meetings gradually became tense and unbearable. It was difficult for everyone.

Instead of providing members with support, the group became

useless. Iya and some other members thought about leaving the group, but Iya thought it would be wrong to give up because of a single member's poor manners. Iya did not want Enu's behaviors to dictate how she behaved.

"As much as we can, we should not allow other people's behaviors to determine how we decide or behave without first listening to the inner voice of our conscience."

Most members remembered the goals of the group and how everybody was cooperating—with the exception of Enu. In general, the group thought of addressing the issue and moving on, but they eventually became divided over the right course of action with Enu.

Iya thought of talking to Enu to help her with her punctuality, but some members argued the group had already done enough. They believed the group had given Enu more than enough time. The majority thought it would not be a bad idea for the group to continue its journey without Enu. Keeping Enu in the group or cutting ties with her put the group between the devil and the deep sea. After months of deliberations, the voice of the majority triumphed. The group decided to cut ties with Enu by leaving her behind and getting rid of her. They excluded Enu from their circle. It was a painful decision for Iya, but the meetings went smoothly to the benefit and satisfaction of all members. The group recovered its original happiness and members were very pleased with one another.

Three months after her exclusion from the group, Enu paid Iya a visit on a Friday evening. Enu was apparently ready to clean up her mess and get back on her feet. She apologized for her poor manners and expressed remorse. She said she realized that the group meant a lot to her only after she left. She missed the group so much and was unhappy without its support. Her business was going down because of the lack of group support. She stressed that the business advice and suggestions from the group were golden. Enu had learned her lesson on punctuality the hard way. She asked Iya to beg the other group members to consider her readmission. Enu promised she would do whatever it took to always be punctual.

Iya was pleased to listen to Enu. She could feel the change in Enu's look and in her voice. Everything seemed to indicate that Enu was ready to clean up her act. Iya could tell Enu meant what she said. Iya reassured Enu of her support and promise to advocate for her readmission to the group. Iya thought she would give the devil its due.

Enu's visit happened to be on the eve of Iya's group meeting. It was Iya's turn to host the meeting. Without alerting the other group members, Iya invited Enu to attend the meeting. Iya told Enu to sincerely present her apologies and remorse to the group at the beginning of the proceedings.

Enu was enchanted with that idea. On Saturday afternoon, she showed up at Iya's house fifteen minutes before the start of the meeting. All the other members showed up at 2:55. They were all surprised to see Enu, but nobody showed any sign of discomfort. No one dared ask any further questions. No one dared interact with Enu.

In opening the session, Iya joked that she had a guest speaker for the meeting. The members giggled politely. Some even pulled faces to deride Iya, curious to see what her next word or move would be. They were all sitting on small wooden chairs. The brown chairs were arranged in a circle. Enu was sitting next to Iya.

Iya turned to Enu with smile after the opening statement as an invitation to speak. Members made faces to make fun of Iya again. Some stared at Enu, expecting her to be haughty.

Against all the odds, Enu did not fall in their trap. She did not disappoint Iya. To Iya's surprise, Enu moved to the center of circle and brought herself down to her knees in tears.

The group was all choked up. Enu's majestic move and gesture took their breath away. Nobody expected that behavior from her. Everyone bent their heads forward and dropped tears. All eyes were wet with tears.

From the corner, Suru could see tears traveling down cheeks and noses.

Iya got up to pass around some handkerchiefs. Everybody got one to wipe what the eyes were full of.

Enu confessed and apologized from her knees. She expressed remorse and promised not to go to the devil anymore. She promised she would do wonders for punctuality. Enu showed clear signs of repentance. It was ceremonial, powerful, and meaningful.

The group could not resist Enu's words and actions. They stood up and showered Enu with applause. Awa knelt down and gave Enu a hug. Other members followed Awa's lead and did the same thing.

Enu was once again welcomed into the group. She felt very happy and was always on time for the meetings. Anytime she was the host, she got the group to start on time and cooked delicious meals that made everybody feel good. She ended up earning the group's respect. Enu regained respect only after changing her ways.

Iya approached Enu to inquire about how she managed to make that U-turn and become so good at punctuality. Enu told Iya that she had learned from her mistakes. She ought to work hard to get and keep whatever makes her happy. Iya and Enu remained good friends until Enu breathed her last breath.

Enu's experience thought Iya a lot about the importance of punctuality. Being tardy is like disrespecting the group you are part of. Being on time is showing respect to the people you collaborate with. When you show them respect, they respect you. When you disrespect them, they tend to disrespect you. Anyone who manages to be on time will earn respect and happiness.

Suru thought his mother would put an end to her storytelling, but she looked very inspired and did not want to stop. She kept on talking while her son listened.

Iya would go ahead and open another chapter of her storybook on punctuality. As if she did not learn enough from her previous experiences, years after Iya and Baba got married, she had to deal with issues of punctuality. This time, it had to do with her small business. Iya used to go to a store every week to get supplies for her business. For months, when she got to the store in the afternoon, she would not find some items she needed. She would leave the store unhappy, but when she was able to get there in the morning, she was able to find whatever was on her wish list—and she was happy.

One day, Iya reached out to the owner of the store for advice. His name was Abu. Abu told Iya that the items were always available in the morning. The store was never crowded in the morning. However, many customers would get their supplies at noon. As a result, most of the good items were gone by the time Iya came to the store in the afternoon. Iya's well-timed meeting with Abu gave her something to think about. The information was an eye-opener. It was extremely difficult for Suru's mother to get to the store in the morning due to her morning routines with her family. She felt happy when she was able to get to the store in the morning because she was able to find all the supplies she needed. Iya decided to design a strategy to find a way to always make it to the store way before noon. Iya's strategy eventually paid off.

Iya went ahead and spoke about her strategy to Suru. To be on time every day, she had to plan her day and activities ahead of time. In the process of talking about her strategy, Suru's mother paused at some point to make sure her son remembered her lesson on planning. Iya had to call upon a daily planner or a calendar for assistance. She told Suru to put his hands on a daily planner and plan his life around the clock. Iya promised to buy her son a daily planner in case Suru did not have one.

"Planning your daily activities gives you enough time to anticipate and time them. Every night, before going to bed, make sure you read your planner to see how the next day is timed and ordered. And evaluate your day every night before going to bed. In the process of your evaluation, think of whatever makes you waste time—and get rid of it. Moreover, a weekly review of your days and activities will maximize your chances of success and sustainability in maintaining your peace of heart and mind. Explore the option of breaking down the amount of time you have and allocate it accordingly to your activities. In whatever you do, take into account the amount of time on your hands and divide it up for use. In a system that puts a lot of demands on you, you have to split up your time according to the length and importance of your activities. All activities might be important, but some are certainly more important and time-consuming than others."

Iya told Suru to divide up his mornings. She told him to try to use three minutes to brush his teeth, ten minutes to enjoy his shower, and five minutes to get dressed. It all added up to eighteen minutes out of thirty, the time on Suru's hands before the morning prayer. That math would imply that Suru would still have twelve minutes to reach the morning prayer without rushing.

"When you begin that type of practice, it might feel mechanical initially, but your body and mind will adapt to it eventually, and you will feel better while improving your punctuality. Remember to always give yourself enough time to reach the location of your activity. Doing so helps you avoid rushing and stressing. Do not wait until the last minute before you leave for your activities. Make sure you avoid the rush of the last minute because it creates stress. If you try to do all that and everything else I told you—and you still feel like you do not have enough time to enjoy your shower—then you do not belong there. You will have to decide."

Suru spent more than two hours listening to his gracious mother's well-spoken sermon on punctuality. He interrupted her time after time to clarify her well-chosen words. They were dense and meaningful.

The mother and son heard a loud bell ringing. Suru explained that the sound of the bell was to signal the end of Sunday games for students. It was also time for all seminarians to get ready for their evening activities. Suru had to go, and his mother had to leave.

Iya gave her son another big hug, and they walked toward the main gate.

Suru bid Iya farewell and watched her leave. He headed to the bathroom like most of his fellows to take his evening shower before their activities resumed. During his shower, Suru kept thinking about Iya's words. Listening to his mother made him think deeply about the value of punctuality. Iya's words and advice were so inspiring. They started creating an immediate turning point in Suru's orientation to punctuality. The strategy Iya spelled out in her talk provided him with inspiration. Suru resolved to adopt her strategy on punctuality, and he was not disappointed. It triggered a shift in Suru's habits on punctuality.

Only a few days after Iya's visit, the strategy started bearing good fruits in her son's life. Suru began to be punctual. Everyone in his social environment started witnessing the changes in his habits. Every morning, Suru was able to take his shower and enjoy it without rushing. He was able to reach the chapel at least five minutes before the start of the morning prayer. Suru became one of the seminarians who showed up first in the chapel in the morning—even before those in charge of the morning prayer sometimes. He was also one of the first students to show up in the classroom. He was mindful of time in all his activities.

It was obvious to everyone in Suru's social environment that something had happened to him, but nobody asked him anything. They were all just full of admiration and respect for Suru. His friends started looking up to him and treating him with esteem.

One day, a classmate and friend of his eagerly asked Suru to explain how he managed to always be in class on time or ahead of time. That classmate's name was Oki. Oki had hard time coming to class on time and was often late.

Suru delightedly talked to Oki about Iya's strategy for punctuality. Oki embraced Iya's strategy, and it noticeably upgraded his punctuality. Oki was grateful to Suru. Some of Suru's teachers also noticed he was the first student to show up in the classroom. They were impressed and marveled at the positive changes in their student's habits. The impact of Iya's advice on her son was profound; the positive changes Suru observed in his habits on punctuality became sustainable. They reverberated all around and well beyond him.

About two months after Iya's visit, Suru was nominated and selected to serve as a permanent timekeeper for the entire seminary. In the seminary, the timekeeper was in charge of ringing the bell to signal the beginning and end of all activities, including waking up everyone for the morning shower. The task was demanding due to its rigorous nature. A timekeeper had to wake up before everyone else and focus on the clock to alert the group. The timekeeper would move with a clock and around the clock, but timekeeping was also considered a noble mission. A timekeeper was an illustration of punctuality. They were expected to always be on time and were role models of punctuality.

The criteria for selecting a timekeeper were excessively rigorous. They included reliability and promptness. Timekeeping was a service assigned only to seminarians who were punctual or reliable. Suru felt honored to serve in that capacity. He also enjoyed the service, which earned him a reputation as a great timekeeper.

Serving as a timekeeper ultimately helped Suru develop good habits of punctuality. Punctuality would progressively immerse his nature and become almost inherent to it. His mother's advice on punctuality changed Suru's life. He learned a lot from it. Iya's experiences on punctuality continue to feed and inspire Suru.

Enu's eye-opening experience taught Suru about the human potential for positive change. We all can do good things. We are all capable of doing what gives us peace of heart and mind if our willingness travels beyond a passive desire and becomes an active will. An active will wants to achieve its dreams for happiness. Change might take us time in some cases; it could be time-consuming and requires patience, but we should always trust in, believe in, and count on our inherent disposition to improve. That was Suru's experience at the beginning of his career as a seminarian. Punctuality remains a challenge for Suru, and it requircs a daily recommitment and willingness.

CHAPTER 10

Nature-Structure Dilemma: Sleep a Lot, Dance, Smile, and Laugh often, Cry as Needed

A few months after Iya's advice on punctuality, Suru felt consolation while thinking of his mother. He was thankful to God for putting her in his life. The insight and advice he got from his mother significantly helped him become more punctual, but he also started developing other questionable habits. Before Iya's visit, Suru was taking a nap religiously, except on the days he was mobilized by force to purge a punishment or due to some other disciplinary issues. However, after his mother's visit, he began to question the usefulness of taking a nap.

On the day Iya came to visit him, Suru did not take a nap. He spent the whole afternoon talking with his mother, including his nap time. And their talk was productive. It made him feel good. Based on that fruitful experience, Suru wondered whether taking a nap was an indispensable thing to do or just a waste of time. He presumed he did not need to sleep during the day. He supposed the day was made to work and not to sleep. Night was for sleeping.

Suru thought he was even getting too much sleep at night and that he needed to make his nighttime sleeping hours shorter if possible. Unfortunately, that was not possible due to the disciplinary rules and regulations of the seminary. Seminarians were required to remain in bed for a number of hours over a rigid time period at night. However, napping was optional in the seminary.

Suru decided to concentrate his attention on ways he would use the time allocated for napping on other activities that would be more useful and rewarding. He was set to design a strategy of sleep deprivation for himself. In the process, he looked for reasons to argue that his afternoon sleep was a waste of time. His efforts were in vain; Suru did not find any sound reason against napping. He found no bad literature on napping. All the information he found highlighted the benefits of taking a nap.

Suru decided to begin to skip his nap in the afternoon. He started using his nap time to study, thinking it would help him save some time to do even better on punctuality and academically. It did not take him long to notice that his afternoons were getting heavier and more difficult to sustain than when he used to take his nap. He also noticed that it became increasingly difficult for him to pull himself out bed in the morning at the sound of his alarm clock. This was challenging because Suru was the timekeeper for the seminary. Moreover, he was getting easily irritated in the afternoon due to sleep deprivation.

Minor differences in group dynamics would trigger feelings of frustration. He was even engaging in conflicts over issues he would usually tolerate. As if these warnings were not clear enough, Suru kept using his nap time for studying. None of the observations made him give up the new habit he was getting into. Instead of giving up his sleep-deprivation strategy, Suru focused on finding ways to improve what he thought were the weak tactics in that strategy. He had a naive goal of strengthening his strategy of sleep deprivation for efficiency and effectiveness. Nothing stopped his new lifestyle until he woke up to the news of his mother's depression.

Suru got the news that Iya had fallen into the trap of depression. It was a long story. Baba told Suru it all started after Iya lost her older brother and went to the village to attend his funeral. Before and after Bao's burial, Suru's mother spent days organizing and coordinating the memorial. After the funeral, Iya was physically and mentally exhausted. Baba said he never saw his wife as weary as she was upon her return from the village. Iya experienced feelings of hopelessness and showed signs of distress.

That period brought misfortune upon her family. It was a difficult period for Iya, Baba, and their children. Baba did everything he could to help Iya get treatment and feel better. Suru got the news as he was getting ready to come home for his summer break. His summer break was miserable. Upon his return home, Suru did not recognize his mother. Iya had lost her traditional enthusiasm and lacked energy. She was submerged by low spirits.

Suru cried time and again. He drew near his mother, kneeled down before her, and wondered what happened.

Suru's sudden presence and the sound of his voice resuscitated his mother's smile and laughter. Iya jubilantly opened up her arms to give her son a big hug. She warmly held Suru tight for a while and said, "Welcome back, son! I missed you so much. Your absence dried me up. Your presence gives me life again."

Suru was amazed at such words; he could not believe the scene. He paused for a moment to wonder about his mother's words.

When Iya regained her energy after seeing her son, Suru's father mentioned that his wife had not smiled in so long. The few times Iya spoke to her husband during her period of depression, her words were either violent or not very sound. Everything around Iya riled her up.

Suru thought his departure for the seminary had contributed to his mother's depression, and he felt guilty. The thought of not returning to the seminary after the summer break crossed his mind, but he did not give it much consideration because he was not comfortable with going back to a traditional college environment. Suru had found a new home in the seminary. In his mother's gracious arms, Suru felt positive energy. Her smile and words contaminated him. He smiled in return and whispered, "Mother, I am happy to be back to you! I am happy to see you! Your life means everything to me. I am glad you feel better."

He thought about putting his mother's health before his vocation by canceling any trip back to the seminary. He wanted to stay by Iya and help attend to her needs, but he also thought Iya would get well whether he was present or not. He was a teenager trying to find a way to achieve his dreams and his vocation. Suru's ego would eventually overcome the thought of giving up or sacrificing his vocation for spending time with Iya.

Suru did not think he needed to spend months with his mother as she recovered. He would bitterly regret his decision later on. While Suru was going through his mental deliberation about going back to the seminary, Iya asked Baba to leave the room. She said she needed to talk to her son privately. Suru's father was reluctant to heed Iya's request, but she insisted. To make his wife feel good, Baba vacated the room. As he was leaving, he told her he would stand by the door in case she needed his assistance. After Suru's father left, Iya made her son sit on a chair next to her bed, and she started telling Suru a long story.

Iya's older brother Bao died after suffering a long illness. Bao was very dear to Iya's heart. She was born immediately following Bao. Her parents had three children. They were two boys and a girl. Iya was the only girl. Her two brothers were older than her. She was the last child. Bao was a good, well-mannered, and beloved man. He was more caring than their oldest brother, Odu. Bao was Iya's closest brother. He was her great advisor. Bao and Iya used to get along so well. They would often share secrets. Bao's death made Suru's mother sad and hopeless. She missed him so much. At the news of her brother's death, Iya was distraught. She rushed to the village by herself. Without her husband's consent, Iya spent several days and nights in the village, coordinating Bao's funeral. Everything fell on her shoulders. Iya was in charge of putting together every piece of her brother's memorial service.

Everybody was crying and wailing, but Suru's mother was making sure everything was ready for the memorial. Iya felt like crying, but she refrained from crying. She felt she did not have the time to cry. She tried to contain her emotions and denied her tears the freedom and right to show up publicly. She pretended she was above pain and sorrow. Iya deprived herself of sleep for more than a week. She was too busy getting everything ready for the memorial. The fast pace of her activities had her concerned about running the risk of a heart attack, but she pushed herself forward instead of listening to the critical alerts from her body. Eventually, her body got weary.

In the process of her storytelling, Suru's mother said she would eventually get better. She knew what to do to recover. She insisted that all she needed to do was rest and relax. She actually started feeling better while telling her story, but at that point, she sighed and coughed.

Baba came in immediately.

Iya asked what her husband was doing around.

Baba told he was bringing her some water. She said he should not mind because her son was there to lend her a hand. Suru took the glass of water from his father's hand and handed it to his mother.

Baba asked his son if everything was okay.

Suru put his thumbs up in response to his father.

Baba vacated the room, and Suru stood next to Iya's bed as she drank the water. After drinking the water, she gave him the cup and asked him to sit back. Suru put the cup on a desk next to her bed and sat on the chair.

Iya continued talking to her son. She went on to lavish some good advice on Suru.

Iya said, "Make sure you always remember to get enough sleep regardless of how busy you get in life. Sleep is a basic recipe for well-being. Happiness requires that we always find time to get a lot of sleep—day and night. Sleep is like a daily potion your body and mind need for happiness. It is like gas that our human tank requires to keep moving on the road to happiness. If you fail to sleep, you are likely to collapse on the road to happiness. Never give up your sleep under any circumstances, including during funerals."

Suru's mother knew what she meant. Iya was paying a high price for what she did during her brother's funeral. She had learned her lesson the hard way.

Iya mumbled a lesson she learned about her brother's funeral. If she were to attend Bao's memorial again, she would behave differently. Out of the twenty-four hours of a day, she would spend more time sleeping than acting, she would be lying down more than standing around the clock. As Iya's introspection continued, so did her monologue. She stressed how Bao loved her so much. Bao would never ask her to give up her sleep for his memorial. Iya wondered why she did what she did. She did not think she did it to please her late brother. Bao would never advise her to do such a stupid thing or anything that would hurt her or jeopardize her health.

Iya did what she did for social reasons. She acted that way at the funeral to please her social environment. She was worried and troubled over so many things, including welcoming and feeding the funeral attendants, consoling mourners, and going around to please everyone. Only one thing was needed: burying Bao. Iya told Suru to beware of the trap of decorum or social pressures. "We should make sure we do not become victims of social or peer pressures. Be mindful that you do not need to please anyone but God and yourself. And God always loves you as you are. The divine Creator wants you to be healthy and happy. Do not do anything that harms you or others. Do not deprive yourself of good sleep."

Suru enjoyed listening to Iya, and she enjoyed talking to him. It was awesome and peaceful.

Iya kept on talking. She alerted her son to the basic need to cry. "Remember to cry whenever you feel like crying. Crying is good for human nature. It helps you release your emotions and feel better. In times of pain, your tears dump your frustrations out of your body. After discharging such toxins, negative emotions, and energy, your heart and mind feel good in the end. Resisting crying is like working to keep all the toxins inside your system. As a result, the system breaks down—and you get sick."

Iya knew what she meant. After Bao departed this life, everyone around Iya kept crying, but she did not cry. It was not that she was not hurt. She was hurt and felt very sad. She even felt like crying. Yet instead of crying, she spent her time consoling all who were crying, and she was running around coordinating the memorial service. She thought she needed to be strong and play an active role of leadership. She was the only girl among her siblings. A large number of things pertaining to organizing the funeral rested on her two shoulders.

Out of respect for her oldest brother, Iya did not explain why she was the only one to shoulder everything. She told Suru it was a tough commitment on her part. However, she managed to portray the character she intended to play by showing a resilient face all the while.

Some villagers and relatives who attended Bao's funeral praised Iya for being so strong. Others congratulated her for taking the lead in coordinating what they called a great and successful memorial service. She was humble, but she felt proud of herself. She dedicated herself to working hard to pay the last respects to her beloved brother.

As Suru's mother continued her soul-searching, she was paying a high price for refraining from crying. She did a disservice to her heart and mind by not allowing her body to cry when it need cry. She prohibited her eyes from tearing when they needed to get rid of the burning tears. She made her heart and mind swallow frustrations and negative feelings when wisdom required that her eyes spit them out. Iya was so wrong. She whispered that if she were to organize her brother's funeral again, she would allow her eyes to pour tears like heavy rains falling from the sky. She would allow her body to release its tears of frustrations in order to feel better and acquire some peace of heart and mind.

Iya stopped talking and burst into tears. Her eyes erupted into tears. She cried and cried. Suru watched his mother crying. At first, Suru's heart was filled with mild emotions, but his emotions would intensify. Iya's tears quickly became contagious. Suru joined his mother in crying. Both of them cried so loud that Suru's father rushed into the room to lend a hand.

Nobody needed to tell Baba about the scene; he understood all about it like a vigilant insider and witness. He reached out, grabbed a handkerchief and wiped his wife's tears and his son's eyes. In that process, Baba started crying himself.

Suru got up to get another handkerchief. It was Suru's turn to wipe Baba's tears. The scene was moving and heartbreaking. Baba's tears looked almost unstoppable and irresistible.

Iya was so touched by her husband's emotions. She confessed her indelible love for him.

Baba responded that he loved her indefatigably and indefectibly.

After Iya and Baba mutually renewed their vows of love for one another through such lovely words, Baba felt better and vacated the room to respect Iya's wishes.

Suru's mother looked at her son and smiled.

Suru smiled back at her. There was a moment of silence.

Iya asked Suru whether he had anything to say. Suru was reluctant; he was more interested in listening to Iya because of her condition. He did not want to disturb her with his thoughts. But he also thought it was a good opportunity to talk to his mother.

Iya immediately read Suru's mind. She intuitively anticipated his move and told him not to hesitate to say what he wanted to say.

Suru felt empowered; he began to tell Iya his thoughts on her condition.

Iya was certainly right on the importance of sleep for human nature. "Whenever you get enough hours of sleep, you feel good and happy. When you do not get enough sleep, you feel vulnerable, angry, and miserable. In the absence of a good night's sleep, everything riles you up during the day. Your lack of sleep results in headaches."

Suru fondly remembered his grandmother's healthy sleeping habits. Her name was Edo. Growing up, Suru was very fortunate to spend some vacations in Edo's house in her remote village. Every day, Edo would wake up with the sunrise and go to bed with the sunset. Whenever Suru ventured by Edo's bedroom around eight o'clock, she was in a deep sleep. Edo's sleeping habits helped her live for 103 years.

Edo's sleeping habits inspired Suru to organize his sleep. Suru learned to stop going to bed late. He learned to give up studying late at night. Edo taught Suru to head to bed as soon as it got dark. Sleep is a great medicine for headaches. Suru's mother was also right about crying. On more than a few occasions Suru did feel better after crying.

Suru's tears cleaned his corporal system by washing away all sorts of toxins, anxiety, and negative sentiments. Crying represents a natural gift with a healing potential for human beings. It can heal us from pain, fear, anger, and blame. Feeling the pain or the emotion and expressing it through spontaneous crying can provide healing to the heart and mind. Crying purifies your heart and mind. The great spiritual and political leaders—including Jesus, Gandhi, Martin Luther King, and Nelson Mandela—did not hesitate to cry. Crying makes you feel good. Refusing to cry or be tough does not reflect strength. Toughness is not a virtue. It has no benefits for the body and mind. It does not grant peace. Instead, toughness stresses the body and mind.

Suru alleged that his sudden departure for the seminary also contributed to his mother's depression. More importantly, he suggested that his youngest sister's absence did not help Iya. According to Suru, Umu going off was potentially a contributing factor to Iya's depression.

Umu was Iya's youngest daughter and last child. She was taken away unpredictably to a foreign country when she was five. She was Iya's right hand. She was so close to her mother. Iya and Umu were doing quite a lot of activities together. Wherever Iya went, Umu would go with her. Wherever Umu went, Iya went.

The dark period of Iya's depression required treatment.

Baba was swamped and pulled in all directions, and it was difficult for him to attend to Umu's day-to-day needs and keep up with her mother's needs. The requirements of Baba's job made things even more difficult. Unfortunately, Suru's father needed that job more than ever. His family was poor, and their financial needs were immense. Suru did not think that provided sufficient reason to send a five-year-old to a foreign country. The thought of getting a nanny crossed neither Iya nor Baba's minds. Having a nanny would have been costly, but it could have been a better alternative mentally.

During Iya's depression, a friend emerged to lend a hand. Her name was Obo. Obo grew up with Iya in Nineb, but she later moved away and settled down in another country called Nobag.

During the period of Iya's depression, Obo was on vacation in Nineb. Obo came to Suru's mother in a disguise. Obo pretended she was going to help Iya's family. She proposed to help raise Umu by taking the little girl with her to Nobag. Obo persuaded Iya that such an option would give Suru's mother more time to focus on her treatment instead of getting the stress that could come from a five-year-old girl and help alleviate her pains.

Obo convinced Baba that such an alternative would help. Obo promised heaven and earth to Umu, including sending her to the best schools in Nobag. Iya was sold on the idea of sending Umu to a foreign country. All this happened while Suru was at the seminary. Suru still wishes he had been present whenever he thought about his parents' meeting with Obo.

Without being critical or seeking advice, Iya and Baba blindly fell into a malicious trap. How could they? Suru could not get it. He recalled his mother's meaningful lecture on making sound decisions. What happened to Iya's great aptitude for making good decisions? Why were his parents so foolish?

Baba felt very naïve. He did not have any second thoughts because he was overwhelmed and made a poor decision. He was aware that one should not make emotional decisions. Suru wondered if his father had lost his mind. He wondered what made Baba lose his common sense. Suru was unsure about what had happened to his father. Baba did not know that Obo had a hidden agenda. Her interests were different from what Suru's parents thought. Obo cleverly managed to appear good to Iya and Baba. She sneakily presented good intentions of assisting them. Suru's parents were mesmerized by Obo's well-turned words.

They found her words sweet and tasty, but her true intentions were bitter and devilish. They were disguised by the spices Obo put in her words. Obo's heart was far from honoring her words.

Obo eventually left and took Umu to Nobag.

Not long after, Iya and Baba started thinking they had made a mistake, but they persisted in trusting Obo as a good friend. It would not take them long to see Obo's true colors. Years passed, and Suru's parents did not get an update on Umu. Iya was worried.

There was not much communication from Obo. She was out of touch. Obo went missing. Iya and Baba struggled to communicate with her. Every time they were able to get an update on Umu, the information was vague and not reliable. Suru's parents had to go through hell to reach Obo and Umu. Eventually, Baba got Umu back. It turned out Umu had been taken away to serve Obo in housekeeping and domestic activities. Umu was never sent to school. She was humiliated and mistreated. Suru's sister suffered a lot. Umu's story was upsetting. Obo got away with it because of the absence of reliable law and order in Nineb and Nobag.

As Suru spoke about his sister, his mother listened carefully and started crying again. Suru gave Iya a handkerchief to wipe her tears. She expressed remorse about sending Umu away. Iya acknowledged the big mistake of sending their daughter away. Their decision was so wrong. It was more egoistic than altruistic. Suru's parents failed to mull over Umu's long-term well-being. Their decision was all about immediacy. They did not anticipate or project well.

Iya thought she ought to apologize to Umu and find a way to repair the harm. If anything, Umu's story enlightened her mother about making decisions. "We should avoid making decisions while we are experiencing extreme emotions, while we are under stress, or while we are under the influence of others—no matter who or what they are. We should avoid making decisions while we are drunk or on certain medications. Any decisions made under such circumstances are likely to be poor and result in unhappiness. The price you pay for them is high and undesirable." Iya cautioned her son not to make the same mistake. She warned Suru to be mindful of the danger of making decisions under stress, emotions, or influence.

Iya realized that her children's presence around her nourished and sustained her happiness. "Children provides a protective feather system to their parents' mental well-being—whether the children and parents are aware of it or not. I suffered for letting Umu go off. It was not easy. Taking my daughter away was like taking off my feathers."

Iya was happy that Suru brought up Umu's story. With an inquisitive smile, she beseeched her son to go farther in sharing his thoughts. Suru understood his mother's eagerness, but he decided to wrap up because Baba furtively signaled that it was time for lunch.

Understandably, the dark period of Iya's depression resulted in her absence from handling her family's day-to-day needs. She withdrew and sought treatment. Iya's absence confirmed her pivotal role in her family. In her absence, her children's lives felt shaky. They all missed their mother's priceless guidelines and precious attention.

Baba was strong, doing his very best, but it takes a team to successfully raise a child. It was difficult for him to run the show alone. Suru's father had to coordinate and respond to his eight children's daily needs. He also had to attend their mother's needs. Baba was brave, but he nearly fainted. He did not hesitate to sacrifice all he could to be present for his children and his wife.

Suru learned that a mother is irreplaceable in a child's life. The role motherhood plays in is golden. We often do not figure it out until a mother is absent from a house. Our mothers are precious and exceptional!

Suru came to the conclusion that his mother was a victim of social structures. Our families and organizations abide by social structures that subjugate and even dehumanize individuals. Social structures propagate a set of traditions, rules, policies, and laws that can lead to sleep deprivation and destruction.

While trying to honor her family's traditions by giving her brother a decent burial, Iya deprived herself of the human need for sleep. She jeopardized her own health. To some degree, we are all trapped by social structures and systems.

A friend once complained to Suru that he was not feeling well. That friend's name was Afo. Suru told Afo to go check with his doctor. Afo promised he would heed Suru's advice, but aware of his friend's sleep habits, Suru also suggested that Afo take time to sleep and rest.

Afo was not in a position to find enough hours for sleep due to his work schedule. Suru then made another suggestion regarding Afo's eating habits. Suru encouraged him to cook his own food and put less salt and sugar in it. Afo was fond of salty meals and sweet breakfasts. Afo did not have time for cooking.

Suru suggested that Afo should exercise a lot more. Afo said he did not have time to exercise. Suru encouraged his friend to meditate. Afo said he did not have any time for meditation. Suru asked Afo what specific activity he had time for. Afo responded that the only thing he had time for was working hard to pay his bills. Suru was not surprised Afo was not feeling well. Afo would certainly not feel well if he did not have time for anything besides working.

"If you have time for working, but no time for sleeping, exercising, cooking, eating healthily, or meditation, you are on an obvious path to get sick. Wellness and well-being are the nexus of all such activities. If you prioritize work to the detriment of all other activities, you slowly exhaust your body and will ultimately kill it. We should always remember that only a healthy mind and body enables us to work. Alas, we often forget that reality. We tend to neglect our minds and bodies by dragging them and working relentlessly. Your health is in the balance you find in doing everything that is required for the well-being of your mind and heart."

Suru thought something was wrong with Afo, but Suru would use the conversation with Afo to evaluate his own existence. He could not believe the results of his self-examination. Suru barely had time for exercise in his weekly schedule. The only time he would push himself to exercise was on Saturday and Sunday. And while exercising, Suru would often rush to finish so he could start the next activity on time or have enough time for the so-called next activity. Though he enjoyed cooking, Suru struggled to find time to cook on the weekends. Suru was aware of the benefits of meditation for his heart and mind, but he struggled to find some time for daily meditation. Though he knew the benefits of sleep for his mind and body, Suru would not make enough time for sleeping due to his daily routines. He would even deprive himself of sleep sometimes to catch up on other activities. Suru might not have enough time for exercise, cooking, sleeping, and meditation, but he would make time to go work every day. He would work every day just to pay bills. The results of his self-examination fascinated Suru. They unveiled that his habits were not different from Afo's. Suru's time was more dedicated to work. He barely had time to take care of his mind and body. Suru was a victim of social structures just like Afo.

Suru's daughter, Ele, once joked her father worked like a machine. Suru took the joke with bad grace; he told his daughter that he was not a machine and would not want to become one. Ele said he should stop acting like one. She explained Suru often rushed to drop her at school and go to work. Ele was right. Every morning Suru would hurry to go, he was always on the go here and there.

Suru enjoyed dropping Ele and her brother and sister to school every morning regardless of the weather. Suru also had some bad mornings. On the bad mornings, his mood was not so great, he woke up grumpy. He would find it laborious to brush his children's teeth, get them ready, give them breakfast, and pack their lunch. By the time he finished getting them ready and packing their bags, he felt burned out. He barely had time to get himself ready and eat breakfast. Most of the time he rushed eating his breakfast. Sometimes, he skipped breakfast to drop his children on time at school. Suru rushed them into the car to make sure they get to school on time. His children did not care most of the time. Ele did not worry about time; she did not worry about being late. At times she only ran her eye over Suru and continued what she had been doing. Ele and her brother, Ovi, made it worse when they did not follow directions. Suru got frustrated sometimes at their behaviors or attitudes. He wondered why his children did not have the grace to be sensitive to time. He wished they were more sensitive to time management. But he often remembered that Ele and Ovi were infants and muttered to himself he behaved the same way when he was their age. Ele interrupted him one morning by saying there was no need to be rushing every morning. She suggested children should be relaxed and natural every morning from the time they woke up through the time they were ready for school. She added, "We should take time to enjoy ourselves and the nature every morning!"

Ele's suggestion reminded Suru how he used to waste time to enjoy taking a long shower every morning while growing up. This made him laugh; he thought Ele was right by natural standards. Unfortunately, society does not allow us to always enjoy nature as we wish to.

On his difficult mornings Suru's ride with his children to school often got stressful. Unhappy with the routine and worried about its potential negative impacts on his health and wellbeing, Suru started thinking of different strategies to boost a positive mood every morning. He tried a series of strategies. One strategy was having the children listen to nice popular music on the ride. It worked sometimes, but not consistently. After a few days of trial Suru found himself back where he started. Ele told him at times that she was tired of listening to music. Her father totally understood. The sound got too noisy and irritated Ele sometimes. She asked for silent meditation instead. When Suru switched from music to silence at her daughter's request, Ele barely observed it. After a few seconds of silence, she became loud and noisy.

One day, Ele eventually performed the miracle. On that day, she gave her father the magic recipe for cultivating a good mood every morning. Suru knew smiling was good; a smile has a lot of virtues and benefits for human body and mind. But he did not know so much about laughing until a lesson from Ele on laughing games. Suru was driving his children to school like he did every morning, rushing and grumpy. Ele suddenly asked him to laugh. He decided to follow her injunction and laughed. His laugh became contagious. It contaminated Ele, Ovi, and their sister Wiwe. They all started laughing with their father. Whenever Suru stopped laughing, the children asked him to resume and do it over and over again. He did, and they all laughed after him and with him. They all enjoyed laughing happily on their way to school that morning. On that ride Suru felt different than previously. He felt good and relaxed. He felt happy. The laughing game just made his day. The good energy he got from it spread through his day in his social environment.

After dropping his children at school, on his way to work, Suru was driving by a zoological park. He suddenly stopped due to a family of geese crossing the road. One of the geese unexpectedly spread its wings and kept on beating them lightly while standing in the middle of the road. It spent about two minutes doing so, without moving. All the cars from both directions of the road had to stop and wait until the geese vacated the road. Suru thoughtfully watched the goose beating its wings. He could tell the bird was enjoying doing what it was doing. Suru was also enjoying watching it. It was a free show, but meaningful. All other people standing by were also watching apparently happy. Watching that spectacle made Suru feel good. It also made him think of what Ele previously said to him on that morning. Ele advised we should not rush in the morning. Instead we should take time to enjoy ourselves and the nature. Suru thought the goose was sending him the same message. The goose forced him to stop rushing and take some time to contemplate and enjoy the nature in its show. It only took about two minutes. But Suru felt good contemplating nature in the goose. It was beautiful and relaxing. He did not go to work late that day.

Upon arriving at work on that morning, Suru shared his laugh story as well as the goose story with co-workers. They were interested in the laugh story. They all liked it. It made them laugh. Some co-workers even promised to try the same thing with their children the following day. They did and they were not disappointed; it worked. Laughing makes human beings produce positive hormones which make everyone happy. Ever since that day, Suru figured out how to start his day happily while driving his children to school. Ele gave her father a good pillar to lean on to start his day, the pillar of laughing for the sake of laughing. In the same process, Suru learned all it takes to make his children laugh, including tickling them. Tickling is good for laughing.

Ele also unveiled to her father the combination of singing and dancing as a pillar of happiness for children. On that weekend, it was Suru's turn for babysitting. He had to take care of Ele, Ovi, and Wiwe in the absence of Lafia, their mother. The children were not following directions. They were all over the place, messing the house. Suru tried everything he could to have them calm down without success. Ele suddenly said to her father, "Let us sing and dance!" Suru followed her daughter's order, and the magic happened. They all became calm and all eyes. Instead of jumping and running around, they started singing and dancing happily. Eventually, they ended up sleeping after a joyful period of singing and dancing.

We can easily become victims of social structures. Mindful of the beautiful scenes of insects and wild animals he witnessed in the backyard of his parents' house as a child—and amazed by how all such animals endorse or enjoy nature—Suru came up with the following hypothesis. Out of all living species, only human beings tend to rebel against nature and push it away. Ironically, we are the most intelligent among all living species. That is designed by existential contradictions.

In many cases, our time is mainly for work and less for taking care of our minds and bodies. We often do not have time to care for our natural selves. We tend to neglect our nature because of structures and systems. We sacrifice our nature to structures. We need our nature so that we are able to meet the requirements of structures. Unfortunately, social structures and systems spin so fast without stopping. They do not even slow down. They are always on. We have transformed society into robotic systems and structures. Such structures and systems tend to dehumanize us because their rhythm is robotic. Many of them are merciless. They have no regard for human health. They drive us all over the place.

They drive nature out of the internal and external environment of human body by kicking the natural out of what we eat or drink. They make us eat farm-raised fish instead of wild-caught ones or artificial food instead of natural or organic food. We should be mindful that we could affect or destroy our natural dimension with what we eat. We become what we eat. If we eat wild-caught fish, we get its natural assets, but if we eat farm-raised fish, we also get its farm-raised assets. A farm-raised fish cannot be a wild-caught fish.

When we eat natural or organic, we remain natural or organic. However, when we eat artificial, we run the risk of becoming artificial. Moreover, structures tend to drive nature away from our dining tables by covering them with bottles of fancy drinks instead of bottles of water. By doing so, they deceive us that water is not good enough. Actually, water is very good for human health.

Suru would postulate that water is the healthiest natural drink the body needs. He would drink water several times a day to rehydrate and refresh his body. Water serves the needs of our health better than liquor. Suru was acquainted with friends or relatives who hurt their health and lost their lives prematurely to liver cirrhosis due to alcohol abuse. Maybe their premature deaths could have been prevented and their lives spared if they were not addicted to alcohol. Structures tend to drive nature out of our bodies with accessories by making nature a stranger in its own backyard.

As Baba was aging, his hair turned gray. Time and time again, some of Baba's friends would exhort him to dye his hair black, but Suru's father would not heed his friends' advice. Baba kept getting suggestions about dying his hair even when he was in his eighties. He once said he would rather abide by natural law and let his hair reflect his age and remind him of the natural cycle. Suru's father would remind his friends that human beings are beautiful and handsome without any ornaments, dyes, or makeup. We are beautiful by natural design. Nature is awesome; it encapsulates beauty. Some structures or systems easily drive that awesome nature out of your body by forcing you to neglect your needs in sleep. They get you to work long hours just to pay the mortgage for a house you cannot even sleep in due to spending your time on night shifts at work. When you neglect your sleep needs, you commit a sin against your health and well-being. Those types of structures and systems do not like to take a break. They do not get tired as we do. In the process, they stress us beyond what we can handle. When we slow down, the social structures and systems eject us and part with us.

All animals are fond of nature; they embrace it. Meanwhile, human beings are retracting from nature by pushing it far away or hurting it. We seem to be uncomfortable with nature. We seem to engage in conflict with nature. We forget we are part of nature. We are made to be natural and to dwell in nature. Nature is vital to our existence. We cannot push nature aside without damaging ourselves. We cannot win our conflict against nature without hurting our health and well-being.

We cannot drive nature away without contributing to global warming or climate change. When we blow nature away, we allow the winds of water pollution, air pollution, and noise pollution to blow in. We cause severe damages to nature through air pollution, water pollution, and noise pollution. We cannot negate nature without fostering the rise and proliferation of new forms of diseases.

Structures often infringe upon some of our basic rights and natural attributes. At times, structures make us deny or neglect our duties or obligations vis-à-vis nature. Nature wants you to do this, but structures want you to do that. When nature wants you to sleep, structures want you to remain awake for work. Structures tend to deprive you of what nature sets up for you.

We need structures for smooth social regulations. The challenge is found in how we balance nature and structure. We ought to find ways to increase the weight of nature in our existential equations for fair balance. We must bring back nature. We should tolerate nature around us and pay more attention to its presence within us. Nature is a vibrant part of who we are. Eating natural, fresh, and organic food is essential for the health of our minds and hearts. Drinking a lot of water is vital to our well-being. So is getting enough sleep. The price we pay for trying to escape nature or pushing it aside is high. Renouncing nature eventually affects our health and existence. Happiness requires that we find a healthy balance between nature and structure. We can creatively find ways to resupply society with natural blood, feelings, and peace. We ought to endorse human nature for happiness. Our peace of mind and heart depends on our ability to humanize society.

From his mother's depressive condition, Suru learned a great deal about some critical requirements of happiness. Happiness requires a lot of sleeping. Not getting enough sleep is refusing to obey the natural demands of our bodies. We cannot disobey nature without running the risk of getting sick. If you deprive yourself from enough sleep, you set up your for disease or sickness.

Happiness correlates with dancing, smiling, laughing, and occasional crying. After Iya's depression, her entire family understood the goodness of dancing, smiling, laughing, and weeping. Dancing, smiling, and laughing relaxes your muscles by helping your body produce healthy hormones. Crying can also be beneficial to your health when it spills out your frustrations. Dancing makes you feel really good.

Baba often took advantage of that knowledge. He would turn the radio on every Friday night and require his family to hit the dance floor. Everybody would take turns on the dance stage for fun, freestyle dancing. They would laugh and sweat. They would enjoy every beat of the music. They felt good every weekend. All week, the family looked forward to their dance party on Friday night.

A smile may trigger muscle relaxation in the self and others. If your smile makes you relax, it also has the potential to make other people relax. Why don't we develop and promote a culture of smiles and relaxation? A smiley culture is necessary for our happiness. Suru would usually feel happy in an environment where people smiled. He did not feel happy when everybody was grumpy. He would hypothesize that it had to do with human nature.

Smiling tends to portray happiness. It is a reflection of happiness. And happiness is contagious. Some people are naturally gifted with smiles. Others are not so gifted, but we all have some potential to smile. Suru would smile easily and spontaneously.

A good friend once joked that Suru smiled to everyone and to everything, including to trees. It was a joke, but it was meaningful. Suru got compliments all the time about his spontaneous smile, including from a number of his students and colleagues. Some explained how Suru's smile empowered them to remain optimistic.

A respected and hardworking businessman in charge of cutting grass around Suru's house once got sick. The man's name was Kini. After a long period of convalescence, Kini came back to work. Trying to check on him, Suru asked about his health. In response to Suru's question about his condition and health, Kini said he was doing fine. In the same breath, Kini added that he missed Suru's smile while he was away.

Suru was blessed with the gift of smiles, and he was grateful to the divine Providence for that great gift. Suru's smile naturally came out of his lips. He easily shows off his teeth. He pushes himself to smile even when he does not feel like smiling. He knows that smiling usually makes him feel good. Suru is better off with smile. His smile is not always spontaneous. Sometimes, it is purposeful. Again, every human being hosts the potential to smile. We only need to cultivate the habit. We need to practice smiling. If we do it often, we get it eventually. Effective communication requires that we often smile. May our faces often radiate or shine in a smile, and we shall be happy!

An experience of severe insomnia during Suru's years of training in the seminary also taught him about the contributions of sleep to happiness. Suru was miserable. He would spend his night in bed listening to the snoring of his fellows next door. The next day, Suru was irritable due to his lack of sleep. He was not happy. Suru was treated with small doses of sleeping pills. After a week on sleeping pills, he got fed up. He decided to stop taking the pills and rely on the natural assets of his body for sleep.

After another week, Suru could not sleep without the pills. He resorted to soul-searching. After a period of self-examination, Suru was able to identify the roots of his insomnia. Suru's insomnia was rooted in anxiety related to quitting the seminary.

After uncovering the source of his insomnia, Suru was able to address it constructively. His sleep eventually came back without the help of sleeping pills. Suru learned not to counter insomnia with sleeping pills. Whenever he experienced sleeplessness at night, Suru would do a self-examination. He would do the self-examination to identify reasons or causes of the insomnia. Once he identified some reasons for his insomnia, he did a meditation. Meditation calmed his mind.

Self-examination and meditation served as tools for granting peace to his troubled mind, but they might not be enough to help bring Suru's sleep back. He would go ahead and drink a big cup of water or milk to rehydrate his body. With that, Suru addressed the needs of his heart.

After addressing the needs of his mind with self-examination and meditation and the needs of his heart with water or milk, Suru would go back to bed. Once in bed, he would wait patiently and optimistically for sleep to come back. It usually worked for Suru. His sleep eventually came back.

CHAPTER 11

Leadership as Authority or Service: Greatness from Humbleness

Iya's depressive condition did not allow Suru to enjoy his summer break. His summer break was supposed to be a vacation, a time for fun and relaxation. Instead, Suru spent it attending to his sick mother's needs and reflecting on her condition. He did not regret spending his summer in such a way. Suru was happy to see his mother and witness her condition improving. Time went by very fast.

After nearly three months of summer break, the time came for Suru to go back to the seminary. He faced a huge dilemma at that moment. He was not sure whether he should go back or remain by his mother's side. Iya was still convalescing. It was a difficult decision to make. Suru thought about it for the entire week before his official date of return to the seminary.

On the eve of his departure, Iya helped her son solve the puzzle. She called him to her room and had him sit down. Iya told Suru she could see he was very disturbed and troubled over the idea of his upcoming return to the seminary.

Suru was surprised his mother was able to read his spirits; he was doing his best to hide his feelings on that issue from Iya. He did not want to add to his mother's depression, but Iya encouraged him to return to the seminary. She stressed that Suru needed to go back because a mission was waiting for him upon his return. Suru did not understand what his mother meant, but he took her words as orders and felt much better. That night, Iya helped Suru pack and get ready for the next morning.

Early in the morning, with his father's assistance, Suru got into a taxi and left for the bus station. Aboard the bus to the seminary, he could not stop thinking about his mother's words about a mission awaiting him. Time and again, he wondered about the mission that was in store for him, but he could not get it.

Upon arriving at his final destination, Suru's fellow seminarians were all excited to see him. They welcomed him warmly. They were from Suru's parish, Saint M Parish. Together with Suru, they spent the first few minutes sharing summer vacation stories. Suru told his fellows about a few of his summer adventures—but not the most important one, his mother's depression. They helped him settle down in the dormitory and took Suru to a nearby kiosk for a very important meeting. In the same breath, they informed him they needed to choose a new doyen or dean to preside over their group of seminarians of Saint M Parish. The previous dean's term had ended, and he had moved on to an upper-level seminary.

The fellows all thought Suru was fit to serve in that capacity. Iya's words on a pending mission crossed Suru's mind. Suru's fellows immediately moved on to casting their votes for him. To his amazement, Suru was elected the new dean of seminarians of Saint M Parish by the end of that meeting. His fellows congratulated him happily.

As they congratulated him, Suru thought about his mother's prophetic words. They became meaningful to his senses. Deanship implied a leader who would be the presiding official over all processes of decision-making for the group of seminarians. Suru would be the official spokesperson for the group. He would be regarded as the most senior member of the group. In the utmost description of tasks involving the dean of seminarians, Suru would be in charge of all the other members of the group.

After their meeting, Suru retreated into his favorite place under the famous mango tree. He wanted to spend some time thinking deeply about Iya's predictive words and the new mission they put on his shoulders. Suru sat on a piece of brick under the mango tree, but he did not look at the brick he was sitting on. He was just happy to be under the mango tree to think and enjoy its shade and the breeze.

A big black ant was resting on the same brick Suru, and he sat on it. The ant stung Suru hard, and it hurt him. Suru's nerves reacted immediately. He jumped up and screamed as if he had lost his mind. It was unexpected. Suru did not expect to have such an unpleasant encounter with an ant. He considered the place safe. He spent a few minutes rubbing his buttock to minimize the pain from the sting and eventually calm down. In that process, Suru quickly looked around. Fortunately, there were no eyewitnesses to the scene.

When he felt good, he decided to climb on the mango tree. Was that the right time to do so? Suru thought it was. He also felt safe on the mango tree every time he went on it. Though he saw a few ants hanging around, none of them had ever stung him before that incident. He thought he was safer in the tree.

Suru sat down on a strong branch and thought about his new position as the dean of seminarians. He thought of all actual responsibilities involved and the plausible implications. The tasks falling upon him seemed immense, challenging, and intimidating. Suru decided to close his eyes for a while and think more deeply about the meaning of leadership. Unfortunately, his reflection did not bear much fruit. It was not that productive because Suru was afraid of falling down with his eyes closed.

He thought about leadership as the ability to lead. Suru remained unsatisfied with his quest of understanding what it meant to be a leader. He reopened his eyes and decided to contemplate how leaders in his immediate and remote social environments led efficiently. Suru pictured two different styles of leaders.

The first type of leaders perceive and exercise leadership as absolute authority. They see leadership as power over others. Their orientation to leadership is that of supremacy, coercive enforcement, and domination. Under their watch, leadership becomes controlling. It controls others more than the self. They exert leadership as a means of self-glorification and subjugation of alterity. What motivates their approach to leadership is only ambition for power and glory as timocrats in the philosophy of Plato.

In that process, leadership turns into commanding and abusing others. They do not foresee any scenario of giving up power. They usurp power or cling to it. They do not believe in any alternative to their leadership and their perception of it. They entrust leadership as entitlement, their natural attribute. They embrace power as private property. Suru could see their portraits in the philosophies of Nicholas Machiavelli, Thomas Hobbes, and others. They are illustrated in political practices by Benito Mussolini, Adolf Hitler, Joseph Stalin, Kim Il-sung, Mao Tse-tung, Josip Tito, Augusto Pinochet, Slobodan Milosevic, Idi Amin, Mubutu Sésé Séko, Jean-Bédel Bokassa, Saddam Hussein, Gnassingbé Eyadéma, Muhamad Kaddafi, and other leaders.

Suru could see them as powerful kings in palaces or kingdoms. They like to be revered and deified. They put themselves above their subjects and require that their subjects treat them in such a way. They cannot survive without the taxes they collect from those subjects. Suru could see them as heads of republics who come into office to stay forever. They barricade themselves behind seemingly eternized state power. They build walls between people and groups. They oppress their people and dictate their rules to everyone. They utilize scary tactics like propaganda, misinformation, exclusion, intimidation, aggression, and mental or physical torture to generate fear and reach their goals. They do not accept or tolerate any opposition. They firmly prohibit political opposition and terrorize political opponents. They cannot stand freedom of expression. They perceive political alternatives as a threat to their survival.

Suru also saw army generals and commanders who use rank to alienate their subjects in how they command or position them in the field. He also saw them in police officers and other law enforcement agents who tyrannize or brutalize local populations and discriminate against civilian communities. Suru saw them in captains who disrespect and manipulate members of their crews. He saw them in relationships where a partner imposes his or her views or will upon their partners, girlfriends, boyfriends, husbands, wives, or business partners.

Suru saw them in households where ladies had no say and were oppressed by their husbands or fathers. He also saw such leaders in our workplaces. They settled down within organizations where supervisors or managers are arrogant or disrespectful. They use their position or title to intimidate, threaten, and mistreat their coworkers. They require loyalty instead of honesty. They replace collegiality with loyalty to them.

If you want to be collegial but not loyal or if you fail to be loyal to them, they judge you as a bad colleague. They rush to judge and condemn their colleagues or subordinates, and they put themselves above laws, rules, and policies. They want their colleagues to be their toadies. They like to be greeted publicly and want people to call them by their title. They mistrust and micromanage their colleagues and subordinates by controlling the process and outcome of everything. They engineer hostility and violence in the workplace. They dump heavy and dirty duties on their colleagues' shoulders and are never ready to help carry such loads. They do not lift a hand.

They are eager to get credits for their coworkers' achievements. They enjoy sitting with dignitaries at the best tables at banquets. They love the reserved, front-row seats at public events. Suru saw them in employers who put in place selfishly designed policies to exploit and subjugate their employees. He saw them in teachers who intentionally disregard and ill-educate some students to meet specific agendas. They believe or pretend they know everything. They are not open to learning from their students and colleagues. They pretend they have acquired full knowledge with their college degrees. They do not practice what they teach.

Suru saw them in trainers who exploit and misguide their trainees. He saw them in athletes who think they have to always win everything and everywhere, in all situations, at all cost or by all means, including by doping. They do not accept losing as an option. Suru saw them in coaches who impose their will upon members of their team for their own interests.

He saw them in advisors who purposefully mislead or take advantage of their advisees. They violate the rules of fair practices and promote the rules of the jungle. They perpetrate misconduct, corruption, misrepresentation, and discrimination. Those leaders emphasize personal success, prestige, grandeur, and aggrandizement. They make a big show of everything so people can see it and praise them. They expect to be praised for everything they do, including wrongdoing. They always want to have the upper hand. Some of them are incompetent or unqualified. They obtain their positions as a result of nepotism, favoritism, or corruption. In that perspective, some of them are thieves or robbers. They literally steal their positions or titles by getting in through the back entrances of fraud or bribery. They get their positions by depriving those who should be entitled to such positions by merit.

They represent their personal interests and the interests of special groups, but they do not serve the interests of the general public. They empty the coffers of the republic and fill up their pockets with public treasures. They take possession of what belongs to the general public. They are also frequent liars. They would give you an order to do something, and when you do it, they deny ordering you doing any such a thing if the consequences of their order are disgraceful or bad. They take credit for it if the outcome of your action is good.

Many of them would not jeopardize their positions or risk their lives for their people. In danger, they run away and abandon their people in order to save their own lives. They are never ready to relinquish power. They grip power and relish it until they die. These leaders do not seem free. They only feel safe within the sort of arsenal of power they barricade themselves within. They do not feel safe without their power. They are always concerned with holding on to power. They are afraid of losing power. They are obsessed with safety and security. They cannot move freely by themselves. They rely on heavily armed bodyguards or carefully designed strategies for their safety. They cannot sleep without being watched over by armed guards. They quickly get exasperated.

In general, their minds are flooded with unaddressed worries and self-conflicts that sink in. They are not happy in most cases. As a result of their lack of peace of heart and mind, they tend to generate injustice, division, conflict, rebellion, and war. Their instable internal environment easily spills over and negatively contaminates their external environment. Most people living in their social environment do not feel happy. They do not have the peace of mind and heart. They do not enjoy the basic needs of freedom. They either engage in perpetual resistance or barricade their sentiments of frustrations. Adolf Hitler certainly struggled with unaddressed internal contradictions that ended up spilling over into his external environment and the international community.

The second type of leader encompasses those who seize leadership as an opportunity for service. This group of leaders includes everyone who perceives and uses leadership as service. They see leadership as service of others. Their orientation to leadership is that of humble service. They look at themselves as humble servants of their people—whether they are in the public or private sector. Under their watch, leadership requires teamwork. It assists others with self-effacement. They exert leadership as a mean of promoting their team and its members. In that process, leadership requires recognition and empowerment of others. They are not attached to power, and they foresee giving it up. They believe in alternatives to their leadership. They entrust leadership as ministry. They relate to power as public property.

Suru could see them in great philosophers and teachers such as Confucius, Buddha, and Jesus. They demonstrate how leadership incarnates service. Suru could also see them in great activists such as Mahatma Gandhi, Martin Luther King, Mother Teresa of Calcutta, and Nelson Mandela. They exemplify leading as serving. Suru saw that style of leadership in a police officer rescuing a lost teenager. He saw that style of leadership in a pontiff washing the feet of prisoners or in Jesus washing his disciples' feet. Suru saw such leaders in firefighters who risk their lives to save a family from a raging fire. He saw that style of leadership in a president who respects citizens' right to religious freedom and diversity. Suru saw such leaders in palaces and kingdoms where kings descend from their thrones to be down to earth with their subjects. They are charismatic and accessible. They put themselves on the same level as their people. They immerse themselves in social equality and participate in public activities.

Suru saw them as heads of states who come to office to serve the interests of all citizens. They build bridges between people and groups. They protect their people. They negotiate and deliberate with citizens over the ruling of the republic. They utilize empowering tactics of honest information, clear communication, dynamic integration, and participation to reach their goals. They welcome resistance and differences of viewpoints or worldviews. They promote political opposition and encourage their political opponents. They advocate for freedom of expression. They perceive political alternatives as a promise for improving the republic.

Suru also saw them in army generals and commanders who use their high ranking to be role models for their subjects in serving their nations. Suru saw such leaders in police officers and law enforcement agents who protect local populations and safeguard civilian communities. He saw them in captains who coordinate their crews. Suru saw that style of leadership in relationships where partners negotiate living together respectfully and freely, whether there are girlfriend and boyfriend, husband and wife, or business partners. He saw it in households where ladies actively and effectively have equal rights and duties with their husbands or fathers. He also saw it within organizations or in workplaces where supervisors, managers, and coworkers serve the team and are not served or worshipped. They happily and carefully emphasize collegiality and honesty.

They trust their colleagues and subordinates and empower the process and outcome of everything. They foster hospitality in the workplace. They share heavy and dirty duties with their colleagues, and they are always ready to help. They make sure all coworkers get credit for their accomplishments. They enjoy sitting at any table at banquets. They prefer the back seats at public events. They humbly prefer to be called by their names and not by their titles.

Suru saw such leaders in employers who put in place selflessly designed policies to promote their employees. He saw them in teachers who respect all students without exception. They are aware they do not know everything. They are open and eager to learn from students and colleagues. They see life as a daily learning process. They practice what they teach.

Suru saw such leaders in trainers who provide their trainees with appropriate skills. Suru saw them in athletes who believe you do not always win. There are times you win or lose, but you just have to do your best. With hope, they embrace any loss as an opportunity for learning, changing, and improving.

He saw them in coaches who negotiate with their teams over strategies for winning. He saw them in advisors who rightfully guide their advisees. They enforce the rules of fair practices and promote integrity and integration. Such leaders emphasize group success and modesty. They do not make a big show of everything they achieve. They do not expect to be praised for everything they accomplish. They tend to be accountable for their wrongdoing. Most of them are qualified and competent.

In general, they get their positions by merit. They manage all public goods with integrity. They serve the interests of the general public. They consciously lead by example. They would risk their lives to save their people. In danger, they stay with their people and are willing to die for them. They are ready to relinquish power. Such leaders are free.

Suru noticed they feel safe with or without power. They are not afraid of losing power. They are just concerned with serving their entourage. They are not concerned with their own safety and security. They move freely by themselves. They do not have to always depend or rely on heavily armed bodyguards or similarly designed strategies for their safety. They can sleep without being watched over by armed guards. They are slow to anger and full of compassion.

In general, their minds are free of worries. They often address their self-conflicts introspectively. They feel happy. As a result of their peace of heart and mind, they tend to generate peace and harmony in their social environments. They advocate for freedom, justice, conciliation, and reconciliation. Their stable internal environment spills over and positively contaminates their external environments. They host and grant the peace of mind and heart. Most people living in such leaders' social environments feel happy. Their constituencies and fellows enjoy basic needs of freedom. They engage in collaboration with their leaders with sentiments of admiration.

Following his contemplation and observations, it became clear to Suru that leadership could be perceived as service or authority. In the perspective of authority, to lead is to direct or command with coercion or persuasion. In the perspective of service, to lead is to show the way by going along or guiding.

Suru decided to try out both styles of leadership. Though he strongly felt attracted to the service style of leadership, he also felt inclined to try the other style of leadership, leadership as authority. His inclination to the authoritative style of leadership was influenced by Suru's immediate environment. His living environment was flooded with leaders of that style. Suru would often find himself in the environment of leaders who perceived and exercised leadership as authority. As a teenager, he was fascinated by some of those leaders at times. In his immediate surroundings, Suru felt that leadership was predominantly about authority, but because this was only a feeling, he thought he would learn more effectively about leadership by having his own experience. In that regard, the opportunity of his deanship would leave Suru to his own devices. He wanted to seize the opportunity as the dean of seminarians to experience how it felt to exercise leadership as authority and as service. Suru was eager to learn lessons about each leadership style. Excited by the thoughts crossing his mind, Suru calmly came down from his mango tree to implement his decision about exercising leadership.

Widely exposed to the authority style of leadership in his immediate social environment, Suru started contemplating and implementing daily what he thought was the dominant orientation to leadership. He would make decisions without consulting and deliberating with his fellow seminarians. They would get frustrated and often opposed resistances. Suru was reluctant to accept any contradicting thoughts from his fellows. This riled them up.

On several occasions, Suru made sure the fellows were fully aware he was the dean, the person in charge. He would take pride in speaking on behalf of the group. Fellows who were eager to voice their opinions did not appreciate how Suru would deceitfully take it out on them; they were not happy with how he monopolized everything, including their voices.

Suru mindfully tried to be a strong leader, but he was not happy. He felt insecure. Monopolizing everything as he did or making sure everybody knew he was the dean actually reflected his inner insecurity. He felt isolated and lonesome. Because his fellows were not happy with Suru's approach to leadership, they did not feel comfortable in his company. They rarely spent time with him. They were defiant and stayed away.

In his lonesomeness, Suru experienced insomnia. His insomnia crisis sounded a loud alarm that he had the wrong orientation to leadership. And he got the message. Suru tried to put on the jacket of the authority style of leadership, but it did not fit. He found it cumbersome. Suru did not enjoy it. He did not like what it made him experience. It was disgusting. He often got upset and made his fellows angry. That approach to leadership often led Suru to perceive his fellows as rivals or adversaries.

Suru created tons of frustration within and around him. He developed intractable hostilities and even engaged in conflicts with some fellows over unsubstantial issues. All the respect fellows had for Suru started vanishing. Some fellows publicly expressed their disagreement and dissatisfaction with his leadership style. Others went as far as almost regretting selecting him as their dean. Suru started experiencing sentiments of disconnection from the roots of his worldview and upbringing. He was not born in a household that perceived leadership as authority. He started feeling dissatisfaction with himself. Suru felt lost. He thought there should be another way to be a leader and be happy at the same time.

In the midst of a sleepless night, Suru sat down and contemplated Iya and Baba's leadership roles in their family. He thought of and looked at his mother and father as leaders. At least, that was how their children saw them. As leaders, Iya and Baba served their children humbly and greatly. Suru's father and mother worked hard to make a living. Iya was regularly in the kitchen to cook delicious meals for her family. She patiently kept her children and her house clean every day. She was doing all that in a spirit of service to her family.

Suru also thought about other related experiences. Growing up, Suru told his friends that his father went to service every time he wanted to tell them Baba went to work. Going to the workplace meant going to service. And early on, Iya taught Suru that leading meant serving. Suru's father had the reputation of being a good leader in his workplace because he was a good servant. Suru's friends used the same phrase of service to indicate that their parents went to work.

Suru learned about the equivalence between service, work, and leadership. To different degrees, all workers are servants—and all servants are leaders. Leadership implies working for or serving the public. It is a service to the public. Regardless of whether they work in the public sector or the private sector, leaders should be servants of the public. They should be serving the public and their people. To be a leader is to serve a team, a group, a community, a city, a country, or an organization.

On that same sleepless night, Suru's quest for understanding leadership as service led him to examine his previous work experience in a restaurant. Whenever Suru served customers well, he felt happy doing so. As a result of his service, his clients felt happy. They expressed their satisfaction by leaving good tips, but whenever he did not serve them well, his clients did not feel happy and complained. They would not give him good tips or any tip at all. Suru would not feel happy either.

His contemplation culminated in meaningful revelations. Leadership translates availability to humble service. To be a good leader, you do not need to overwhelm people. You just need to serve them. You do not need to be above people. You just need to be with them. Great leaders are humble, and humble leaders are great. Greatness in leadership springs from smallness or humbleness. Humble leadership effectively communicates with compassion. Those revelations triggered a paradigm shift in Suru's orientation to leadership. This drastically changed his exercise of leadership.

Inspired by what he would call an epiphany on how to lead in service, Suru got his act together and stepped up to do wonders for leadership. And it paid off. Suru immediately started consulting and deliberating with fellows in all decisions. He no longer made any decisions for the group without consulting and deliberating with his fellow seminarians. His fellows would happily collaborate with Suru in all decision-making processes. They all felt good, and Suru felt good as well. He would reach out to fellows whose ideas contradicted his, including the spoilers. He would help them feel integrated in the group as valuable actors. This empowered every member of his group.

Suru was happy to delegate fellows to represent the group. He made sure leadership in the group was shared and rotated from him to other group members. It collaboratively shifted from one individual to another. Each member took a turn to speak on behalf of the group—without exception. The practice alleviated Suru's duties. The process was inclusive of everyone. The fellows who were eager to voice their opinions did so and felt welcomed.

Suru was mindful to be a leader at the service of the group, and he felt safe doing so. The group felt happy, and Suru was happy. His deanship was light to bear. He felt accepted by his fellows. Many of them wondered what had happened to him. Some of them confessed that they were happy with his new approach to leadership. They felt comfortable in his company.

As a result of the change, Suru's nights became calm. He slept deeply every night in that period. He felt peace in his heart and mind. He put on the service style of leadership, and it fit so well. Suru enjoyed it. It tasted good. It helped him gather and not scatter his fellows. That approach to leadership led Suru to perceive his fellows as valuable assets for their group and not as threats. Around the clock, he would negotiate with them.

Suru respected his fellows' views, and they respected his. All members learned to disagree and agree respectfully. Despite their differences, they learned the art of getting along by working together. Everyone felt good. The greatest lesson Suru learned as the dean of seminarians of Saint M Parish was that leadership contributes to irrigating the heart and mind with peace and happiness. Leaders who truly serve people ultimately water or oil themselves and their social environment with peace and happiness.

Leadership is like leading a ship. Depending on the type of captain you have, you will be happy or unhappy on your ship. If your captain is there to humbly and happily serve you throughout your journey, you will enjoy happiness on your trip. However, if your captain is grumpy and authoritative, his unhappiness will affect you to some degree. If your leadership sinks in unhappy feelings, your ship will ultimately sink, but if your leadership floats in the ocean of happiness, your ship will float on the waves of happiness. We are always capable of turning the ship of our existence in the direction of leadership that serves. Over the years, Suru kept that lesson like a golden treasure. Ever since, it has been reflected in his experience of leadership. It became the source of Suru's orientation to leadership regardless of the leadership position.

That change in his orientation to leadership profoundly impacted Suru's leadership as a teacher in the classroom and beyond. When he taught English and religion courses in Saint J Seminary in Nineb, Suru would use class discussions to confess to his students that he was among them to serve each and every one. He would raise their awareness on how meaningful their presence in the classroom was to his presence among them. He would alert them that their presence justified his presence and his teaching.

Suru often made it clear he would not be a teacher if there were no students. Any teacher is a teacher only because of and in the presence of students. In the absence of students, all teachers become irrelevant. Suru learned to treat all students with respect and dignity. He would challenge students with ground rules of respect and politeness toward all members of the class. He used his lectures to inspire them with philosophical thoughts. Suru welcomed all questions and stimulated students to listen reflectively. That practice empowered his students to engage in discussions and feel safe and happy in the classroom. They felt happy, and he felt the same way.

Suru carried that practice of service-style teaching across time and space in his classes in a number of institutions of higher education. He would later root that practice in the philosophy of *Ubuntu* (I am because we are) as the backbone of his teaching. In general, Suru's teaching methodology relies on blending the philosophies of *cogito ergo sum* (I think, so I am) and Ubuntu. *Cogito ergo sum* is from French philosopher René Descartes ("I think, so I am."). This philosophy emphasizes the importance of a rational ego in the learning process.

Ubuntu comes from the Xhosa language. It means "I am because we are." This African philosophy conceptualizes the importance and weight of the community and society for individual learners. Suru operationalizes such philosophies in the classroom by utilizing techniques of communicative teaching. His communicative teaching contrasts the perception of teaching as a one-way interaction where teachers only dump lectures on students and strive to meet the needs of a curriculum instead of actual student needs.

In communicative teaching, Suru exemplifies teaching as a two-way interaction between teacher and student where the teacher sends a message and then stimulates and welcomes the student's response. As such, communicative teaching is a student-centered process. It is a teacher-and-student-driven process. Its well-rounded outcome is rewarding for students and teachers. It facilitates teaching and learning. It allows the teacher to work with the personality of each student to meet their specific needs.

Working with a student's persona requires getting to know students by names and personalities. Knowing students' personalities allows the teacher to better understand the group dynamics inside the classroom and beyond. More importantly, it raises the teacher's awareness of individual needs and how to address such needs constructively and meaningfully for effective outcomes in teaching and learning.

Communicative teaching requires reflective listening. It also requires flexibility in class design and class planning. A student reminded Suru of what it meant to be flexible in class design and planning. The scene occurred in a course on research methods. For that class, Suru was using PowerPoint presentations for lectures. He would post lectures online for students about forty-five minutes before class to make sure students did not neglect other reading materials. Suru wanted to make sure they took the time to complete all the course readings. His experience showed that posting lectures days before the class session deterred students from completing their course readings.

Students were content with the posted lectures, but they neglected to read other assigned course materials. Suru explained his intention in that research method class, and the students seemed to accept his explanation, but after the class ended, a student came to Suru to express his thoughts on the issue. That student's name was Osi. Osi indicated that Suru's posting of the lectures forty-five minutes before class was not helpful. Osi made a case that he needed more time to print the lectures and use the printout to take notes in class. Osi presented other arguments to advocate for his case. He ultimately suggested posting the lecture on the eve of class to meet the needs of all students.

After carefully listening to Osi, Suru thought his student's arguments were relevant to meeting his students' needs. He promised Osi that he would start posting lectures on the eve of class. Osi became visibly happy and enthusiastic.

Suru's interaction with Osi could supply any teacher with a takeaway. It does not take much to be flexible in class design and planning; we just have to be willing to meet students' needs. Communicative teaching makes teachers balance standard curriculum requirements and actual student needs. It promotes the recognition of student identity and student empowerment.

Communicative teaching reminds teachers that they cannot not be who they are and do what they do without their students. In communicative teaching, students' identities make teachers mindful of their own identities. Communicative teaching allows room for disagreement with teachers. It allows teachers to show compassion to their students. Communicative teaching makes us teach with our minds and our hearts. In communicative teaching, the heart seasons or spices up what the brain cooks to make it taste good, be healthy, and feel attractive to our senses.

In the process of communicative teaching, Suru works to create an atmosphere of family in the classroom. This allows him to call all students by their names and recognize and empower each one. Students relate to one another in ways that facilitate the learning process for constructive and sustainable learning outcomes. Such techniques emphasize critical thinking in learning and create a happy ambience in the classroom for collaborative learning and student success. Ubuntu in teaching and learning means: I am a teacher because you are students, and you are students because I am a teacher. I am in the classroom because students are in the classroom. I am in the classroom to serve my students. This implies humble dedication to all students and full attention to each student.

By relying on such philosophies in recent years, Suru's orientation to leadership as a humble service has translated to availability in the classroom and beyond. He happily taught a range of undergraduate and graduate courses in a variety of institutions of higher education in Nineb and beyond. Suru was flexible and available to create, develop, and teach any course whenever he was allowed or requested to do so, blending philosophies of *Cogito ergo sum* and Ubuntu with techniques of communicative teaching. Such philosophies and techniques allowed Suru to engineer healthy group dynamics in the classroom for humble collaboration in teaching and learning. His ultimate goal was to make learning meaningful, enjoyable, and tailored to students' needs. As echoed by student evaluations and testimonials, Suru's teaching was a student-centered process.

As a teacher serving students, Suru's teaching was driven by student-centeredness. He would conduct his classes in compliance with organizational norms, policies and guidelines. He would record student attendance and participation consistently. He would show tangible sensitivity to students' difficulties with the course load in the classroom and beyond. He would be available for student consultations beyond the classroom during office hours. He would grant some extra attention and resources to students when appropriate. He would provide constructive and timely comments on students' essays, papers, quizzes, or exams.

Suru would keep students informed about their progress. He would conduct formative evaluations in class as the semester unfolds. He would post the final grades by the deadline. He would teach the course according to the syllabus by providing a clear and well-timed lesson for each weekly objective. He would provide well-ordered instructions on how to participate in course learning activities.

Suru was prepared and organized for class. He would highlight the learning outcomes by enhancing key points in lectures using PowerPoint presentations. He would often repeat announcements to elaborate about course contents and expectations. Suru would ensure grading criteria and rubrics were well-defined in the syllabus and clearly explained in the classroom. He would participate actively in class discussions through facilitation and by using techniques of appreciative inquiry. He would empower individual students to appreciate and build on their own intellectual assets as well as their classmates' assets.

Suru would encourage open dialogue and collaboration among students. He would brainstorm discussion topics to increase student interest in critical issues. He would integrate videos and new technologies to stimulate students' attention. He would encourage students to use a variety of information sources, including required course reading materials. He would provide students with information on current and recent events relating to course content. Suru would start his class sessions with provocative and inspiring thoughts of the day in connection with the course's weekly objectives to stimulate and motivate students.

Suru would incorporate all sorts of learning activities that would help students combine theory and practice through research. Through simulations, class presentations, panel discussions, and debates, he would provide students with opportunities to test and apply knowledge. He would ask questions that stimulate students to think critically about the subject matter.

Suru would develop scenarios and solutions to course problems that could be applied. Through guest speakers and practical cases, he would present students with the opportunity to network and use the knowledge gained from class in real life.

All such methods contributed to making Suru's teaching very effective per all standards. Suru made the orientation of his courses dynamic, taking into account recent developments in local, national, regional, and world affairs. His courses provided ad hoc case studies to blend theory and practice. Students' final evaluations for all courses were summative evaluations. The summative evaluations focused on assessing the course process and learning outcomes at the end of each semester. Each student was allowed to use quantitative and qualitative measures to evaluate the course process and learning outcomes. The quantitative evaluation was done using specific measures. The qualitative evaluations were reflected in student narratives. Evaluation data were collected in his absence to make sure he did not affect student responses or evaluations.

Suru's orientation to teaching was rooted in his spirituality of service. Suru's spirituality of service is echoed in the philosophy of Ubuntu: "I enjoy existence by serving others." So is Suru's overall administrative work ethic. Suru was once an academic program administrator. In such capacity, he worked with students and colleagues in that same spirit of humble service. His ears and eyes were all receptive. He welcomed everyone's input. He humbly consulted with students and colleagues for decisions on the orientation of the program he managed. They collaborated on most decisions regarding the program. They all partook in deliberations over significant decisions. Suru also relied on an open-door policy and other strategies for organizational development to humbly listen to students' needs and take them into account as much as he could.

Making students successful and happy was Suru's ultimate goal in serving them. Making students happy made Suru happy. A number of Suru's students would confide to him they were excited and happy to attend his classes. In return, Suru would confess that serving them was also rewarding; serving them made him happy. Suru's experience taught him that teaching and learning blossom into happiness only at the crossroads of teaching and service. When perceived and undertaken as humble service, teaching radiates into happiness for the teacher and student.

In addition to his students, Suru's colleagues would often laud him for his lectures. Suru was enthusiastic while teaching. He was passionate about the topics of his courses. He taught with self-assurance and persuasion; he taught with expertness, and he believed in what he preached. His lectures were inspiring. Attending Suru's lecture would likely make you adhere to not missing any of his class sessions.

His enthusiasm was contagious. Listening to him makes you feel good. He was a gifted speaker and a talented communicator, but Suru was aware that his strength could turn into his weakness sometimes. If you allow him, Suru can entertain you all day with long talking points. Suru is very talkative. The good news about this is that you will not get bored listening to Suru. He knows how to catch the attention of his audience with a melodious accent and tone. His arguments resonate relevance. They go straight to the point, but listening to Suru also has a downside. His talk hosts the potential to prevent you from moving to your next activity or making it on time. Attending Suru's lectures could make you late to your next class. His students know him well enough to alert him about the time. Suru often exhorts them to remind him to wrap up his lecture ten to fifteen minutes before the end of a regular class session. Students happily collaborate on that.

Beyond the school environment and workplace, Suru has learned to be mindful to exercise leadership in his family as humble service. He has learned to perceive his title of father as that of a leader. As a father, he leads by consciously serving his children daily. He loves them and dedicates his time and energy to them. He is present to them and their needs. He works hard to provide for their basic needs. He packs their lunches and gets them ready for school every day. He drops them at school every morning, and he picks them up from school every evening. He helps them do their homework and reads to them every night.

Suru does not let his children sleep without covering them with warm blankets, kisses, and good night wishes. He makes sure to attend their school programs. He takes them to medical appointments as needed. Every week, he runs around different stores to buy groceries for his family. Suru spends some time playing and laughing with his children on weekends and holidays. He celebrates their birthdays delightfully. Their happiness reflects his.

Suru has also learned to perceive his title of a husband as that of a humble leader. What could Suru tell you about the love of his life? How does he frame in words what he needs to tell you about Lafia? What do you need to know about their connection? For now, he can only tell you so much on that account. He promises to tell you more later on.

Suru loves Lafia and devotes himself, his time, and his energy to her. He spends quality time with her—days and nights. At home, at work, and beyond, he remains mindful of her loving presence. Suru and Lafia negotiate their togetherness daily to enjoy their life-sharing experience in time and space. He consults with her on all personal and family decisions, and they both collaborate in every decision. He appreciates her love and teamwork for their family.

Suru helps make breakfast and takes turns cooking lunch or dinner for the family. He also helps wash dishes, does laundry, cleans bathrooms, removes and replaces trash bags, sweeps and mops the floor, and vacuums the carpets around the house. Suru likes to spend some of his weekends fixing or repairing things around the household. He enjoys trimming trees and bushes to keep his backyard and front yard clean from dirt and snakes.

Lafia is scared of any snakes wandering around in the backyard or front yard. She tends to blame Suru for any snakes that show up. He makes sure to keep all snakes away by keeping all spaces clean.

Every year, Suru commemorates Lafia's birthday with flowers, cards, gifts, and a devoted presence. He stands by her in times of joy and in difficult times. Their life together has taught Suru that his leadership as a husband ought to patiently translate into utmost services in times of tribulations. He reminds Lafia to frequently exercise and take care of herself. He takes her to medical appointments. He knows all of Lafia's doctors. Suru's services to his children and wife make them happy. And this makes him happy as well.

When leadership becomes service, it engineers happiness or peace within your family and beyond. Leadership that is service gratifies you and your environs with happiness. At least, that is what daily life teaches Suru. He has learned and experienced such meaningful reverberations of the service-style leadership on himself and on his entourage in the midst of his interactions—from all angles of his social environment.

CHAPTER 12

From Competition to Collaboration and from Resistance to Negotiation

A few years after Suru got his memorable epiphany on leadership as a service, he completed his training at the minor seminary of Meji. The boat of Suru's training for priesthood had to sail to D Seminary of Rako to continue his studies. D Seminary was located in the northern part of Nineb, in a city called Rako. Suru's first trip to D Seminary was amazing. He still remembers that beautiful voyage. It was his first journey on a train, a relatively long trip.

On the day of that trip, Suru woke up early in the morning. Iya and Baba recruited a taxi to take their son to the main train station. They started loading the cab with Suru's bags and suitcases. The taxi quickly got filled inside with Suru's belongings. There was barely space for any human passengers besides the driver and the front passenger. Yet after ascertaining the taxicab had enough space for Suru and his luggage, Iya noticed there was still space for a person of her size to fit in back.

Baba would not go to the train station with Suru; he was already running late for work.

Iya decided to take the narrow spot inside the cab. Suru's mother joyfully joined her son inside the taxi by squeezing her thin body inside.

Suru was sitting next to the driver and watched as Iya sat next to his large suitcase. The driver had no other option but to keep that suitcase in back since the trunk was jammed with Suru's other suitcase and bags.

After a few minutes of chatting, the taxi dropped them at the main station. Patiently, Suru's mother helped her son go through a series of formalities until Suru was able to board the train. Before letting him get into the train, Iya granted Suru her best maternal advice and reassured him of her maternal prayers.

Suru gave his mother a very emotional hug with words of love and goodbye. Once inside the train, Suru was surprised the seat he was assigned was more comfortable than most car seats he had sat on. It was his first time on a train, and he did not have much to compare with.

The captain said, "All aboard!"

The train departed. Suru missed some important signals from the captain due to a bad speaker. His seat was comfortable, but the sound system was not so great on that train. Suru did not worry too much or complain about it. Who would he complain to? He was amazed by what he could see from his window seat. He saw some beautiful parts of Nineb as the train was crossing rural areas from the south to the north. He watched and admired the nature in its beauty, the changing vegetation, its habitants, the flowing rivers, and all kinds of people. The train went across dense forests, thick bushes, and grassy lands.

The size and height of young and old trees took Suru's breath away. He watched herds of deer elegantly running away as the train got near. He contemplated eagles flying far away in the sky to escape from the noise the locomotive was making. He spotted cows and sheep grazing peacefully in green valleys.

Suru also paid attention to how he felt when the train slowed down and how it felt when it picked up speed. He was pulled between mixtures of high and low emotions. At every stop, Suru was glad to get up, stretch his legs and arms, and chat with other passengers. And he felt good. His heart was filled with compassion for the poor he encountered in the countryside. Suru felt powerless about their lack of fundamental needs for food, clothes, shelter, and education. He felt bad that he could not do anything to put clothes on the toddlers crawling or running naked in the countryside, but he was impressed by the candid smiles on their faces as they waved their hands to welcome or say goodbye to the train.

He witnessed farmers running out of their shaky huts as the train got near. The powerful noise of the locomotive was enough to make their shacks shake. Suru felt bad for those poor mothers selling groundnuts by the railroad: they only relied on a few cents to survive daily. All such scenes made Suru realized how privileged he was. He called into question everything he took for granted.

Suru became more aware of the extent of the dreadful poverty in Nineb and the urgency of helping the poor as his mission. The locomotive kept moving from one village to another, from one town to another, until it reached the city of Rako, its final destination. Upon arriving in Rako, it was late in the evening. It was dark inside and outside the train. Thankfully, the darkness was challenged by spotlights and flashlights. Such lights were enough for all passengers to find their way out of the train. Before getting out, Suru sat back quietly in a dark corner for a few minutes and thought about a powerful message he got on that trip: everyone should embrace the mission of helping the poor to make the world a happy place for all. Such a mission should be seen as an urgency by everyone in a position of leadership. Good leadership should be determined by its humble and generous service to those who are poor or needy.

His understanding of leadership as service successfully impacted Suru's last years of study in the minor seminary of Meji. By the end of his training period at Meji, Suru felt humble. He was admired by many of his fellows as a good leader and role model, but he kept struggling with other existential challenges.

One challenge became obvious and dominant during his time at D Seminary of Rako. It had to do with Suru's inclination toward resistance and competition rather than collaboration. Suru was a champion in competing. He was a partisan of resistance. He would take pride in competing with others and resisting just for the sake of doing so. Without taking enough time to think critically before deciding on his position or course of action, Suru was quick to compete and resist. It did not matter whether what he had before him was good or bad. To say the least, he was trapped within his thoughts and initiatives of competing with others and resisting others in so many things, in so many ways, and around the clock. Suru did not have a clue why he was so into all that. He thought that pattern of behavior was to his advantage. He made no sense. Yet he felt powerless refraining from it. It was like an addiction! Suru could not stop competing and resisting. He was stupid in that time frame.

Suru enjoyed studying alone when preparing for his tests and exams. This was in part due to his penchant for competition. He was always competing with his classmates to get the highest score. Suru wanted to be seen as the best student in the eyes of everyone. He felt like he was better off hiding his study tactics to his fellow students to be the best student in class. He would resist all impulses and invitations to study with classmates, but he was doing well on his tests to some degree. His scores were well above average. Though most of his test scores were high, they were not always the highest.

Suru's performance was not sustained. Sometimes he would get the highest score, and other times, his score was just high. Other classmates would get the highest scores to Suru's dissatisfaction. Every time he failed to get the highest score, he was disappointed. His disappointment led him to conduct a self-evaluation of his performance and study techniques. Suru's goal was to improve his tactics in order to always get the highest score. He would later see that remote purpose as a naive illusion of an egocentric teenager!

In the course of his self-evaluation, Suru observed that it took him hours to review course materials when studying for his tests or exams. Because he was studying alone, he had to review everything by himself. He also observed that he easily got tired in the process of studying for his tests. It was very difficult doing it all alone.

Due to the fatigue from studying alone, Suru was often irritable and frustrated with fellow students over what he would later consider to be minor issues. His bad temper was spilling over in his social environment. Suru was taking it out on his fellows. He was quite suspicious; he would quickly complain about attitudes or behaviors perceived as offensive and yell at classmates on the playground or in the hallway. As a result, fellow students were staying away from him to avoid conflict. They were trying not to rile him. He was also trying to avoid them in that period as much as possible.

It was a dark period of self-inflicted isolation. Suru felt isolated and unhappy sometimes. He was hit by an infectious malady. He studied in remote areas under mango trees, and the mosquito bites knocked him down with a severe malaria. He became bedridden. The malaria kept him in his bed for a week. He was on malaria medications.

The illness provided Suru with the opportunity to reflect on malaria in poor countries. He became aware of how millions of people were dying around the world. With his infection, Suru almost made the list of those people. He had no idea how a disease that was eradicated in some rich countries was still rampant in poor countries. Malaria continued to damage poor countries in part due to a lack of goodwill and collaboration between poor countries and rich countries.

Suru suspected that a collaboration between rich and poor would result in finding ways to eradicate malaria, but the pharmaceutical companies seemed to be using malaria as a means of making money in the backyard of the poor, which was the case with other infectious diseases. Medications to remedy malaria are expensive for poor people. Suru thought the pharmaceutical companies supplying malaria medications resembled nephrologists trying to treat patients suffering from chronic kidney diseases with cycles of dialysis while their conditions required a kidney transplant. Dialysis is certainly helpful, but it does not address the issue once for all. The patients would be required to keep getting it again and again. And dialysis is not cheap. A kidney transplant is expensive, but it takes care of the patient's problems better than dialysis. Similarly, malaria medications are helpful, but they do not take care of the structural roots of the problem. Finding ways to uproot malaria for good would serve the poor better. Human beings certainly have the brain power to uproot malaria from poor countries under the hospices of goodwill and collaboration.

Suru's self-examination also unveiled the dynamics of his academic scores. It turned out that he got the highest scores on the midterm exams but not on his final exams. Suru's midterm exams occurred when his mind was still fresh and his body was full of energy. The final exams occurred when he was mentally and physically exhausted.

Suru also noticed a group of classmates whose performance was sustained throughout the semester. That group of students were always studying together and managed to always get the highest scores on their midterm exams and on their final exams. The students in that group were always smiling and laughing; they were well-tempered and well-mannered. Efo explained to Suru that they would take time to advise every member of the group not to get in trouble with anyone. They were studying together and playing together. Efo's group invited Suru to join their study group more than once. Every time they tried, Suru declined their invitation for egoistic reasons. Efo's group was made up of the students Suru was competing against academically. Time and again, he resisted their invitation to become a member of their group, but at the end of his self-examination, Suru decided to give it a second thought. *There might be something good about collaboration. Collaboration might be a worthy experiment.*

A day after his self-examination, Suru asked to join Efo's study group. To Suru's surprise, the group welcomed him immediately. He experienced shame and excitement. He was ashamed for taking so long to join them, but he was excited to join a group of elites. This happened at the end of the first semester of the academic year.

The following semester, after he started participating in the meetings and activities of Efo's group, Suru recorded a clear improvement in his wellness and academic performance. He was happy to enjoy the company and network of friends he was studying and playing with. The extreme and chronic fatigue syndrome Suru previously experienced while studying went away for good. He no longer felt any fatigue while studying for tests.

As a group, they split up tasks. Everyone was given a chapter or a topic to review and present to the group. Everyone was trusted to do a good job. Everyone was accountable to the group. Everybody was doing a good job. They all knew their rights and responsibilities vis-à-vis the group. They took their duties seriously. More importantly, they learned how to negotiate.

The collaboration helped improve Suru's negotiation skills. It taught him so much about the importance of negotiation. Suru would not hesitate to tell stories about members' ability to negotiate in the group. One week, as the group was reviewing for a final exam in philosophy, they got caught in distributive traps. Following their regular review process, they split a chapter into eight parts to match the number of members of the group. They assigned a portion of the chapter to each member to read and present to the entire group.

Suru was usually assigned the task of presenting the introduction. He was fond of starting the presentation cycle. As a result, his presentation usually came first. However, that week, his classmate who usually presented the conclusion had a conflict. His name was Yabi. Yabi was scheduled for an important meeting with the director of the seminary at the time of his presentation. Yabi did not have any intention to ask the director to postpone the meeting due to a group review for final exams. His only option was to negotiate with the study group.

Yabi brought his concern to the group. Together members explored a series of options. They tried to switch or postpone the review. It was difficult due to numerous factors, including the time constraints in their regular daily schedules.

Following a series of deliberations, they figured out it was impossible to have all of them together for a review at a different time before the final exam. Yabi asked the group to allow him to read and present the introduction that week instead of the conclusion of the chapter. Doing so would allow him to attend the presentation and still be able to catch up with his meeting with the director.

At first, Suru was not very excited about that idea. His proclivity to resistance came across. And he thought he had good reasons to resist Yabi's suggestion. Suru enjoyed reading and presenting the introduction or beginning of chapters and articles. He preferred going first in group presentations.

Prior to the discussion, Suru had read the introduction and was ready to present it. Suru paused to think about the right course of action in that situation, but everybody quickly turned to him and asked him to voice his opinion on Yabi's suggestion. The other members knew that Suru's opinion was critical in that case. If he would agree to switch his order of presentation with Yabi, the problem would easily be resolved. However, if Suru were to oppose trading his introduction with Yabi's conclusion, then the group would be left with a tougher decision-making process. The group was faced with a dilemma.

Suru tried to put himself in Yabi's shoes, and he asked the group to allow him some time to think about it. Suru went over the chapter and focused on the conclusion. After skimming the chapter, Suru was not eager to present the conclusion. He came up with a new idea. Suru suggested that every member should read the entire chapter and present any aspect of the chapter that would touch them either because they agreed with it or disagreed with it—or simply found it meaningful.

The group cheered up at that thought and welcomed the idea warmly. They all thought it was the best option for their group and a win-win for every member, including Yabi. Actually, Yabi gave Suru a personal handshake for what he called a bright idea and a win-win solution. The implementation of that idea brought joy and happiness upon all members without exception. Yabi was able to keep his assigned conclusion, and he was also able to present first. His presentation to the group emphasized what he thought was meaningful in the conclusion.

After his presentation, Yabi left for his meeting with the director.

Suru presented next by commenting on a sentence from the introduction he thought was significant. The other members of the group took turns highlighting different parts of the chapter they agreed or disagreed with. They spent time clarifying concepts that needed clarifications. At that moment, they all realized that the chapter at stake was short and easy. They came to the conclusion that the order of their presentations did not have to follow the sequence of the chapters in order to understand its content. It did not matter who presented their assigned part of the chapter first. What mattered was having a good understanding of the contents of the chapter. Understanding could be reached using different techniques.

Members were able to keep their reviews as scheduled, and Yabi was able to meet with the director following his participation in the review. All members of the group scored high on that final exam in philosophy. Based upon the negotiation process, the group dynamics got even better. Subsequently, the group changed its traditional method of study by adopting the study method Suru suggested as its standard method, which required everyone to read and present the part of the reading they connected with. It was magnificent and beautiful.

Suru discovered a rainbow in teamwork. In the process, he was inspired by the players' collaboration in soccer and basketball teams. It takes collaboration for a soccer or basketball team to win. In a sense, no matter how good individual players might be, it would be nearly impossible for them to win it without working together. Any individual who might try to win it alone would run the risk of exhaustion and self-destructruction.

Overall, Suru's experience collaborating with members of the study group affected his being and doing. He was able to sustain a good mood throughout the semester. He was able to sleep well. He was smiling and laughing a lot. Suru was chatting constantly and happily with his fellow students. He was a being in relation with others as Aristotle put it in his philosophy, which Suru was studying in that period.

He was happy to relate to the alter ego in his fellow students.

That experience taught him that human beings can collaborate successfully in the midst of their differences. That experience would forever enlighten his perspective on collaboration for constructive group dynamics in the workplace and beyond.

We are so different in the workplace. The workplace reflects an amalgam of human differences in background, race, gender, religion, generation, and culture. We need one another for effectiveness in the workplace. High performance or productivity in the workplace depends on collaboration. Individual success and the success of the workplace depends on a degree of mutual tolerance and collaboration. In a sense, even our health depends on how we collaborate with others. Collaboration makes us not to carry the burden alone. This reduces stress levels, which triggers bodily mechanisms to produce good hormones for health benefits. In that process, collaboration utterly contributes to our peace of mind and heart. That perspective on collaboration inspired Suru's professional approach to teaching and learning.

As a teacher, Suru would often remind students of his perception of teaching and learning as a rendezvous of giving and receiving. In addition to interactive lectures, he would generate frequent class discussions to stimulate student participation. Suru would organize creative group presentations or simulations to foster students' contribution to the process of teaching and learning. In the process, he would often remind them everyone had something to contribute to teaching and learning. Such venues provided students with the opportunity to learn from one another; they also allowed Suru to learn from students.

Suru would also design panel discussions and debates to encourage disagreements over arguments, mutual respect, and mutual learning. Suru learned to collaborate with students over their specific interests and the general interests of the class. Without creating any double standard, and mindful of his philosophy of no student left behind, Suru learned to focus on the needs of individual students in his classes to help each and every one achieve success in the course. Thankfully, he has been blessed with teaching relatively small classes. On average, the size of Suru's classes ranged from twenty students to thirty-five students. In such small class environments, he learned to transcend his positions in order to emphasize mutual academic interests.

When a syllabus requires that students complete five assignments on specified dates in order to succeed in the course, Suru remains mindful there may be students with a different position. They may think that their life situations would not allow them to complete the required assignments on the indicated dates. Faced with such students, Suru would look beyond their position and engage in collaborative problem-solving over a common academic interest. That common interest was usually for everyone to succeed in the class. The process often led Suru to discover that most students had good reasons behind their positions, including serious time constraints, disease or deaths of family members, or other family emergencies. As long as they were willing to collaborate, and as much as they would allow him, Suru would work with them to look beyond their respective positions and focus on their mutual interest in succeeding in the course. He would often cooperate with them on finding workable alternatives for the completion of their assignments at a time that would be good for them and for him. It was not always easy, but in most cases, the process resulted in mutually satisfying outcomes for all parties involved.

Collaboration makes humankind work together for mutual gains; it helps construct and regulate our interactions in a win-win perspective and is more effective than resistance or competition.

Think about how many car accidents and road violence result

from a lack of collaboration among drivers as they compete on the road. There are numerous traffic accidents due to senseless lack of collaboration among drivers. They fail to collaborate on the road and run the risk of a traffic accident when they go beyond the speed limit, fail to stop at a red light, or do not yield. They fail to collaborate with other drivers when they drive drunk. When you are on the phone while driving or crossing the road, you fail to collaborate and risk having an accident.

You fail to collaborate when you text while driving or crossing the road. If you cause an accident, you become a loser. In the worst-case scenario, you either lose your life or someone else loses their life due to your lack of collaboration on the road. In a nonfatal situation, you lose your time. If you were trying to reach your destination on time, in case of an accident, you would have no other choice than to wait for law enforcement to complete all related formalities. And in the end, you would not be able to reach your destination on time. In either case, when you cause a traffic accident, you will not be happy. Neither will be any other parties involved in that accident.

Harmony reigns on the road when drivers collaborate with one another by yielding and respecting traffic regulations, traffic lights, and speed limits. Such collaboration allows everyone to reach their destinations safely and happily in many cases. As we work together, we recognize one another with mutual respect. In that process, we learn from one another, we enrich one another, and we become stronger, safer, and happier as a team and as individuals. Collaboration brings the best out of us as individuals and groups; it brings us harmony or peace on the road and beyond.

Suru's contemplation of road collaboration made him think about collaboration on a much larger scale: society at large. In the process, Suru became aware that he was wearing a colorful shirt. That shirt looked awesome. Suru did not design or make the shirt. Somebody else did. All Suru did was buy and wear it. He would not have that shirt if nobody had made it. Subsequently, Suru had the same thought about his trousers, his belt, his socks and shoes, his watch, and his glasses. He also thought the same thing about the coffee his friends drank every morning and the dark chocolate he enjoyed every once in a while.

When Suru became aware of how much he depended on artisans and farmers, he trained himself to be mindful of and grateful to all farmers and artisans who produce what he wears and eats. Whenever Suru wears something, whether it is his shirt, or his trousers, or his belt, or his socks and his shoes, or a watch, or even his glasses, he would think of the tailors or whoever made them. He thinks of those who shipped them out of factories as well as the merchants who bought them and sold them. He takes a moment to contemplate and admire the chain of collaboration.

In his heart, Suru often expresses his gratitude to everyone involved in the process because he depends on them to a great extent. And every time he does, Suru feels humble. He feels he really needs others. He needs their work to have his shirt, his trousers, his belt, his socks and shoes, his watch, and his glasses in order to go to work or to function. He cannot do much without their talents and contributions. Suru is not a tailor, a shoemaker, or a technician. He cannot put together a watch or design or make glasses. If Suru were to learn to do that, his life would be hectic and miserable, and he would still need help on other fronts. We just cannot do it all alone. Thinking of such farmers and artisans and being grateful to them also makes Suru feel good. He feels happy he can rely on others.

What if we think of such farmers whenever we drink tea and coffee or eat chocolate? What if we are mindful of those brave artisans every time we wear our shirts, our trousers, our socks and shoes, our watches and glasses? What would we lose by thinking of them? We certainly would not lose anything. On the contrary, we might even achieve something great. Maybe, when we think of them, our awareness of interdependence and collaboration would increase. Perhaps we will show more concern for the poor conditions in which some of them work to grow coffee and cocoa or to produce the clothes and footwear we enjoy so much.

If we think of those farmers and artisans more often, we will feel good in what we do, they will also feel good in what they do, and we will all be happy together. Our happiness depends on their happiness and vice versa. No one can do it all alone. Suru has learned and understood this by experiencing it firsthand. He has also learned to be mindful of it in every aspect of his life. Suru needs others to be who they are and do all the good things they do for his use so that he can be who he is and do what he is meant to do in society. We are different, but we all need one another in a dynamic togetherness and relation. We ought to negotiate our living together by collaborating. We need to collaborate on all accounts in society for happiness. Other people impact or contribute to our being and doing.

There is something beautiful like a rainbow in teamwork. A rainbow is made of different colors. When isolated, each color is unique, monotonous, and boring in a sense. Brought together, the colors collaborate to produce a harmony reflected in the rainbow. Indeed, the rainbow is attractive; it radiates beauty and peace. It vividly highlights the relevance of each color and emphasizes the interdependence of all the colors. The rainbow cannot be in the absence of one of the colors it is made of; to say the least, its harmony would be tarnished. Human collaboration reminds us that we all depend on one another. Our social togetherness makes it a requirement that we all need each other for happiness. Nobody can do it alone in the pursuit of happiness. No country can truly be happy without the other countries. No country will succeed happily in isolation. In isolation, we run the risk of exhaustion, self-destruction, and extinction. In the absence of collaboration, we are overflowed with the venoms of competition and resistance. Competition and resistance help kick-start flares of mutual destruction by all odds. When we relentlessly let off flares of competition and resistance, the odds are we end up destroying ourselves and others. We need others to survive and to sustain happiness. We ought to collaborate in order to harmonize our differences in worldview, generation, gender, ethnicity, race, nationality, ideology, religion, value, and culture.

Immediately following Suru's enlightenment on collaboration and negotiation, it was summer break. All seminarians vacated the seminary to join their families or relatives. Suru went home to spend time with his family. His relatives were going through a turbulent time. Baba's older sister was not happy with her daughter's choice of boyfriend. The aunt's name was Wahala. Her daughter's name was Eke. Wahala alleged that Eke's boyfriend was not a good choice. The boyfriend's name was Ido. Wahala did not want to see Ido around. She had no substantive argument or clear evidence to back up her claim about Ido.

Eke tried hard to talk to her mother privately. She explained to Wahala how Ido was a good man with a good heart and mind, but Wahala would not listen to anything. At the age of thirty-five, Eke was still single in part due to her mother's animosity toward literally every man who came into her life. Wahala would always find something wrong to disqualify every man who loved Eke and whom Eke loved.

Eke loved and respected her mother. As a good child, she was listening to Wahala carefully; she did her best to heed her mother's advice and warnings. Eke would do anything she could to please her mother. As a result, Eke had been breaking up with her boyfriends—one after another. She could not stay in a relationship with a man. She could not move on. Her mother was so attached to her. Wahala would even go as far as lying or trapping boyfriends in order to get rid of them or make Eke give up on them.

Unfortunately, Wahala was using Eke's respectable manners against her daughter. She was violating Eke's relationship and privacy. She was abusing her daughter. Eke would understand her mother's game after Wahala lied about a boyfriend and fiancé who Eke once loved dearly. That fiancé's name was Labi. Wahala said that Labi was already a married man and had many children before meeting Eke. She even skillfully manipulated another lady by the name of Iti to stand up against Eke and pretend she was Labi's wife.

Without checking other opinions, Eke confronted Labi and called him a liar and other names. Labi felt humiliated; he did his very best to prove he was innocent, but Eke would not believe him. Instead, she naively believed in her mother's words and took them for gospel.

Disappointed, Labi went his way and moved on with his life. He was a decent and honest man who deeply loved Eke and had wanted to create a lovely family.

A year later, Eke found out her mother had lied and was wrong about Labi. Labi had never been married before meeting Eke. He had no children. Eke was distraught, and she tried to apologize to Labi for her mistake. She tried to amend as much as she could, but it was too late to get a second chance from that nice man.

A year after Wahala tried to destroy Labi's reputation with a despicable lie, he found the woman of his dreams. Labi won that woman's heart and mind. Her name was Osi. Labi was happily committed to Osi, and Osi was happily devoted to him. They had a happy relationship. Osi happened to be Eke's old classmate. They all went to school together, including Labi. Eke felt happy for Osi and Labi, but she felt bad for herself. Eke became bitter with her mother. From that moment on, she decided to keep her mother away from her relationships.

Wahala still managed to melt into her daughter's life. She was trying to control Eke's relationship with the new boyfriend who she alleged to be a bad choice. Learning from previous experiences, Eke was aware that her mother's ultimate goal was to have her new relationship with Ido melt down. At the age of thirty-five, Eke no longer wanted to allow Wahala to push her relationship to a melting point. She cherished that new relationship so dearly, but her mother would not give up. To avoid any meltdown in her relationship with Ido, Eke complained to Baba. Suru's father was Wahala's brother and Eke's uncle. Eke knew Wahala respected Baba. Wahala trusted Baba's judgment on almost everything. She might not listen to anyone, but she would listen to Baba.

After carefully listening to Eke's complaint, Baba called in Wahala to hear her version of the story. When asked, Wahala explained to Baba that Eke's boyfriend was from different ethnic background and religion. She wanted Eke to find a boyfriend from their ethnic group.

Upon hearing Wahala's arguments, Baba tried to intervene to help transform the conflict between Wahala and her daughter. Baba tried to remind Wahala to remember he and Iya were from two different ethnic groups and were happily married.

Wahala sighed carelessly. She despised Baba's perspective. After a moment of silence, she replied that Baba and Iya were in a different situation. She struggled with that answer, and Suru thought it was weak.

Suru could hear everything from his room because his room was adjacent to the living room where Baba and Wahala were having their conversation. Without challenging Wahala on her weak reply, Baba tried to coach her on managing her emotions vis-à-vis Ido, but Wahala did not want to hear anything of that kind. She resisted to Baba's exhortation to soften her position.

Wahala did not welcome Baba's invitation to put Eke's interests first. Wahala ultimately got upset and left Baba in the room unapologetically.

Eke did not want to let her mother have a hold on her relationship any longer. She was no longer willing to hear any warning from her mother. She was unwilling to heed any advice from Wahala. Eke was fed up with Wahala's perception of her love for Ido. Her mother's perception of Ido did not reckon with her feelings. Per Eke's account, Ido was a quiet boy. He was Muslim. He was a very respectful and decent man. He was hardworking and focused. Eke was deeply in love with Ido. She considered him the love of her life, and he loved her in return.

An informal and unexpected meeting between Baba and Ido would confirm everything Eke said about Ido. It was on the occasion of a banquet hosted by Baba's friend. The friend's name was Bayo. Bayo invited Suru's father to join a feast he organized to celebrate his newlywed daughter. The daughter's name was Masi. Masi was Eke's friend. She invited Eke to join the party. Ido accompanied Eke to the party. They joined the party without knowing that Baba was also invited. Eke was pleasantly surprised to see Suru's parents at the banquet.

Baba and Iya honored the invitation, and Suru also decided to go with them. It was a golden opportunity for Eke to introduce Ido to Baba and Iya. Ido was very respectful, and he bowed down as he greeted Suru's parents. Baba wanted to make sure Ido was not just acting. He seized the opportunity to watch Ido throughout the feast.

As guests of all ages and genders crowded the feast happily, Ido was calm and polite with the crowd. He volunteered to help distribute plates, spoons, forks, knives, and glasses to all the guests. Ido also humbly volunteered to help serve the food by carrying it around. Suru's parents found such behaviors extraordinary. After he completed waiting on the guests, Ido came back to sit next to Eke, but his seat was taken by another guest. Eke tried in vain to save Ido's seat while he was waiting on guests, but there were too many guests who needed a place to sit.

At some point, Eke thought it would be unfair to have a chair vacant when so many people needed a place to sit. She gave up her boyfriend's seat, and it was quickly occupied.

When Ido showed up, Eke winked at him to signal that his seat was taken. Ido winked back at Eke. Abo, the new occupant of Ido's seat, understood the message and tried to get up to allow Ido to sit next to Eke, but Ido promptly beseeched Abo not to vacate the seat.

Ido quickly grasped a broken piece of wood and sat comfortably on it next to Eke. He was affectionately holding his girlfriend's hand. It was beautiful to watch. Everybody witnessing the scene marveled at Ido's acts. Nothing in his acts was fake; they all spontaneously and genuinely came from the bottom of his caring heart and good mind.

Ido was devoted to Eke, and Baba agreed with Iya on that. A witness of the scene went to tell the whole story to Bayo, the host of the banquet. Upon hearing the story, Bayo was impressed. Bayo invited Ido and Eke to sit at the table of the guests of honor. It was a pleasant surprise for Ido and Eke. They gladly accepted the invitation and joined the table to a standing ovation from the other guests. Ido's attitude and actions brought him honor in the presence of all the other guests.

Upon watching Ido's behavior, Suru's father resolved to exhort Wahala to give Eke a chance to move to the next level with Ido. Baba's timely observation of Ido resulted in a very good impression. Ido made an excellent impression on Suru's parents, but Baba did not know how to approach Wahala about the issue. He communicated with Iya about the situation and sought her advice. Iya told Baba to call a family reunion for collaborative problem-solving through dialogue. Suru's father decided to heed Iya's suggestion within a month.

The conflict between Wahala and Eke escalated. Eke smartly moved out of her mother's house, far away from Wahala, and into another neighborhood without breathing a word to Wahala about it. Unaware of Eke's whereabouts, Wahala was lonely and depressed. She enjoyed her daughter's presence and being around her under the same roof. She could not stand Eke's absence or disappearance. Wahala was bewildered.

Eke did not tell anyone about her new neighborhood except Baba. She warned Suru's father not to tell anybody. She trusted Baba and was aware of how good he was at keeping secrets. She unveiled the motivations of her decision to Suru's father. Her goal was to stay away from Wahala in order to enjoy her existence with peace in mind and heart. Eke felt she was better off away from her mother.

Baba kept the secret. After spending three miserable weeks searching for her daughter in every corner of her neighborhood, Wahala rushed to Baba for help. She was aware Eke trusted Suru's father and would resort to him before any major decision. She hoped Baba would know her daughter's whereabouts.

Suru's father knew it, but he refrained from telling Wahala he was aware of Eke's decision and whereabouts. Instead, Baba took his time to listen to Wahala's complaint and her request for help. Wahala explained to Suru's father that she was deeply sorry for making Eke's life despondent. She would pay any price to bring her daughter home. Wahala was ready to do everything Eke would require to come home. Wahala would accept all conditions her daughter put forward.

Baba gladly welcomed Wahala's offer. He seized the opportunity to unveil his intention to call for a family reunion to address the issues.

Wahala desperately agreed with Suru's father on the need for a family reunion to solve the problem.

Baba and Wahala finalized a date for the reunion. Baba informed Eke and other relatives about the schedule for the family reunion. They all agreed to have a family reunion to deal with the issue. Eke would be willing to attend the meeting and move home if her mother would leave her alone and respect Ido. She obtained a guarantee from Baba that her needs would be met.

Wahala and Eke asked Baba to facilitate the discussions at the family reunion. They both trusted him. The parties trusting in the facilitator is a critical determinant of success in any family reunion. Baba's house was selected as the venue for the family reunion. Most family members were fond of the trees in his backyard. His house also had enough space to host all the participants. Iya was a good cook, and everyone would enjoy her cuisine during the proceedings.

Suru's uncles and aunts brought some of their children. Suru was extremely happy to see some of his cousins. Tasked with the responsibility of facilitating the meeting, Suru's father introduced the meeting without delay. Baba first welcomed the participants and presented the ground after a brief introduction of each participant. The ground rules revolving around attitudes of respect and politeness were operationalized. Participants would listen respectfully to one another. They would take turns talking. They would patiently wait for their turn to talk.

Baba allowed the two primary parties to present their issues. Wahala took advantage of traditional rules of seniority and quickly went ahead with her concerns. She expressed her frustrations with Eke over her choice of boyfriend. She did not want to see Eke with a man from a different ethnic group and religion. Wahala got emotional and stressed that her position was out of love for Eke.

In a gracious gesture of compassion, Eke handed a white handkerchief to Wahala to wipe her tears. Participants welcomed Eke's gesture with applause and words of admiration. Empowered by her daughter's gesture, Wahala explained that she wanted her only daughter to be happy in her marriage.

Suru watched and listened to Wahala remotely from his room, and he wondered if his aunt was happy in her marriage. Wahala was often complaining to Baba about her husband's domestic violence. Ebu was often drunk and would yell at Wahala or even batter her. Wahala's position mirrored the culture she was a product of. Her parents were from the same ethnic group. Her husband was also from that same ethnic group. Most of her siblings were married to people from the same ethnic background. Wahala was also a product of her generation. Wahala was a core traditionalist, and she was always doing her best to enforce traditions.

As Wahala made her case, the attendants respectfully listened to her. Without breathing a word, Eke carefully and patiently listened to everything her mother had to say. Then came the time for the daughter to make her own case.

Eke started by appreciating her mother's concern for her happiness. She energetically built her arguments over the same concern. As a pure product of her own generation, Eke tried to prove to Wahala what happiness meant to her. Eke explained how her happiness could not be anything more than how she was feeling with her Muslim boyfriend. In short, Eke felt the peace of heart and mind with that man. With Ido, she was feeling good in her heart and mind. Eke reiterated that the two years she spent dating Ido were the happiest of her life. She indicated she envisioned her married life in the perspective of those two years with Ido.

Wahala kept whining and sighing as her daughter continued to tell her story to the audience.

However, Eke fearlessly enhanced her goal to be happy with her future husband. Wahala tried to stop her by implying that two years were not enough to know and select a husband, but Baba was fair and firm in reminding Wahala to respect the ground rules by listening to Eke silently.

After Eke's storytelling session ran to the finish line, Suru's father tactfully asked everyone in the audience to share their thoughts about what they had heard. All participants spoke out. The process took the form of brainstorming and sharing information. Using paraphrasing and reflective listening, Baba carefully reframed the issues and interests of both parties. It became clear to all the participants that both parties' common interests rested in Eke's happiness.

Eke stated she was happy with Ido. Participants backed Eke's statement by indicating that she showed clear physical and mental signs of happiness with the enthusiasm and compassion she displayed at the gathering.

Using typical cases of friends and relatives who were happily married, Baba tried to help Wahala understand that one can be happy in interethnic, interracial, or interreligious marriages. In a move that some participants did not expect, Baba went on to cite his own case. He bluntly explained how he and Iya were happily married even though they were from different ethnic groups. Suru's father enhanced the notion of mutual love and respect as the first building block and impetus of a happy marriage.

Iya stood in agreement with him to a standing ovation. Everybody else followed her lead happily. Wahala reluctantly stood up to applaud as well.

Eke fell on her knees before Wahala. She tried to reassure her mother she was very happy with Ido. Tearfully, Eke begged Wahala to believe in her.

In seeing her daughter's teardrops, Wahala emotionally decided to pay Eke back in the same coin. She leaned forward, stretched her right hand, and wiped her daughter's eyes with the handkerchief. Wahala pulled Eke's hands to make her stand up. After Eke stood up next to her, Wahala gave her daughter a big hug and whispered her apologies.

The crowd jubilantly responded with sustained applause. That instant was mesmerizing and powerful, and it generated happy feelings within the hearts of the participants. And their minds seemed to be in harmony with their hearts. It felt like everyone involved in the family reunion experienced the passage of a refreshing breeze of peace in their hearts and minds.

Eke was very happy in her relationship. The deliberations convinced Wahala to give Eke a chance—or at least the benefit of the doubt. Wahala nodded, and all the participants praised the mother and daughter. Delighted, Baba stood up and congratulated Wahala and Eke.

Suru thought the meeting was all over, but no, it was not.

While Baba was congratulating the two parties, Iya found her way to Suru's room for assistance. Apparently, she needed her son's help with some items. Suru was in his room because he was not allowed to participate in the meeting. Baba thought Suru was too young to participate in the discussions. Suru was about fifteen years younger than Eke. Baba also put forward sensitive issues of confidentiality to send Suru away to his room.

At first, Suru was disappointed. He was curious, and he expected to partake in the discussions. It did not take long for Suru to figure out that withdrawing to his room was not so bad. From his room, Suru was able to hear all their discussions. He could even see some of their actions depending on his position in his room. Baba probably forgot that Suru's room was adjacent to the family room. Suru managed to listen to the conversation. He was certainly invisible to the crowd, but he felt like he attended the meeting

Suru even stepped out to use the bathroom every so often. The bathroom was across from the family room. The walk to the bathroom would give him a good view of the participants, their reactions, and the smiles of some participants. Suru was just pretending to go to the restroom. He tried not to distract the participants in the process. Suru was discreet in his movements and respectful of the meeting, but he managed to come out to witness every ovation. Baba's position did not allow him to see any of his son's movements. The meeting took several hours.

Iya urged Suru and Femi to help pass some cups around. Each cup was filled halfway with drinking water. Every participant got a cup. Suru was not sure what all that was about. He quietly asked his mother as he went back to the kitchen to return the empty trays.

Iya whispered that the participants were about to conclude the meeting with the final ritual of reconciliation. Suru was not sure what his mother meant, but he saved his breath. By the time he went back to his room, the participants were all heading to the backyard with everyone holding a cup in their right hands. In no time, they formed a circle.

Baba provided some guidelines and explained the meaning of the ritual. Each participant would rinse their mouth with some water from their cup and spit it out on the ground. Suru's father insisted nobody should swallow the water. He explained the symbolism of their circle. The circle indicated the participants all belonged together. Everyone was part of the group and should feel comfortable and happy. He warned that conflicts would often bring divisions in the circle. He asked the participants to trust in their potential to transform and transcend conflict by always working constructively to recreate the circle. He explained the symbolism of the rinsing and spitting. By rinsing their mouths with clean water, the parties would attest to their readiness to cleanse their hearts and minds from conflicts in order to make some room for the other party in their hearts and minds. By spitting out the water, the parties would demonstrate their willingness to reject hatred and conflict in order to embrace forgiveness and reconciliation.

After Suru's father put a final note to the guidelines and explanations, the participants unanimously and symbolically rinsed their mouths and spit the water out on the grass. The green grass happily welcomed the water, which quickly permeated the muddy soil and disappeared.

Wahala publicly displayed signs of remorse and formally apologized to Eke. She later apologized to Eke's boyfriend. It was such a moving moment that even Baba cried with joy. After that final ritual of reconciliation, the participants became extremely animated. They were chatting, laughing, and chanting. Eke and Wahala sang an entertaining song about forgiveness and reconciliation. With such jubilations, the traditional silence often recorded in Baba's backyard dissipated. The scene was fun to watch.

Femi and Suru were still watching when Iya rushed back to them for assistance. She needed their help to pass around plates and silverware. Suru understood it was time to celebrate and eat. He gladly helped his mother set up the table and get everything ready. Suru enjoyed eating. It would be hard to resist his mother's cuisine. The participants enjoyed Iya's rice and beans with baked fish and spinach on the side. It was a delicious meal.

A year later, Eke happily married Ido, the husband of her dreams.

Wahala reiterated her apology to her daughter and son-in-law.

They gladly accepted her gesture. After the birth of the happy couple's first child, Wahala became the best grandmother for her grandson and the couple's closest friend. Eke and Ido were very happy in their marriage.

Five years later, their relationship was tested by the challenges of parenthood. As they began to feel the heat from parenting, they experienced disagreements over how to raise their children. They started facing other issues. Their love for one another turned sour and shaky.

Eke immediately asked Iya for advice. Eke admired and trusted Suru's mother as her advisor and mentor. Ido was particularly respectful of Iya, and he trusted her. Upon becoming aware of their situation, Iya invited Eke and Ido to a private meeting in Baba's backyard.

They both showed up for the meeting on a Saturday evening. They comfortably spent over an hour in discussions in a remote corner of the backyard. All Suru was able to hear from distance were laughs. Apparently, it all went well. It turned out that Iya used the opportunity to listen to both parties tell their stories. She invited them to share their love story from its very beginning. And they did. They were certainly far from expecting Suru's mother to factor that part of their relationship into the meeting, but they did not hesitate to take turns sharing their love story.

Eke and Ido remembered the incredible beginnings of their love. Eke remembered how she was attracted to her Muslim boyfriend due to his good heart and manners. Ido shared how Eke's spontaneous smile made his heart start pounding. Eke became highly emotional in the process. She cried bitterly as she shared her struggles with her mother.

Ido instantly kissed her on cheek and gave her a big hug. Iya watched their gestures with admiration. They both remembered how they swore to always stand by one another regardless of their challenges.

As they talked about their first encounter and the beginning of their love story, they started feeling positive energy. They laughed. Lots of good memories came out after warming up and energizing their hearts and minds. Their mouths clearly spoke what their hearts were full of. The good energy warmed up and spiced up their relationship for their peace of mind and heart.

Suru's mother listened to them with admiration. After carefully listening to them, Iya invited Eke and Ido to never forget to lean on the main pillar of their relationship, which she called the beginning of their love story. She encouraged them to always remember that beautiful beginning, especially during challenges and difficulties. She warned them how difficulties would always arise due to human weaknesses and limitations. They would come and go and come back again. Iya reminded Eke and Ido that they were both wonderful people, but neither of them was perfect. They were two imperfect people who selected to live together in a marriage. She encouraged them to be patient with one another and remember the launch of their love in times of weakness. Iya also gave them credit for seeking her advice.

Eke and Ido went to Suru's mother for advice and redeemed their marriage. Wherever there is marriage, there is conflict—just as conflict springs up wherever there are people. Relationship is like a rosebush. It certainly bears beautiful roses, but it also bears thorns. The thorns of a relationship can sting and hurt both parties in that relationship. When we embark on any relationship, we should not expect only roses or flowers. We should also expect thorns. Whenever the thorns in a relationship hurt us, we should be mindful of the roses as we feel the pain. Beyond the pain, we should learn to contemplate the beautiful roses within our reach. Couples will always have to deal with conflict.

Fatou was in her third marriage, and she said, "If I knew what I now know about relationship, I would not have divorced my first husband!" Every time she remarried, she got caught in the same issues that triggered her divorce with her first husband.

We can never be in a perfect relationship. We should never expect a perfect marriage. We are human beings. And human beings can never be perfect. A relationship will never be perfect, but you can make it successful and fairly happy. Spouses ought to find constructive ways to reconcile their differences if they want to remain married. In a relationship, whenever we are unable to talk about our issues in a face-to-face meeting, we may be running the risk of divorce. To maximize the chances of redeeming our relationship, it is a helpful decision to have recourse to people we trust for advice and help. Their advice may help us remember the beginning story of our relationship. Maybe the positive energy radiating from such a story will galvanize us to pass our negative feelings in times of conflict.

The start of a love story radiates the potential for transforming conflict and divorce. In times of conflict, couples tend to forget the beginning stories of their love, their first dates, and the romance. If we are mindful of our love stories and trust in our potential to recreate them in times of conflicts and beyond, maybe our divorce rates would slide down. In times of existential contradictions, couples would certainly gain a lot from negotiation and reconciliation if they could remember the feelings they experienced at the beginning—and if they are hopeful and willing to recreate such feelings and move past the negative feelings.

Eke and Ido instantaneously awoke to their potential to rekindle the light of their positive feelings and rehydrate their love for one another. They became mindful of resorting to the transformative potential of their love story to navigate successfully through the waves of existential contradictions intrinsic to marriage. Time after time, they capitalized on that strategy to live happily together.

Just like Eke and Ido, countless of couples find themselves in relationships where love transcends racial, ethnic, religious, and gender groupings. However, their love often encounters social obstacles owing to racial, ethnic, religious, or cultural differences. As a result, their love is often under pressure, hidden, or jeopardized. Suru would hope they could find some support and inspiration in Eke and Ido's story. We should never give up on love. For in its happy nature, love does not know or speak the language of race, ethnicity, religion, or culture. Happiness in love only speaks the language of the heart.

Collaboration ultimately implies negotiation. Negotiation is dialogue or mere talk. Dialogue constructively bridges our differences in position, in worldview, in culture, in generation, in ethnicity, in race, in gender, in nationality, and in religion. It allows us to negotiate our coexistence or living together for mutual and valuable understanding. Negotiation requires effective communication. Effective communication implies showing compassion to others and giving them the benefit of the doubt. Giving them the benefit of the doubt is believing in their potential to do or be good.

If we are able to find tactful and respectful ways to communicate with others and let them know how we feel, they may apologize for their mistakes. A supervisor had a conflict with his colleague. The supervisor's name was Yeki, and the colleague's name was Akoue. Akoue was very professional and good at her job. She felt like her supervisor was very disrespectful of her. Akoue shockingly remarked in some email messages that Yeki would address male colleagues respectfully with concepts of politeness such as "please." In those same messages, Akoue would be the only colleague to get an order without "please." Aware she was the only female on the list, Akoue often got upset or frustrated.

Yeki would yell at Akoue while giving her orders. Every once in a while, Akoue would yell back at him, and the situation continued to escalate. Akoue spoke to her husband about her frustration. Her husband's name was Ero. Akoue considered resigning and finding another job, but she liked her job except for her frustrations with Yeki.

After listening to Akoue vent, Ero told Akoue to ask for a meeting with Yeki. The meeting would be in the presence of a third party. Akoue heeded her husband's golden advice and met with Yeki in the presence of their common administrator. Akoue had previously briefed Emi about the situation.

At the meeting, Emi listened to Akoue's concerns about Yeki. After carefully and silently listening to Akoue's complaints, Yeki apologized for his mistakes. He showed regret and remorse for his offensive messages. He indicated that he did not intend to be mean. He promised to be more careful in the future. Yeki shared how he also got frustrated at times by Akoue's attitudes and behaviors. Yeki felt Akoue had no respect for his authority. He went on to present evidence to back up his perception, including how Akoue would yell at him sometimes.

After carefully and silently listening to Yeki, Akoue apologized. She promised to be more cautious in the future. The meeting ended with a warm handshake between Akoue and Yeki. They both felt better. From that moment on, their workplace relationship transformed. Yeki and Akoue became very respectful of one another. The ambience in their workplace improved.

Akoue would later confide to her husband that she was surprised when Yeki apologized. From what Akoue knew of Yeki, his apology came as a surprise to her. Akoue had thought Yeki was too full of himself, a man who would not apologize for any misconduct, and a sort of heartless patriarch. After the meeting, Akoue's perception of Yeki drastically shifted. Knowing Yeki had the potential to recognize his wrongdoing and apologize made Akoue feel better. She realized her supervisor also had a heart that could be hurt. She understood she was working with another human being. If we meet and talk, we might be able to sort out our differences.

Suru's path once crossed with that of an old couple in their eighties. The husband's name was Yaya, and his wife was named Yabo. Yaya and Yabo were celebrating their sixtieth anniversary of marriage. Marveling at how happy they were, Suru asked them about the secret of their happy marriage.

Yaya said, "My son, you have to talk—and talk it out!"

Yabo smiled and looked at her husband. "Yaya! You actually do not like to talk, but I make you talk anyway!"

Yaya could not disagree with Yabo. He giggled and whispered, "Someone has to initiate the talk!"

The old couple's input was meaningful for Suru. For any human relationship to be happy, we need to talk—and someone in the relationship has to initiate the talk. Growing up, Suru became aware that marital life is all about negotiation. Suru often saw his father negotiating with his mother over many things, including their schedule.

Suru remembered an intense negotiation between Baba and Iya. It was over the right time to go bed at night. Due to Baba's work schedule, he would prefer to go to bed at eight thirty and wake up early. Suru's father enjoyed those three hours of sleep before midnight and would not trade them for anything, but Iya would go to bed at nine thirty due to her daily activities. She enjoyed the three hours of sleep from four until seven. Whenever Baba was up in the morning, his movements disturbed his wife's sleep.

Iya suggested Baba was too noisy. Suru's mother also associated the problem with the fact that Baba was waking up before her. More than once, Iya invited her husband to rearrange his schedule to remain in bed longer, but much of Baba's work schedule did not depend on him. Baba was required to be at work early. Iya did not want to believe that. She did not seem to understand her husband's argument until after they sat down and talked about it on a Saturday morning.

As they talked about the issue, Baba and Iya managed to identify the main source of the noise that was disturbing Iya's sleep. It turned out the noise was mainly coming from the bathroom while Baba was taking his morning shower. The problem was not Suru's father waking up early; it was the morning shower. Instead of taking his shower every morning, Baba decided to take his shower before going to bed. Iya was very pleased with that solution.

After Baba and Iya found a common ground in that solution, its implementation granted both of them peace of mind and heart. Baba was able to wake up early without disturbing Iya's sleep. Their negotiation over that issue helped Suru's parents transcend their positions and focus on their interests. Iya's initial position was an invitation to Baba to change his work schedule to remain in bed longer. Baba's initial position was to take a shower in the morning.

Iya's interest was getting enough sleep without being disturbed by her husband. Baba's interest was going to work early without disturbing his wife's sleep. The negotiation process allowed them to move away from their positions and embrace their interests. In the end, Suru's father was still able to wake up earlier for work without disturbing Iya. Suru's mother was able to get enough sleep without making Baba change his work schedule. And they were both happy.

Daily human existence is a nexus of negotiations. Negotiations may ultimately help reconcile differences, including the differences that seem irreconcilable. Negotiation could help reduce the high divorce rates trapping so many families. A successful negotiation grants its parties some peace of mind and heart.

CHAPTER 13

From Authoritarian Rule to Democratic Freedom

In previous chapters, Suru saw leadership as humble service and not authority. He also got the message about the importance of collaboration with others. In the chapter on leadership as humble service, Suru alluded to the environment where he grew up. He indicated his environment perceived and practiced leadership as authority. Suru mentioned how he was exposed and affected by that environment of his childhood and adolescence. The venue of this new chapter serves to substantiate what Suru meant then.

Here is the place to elaborate on the country where Suru grew up. For he grew up in a small country called Nineb. The goal of telling you more about Nineb is twofold in the context of this book. First, Suru intends to show the readers how the political environment in the country of his childhood corrupted to some extent his early perception of leadership, but he also wants to show something more important than that.

While Suru struggled with his understanding of leadership and worked hard through self-examination to transcend his contradictions and shortcomings on that account, at about the same time, the country of his childhood dealt with similar contradictions. Nineb strived to shift from a dictatorial and single-party rule to a multiparty democracy. What happens in our social or political environment certainly has some impacts on us; children tend to respond to conflict in the same way the environment responds to it.

Before Suru's eyes, Nineb successfully achieved participatory democracy through a national conference. This chapter primarily intends to further conceptualize the national conference as an opportunity for individual and collective self-examination for all citizens of Nineb. Suru happily and carefully witnessed the transformation process. What trend of contradictions trapped Nineb? How did it happen? Suru witnessed contradictions and conflict escalation that resulted in a national conference and democratic freedom in Nineb.

The goal here is less to pinpoint the geographical location of Nineb on a map. The goal is more about sharing Suru's experience of that tiny republic in terms of its contradictions and self-examination. Nineb is a country where people may be materially or financially poor, but in general, citizens of Nineb are rich in the spirit of hospitality.

Nineb is a land of hospitality. Its people are friendly and welcoming to everyone. They might not have much, but they will welcome you into their homes and share the little they have. The odds are you will not need an invitation before you join a party in Nineb. In most of the families Suru has known and visited, you do not need to announce your arrival before people welcome you to share their dinner with you.

The country is built on a tradition of community and interdependence among its people. The entire community would help raise your child with you. Growing up in Nineb, Suru was free to move from door to door or from household to household in his neighborhood. And Suru's parents did not need to worry about people doing any harm to their children. In general, everybody was nice and kind. Suru knew all the neighbors, and they all knew him. He often ate lunch or dinner at neighbors' tables with his parents' consent—and even without his parents' consent sometimes. Distrustful of their government, the communities would rely on local capacities to assist their people. In Nineb, your community is perceived as your first succor.

The political timeline of Nineb presents a creepy journey paced with contradictions. After its independence, the republic of Nineb was churned by political and economic turbulences. In the early postindependence period, its political leadership was unstable. Military coups succeeded one after another. The economy was fragile. The last successful coup saw the emergence of a repressive regime. That regime opened the door to a series of contradictions in Nineb. Citizens would be pulled between oppression and freedom. Citizens would hope for light in the valleys of shadow and desperation. They would strive for liberty under the structural chains of ideological captivity. They would aspire to freedom under a regime that repressed their basic human rights. They would hope for political inclusion under a regime that excluded them from political participation. They would ultimately successfully redeem themselves from the captivity of repression.

Upon usurping power, the authoritarian regime adopted a hardline Marxist ideology. The regime did not hide its intention to cut ties with the West. It blamed its political and economic problems on the West. Its adoption of Marxism put the regime at odds with the West. This came in opposition to the capitalist model of development that the country initially embraced. The two contradicting ideologies at stake hid two antagonists that represented the Western capitalism and the Soviet socialism.

The conflicting parties in Nineb held tenets of both ideologies. The leader of the Marxist camp was named Oga. Oga's military regime was a dedicated proponent of Marxism and Leninism. Oga and his camp confronted civilian leaders who were supporters of capitalism and multiparty democracy. This shed some light on the Marxist regime's intention to establish strong relationships with the Soviet alliance. The West was not happy with that move, but the authoritarian regime enforced a single-party rule and dismantled all opposition parties. They monopolized political power and concentrated it within military hands. In doing so, the military junta intended to exclude civilian leaders from political participation.

Under Oga's watch, the army ousted all civilian leaders from political office to showcase that the military was capable of running the show of political affairs. However, soldiers' motivations clashed with civilian leaders' perceptions of political office. Civilian leaders leaned on the tradition the army should stay on the sideline of political affairs. Moreover, the autocratic regime banned the freedom of expression. The national radio and television were abruptly transformed into seasoned tools for political and ideological propaganda. They served to indoctrinate and spread the culture of Marxism and Leninism in the republic of Nineb.

In the absence of a check-and-balance system, the authoritarian regime exploited the control of the media. They enforced a merciless and arbitrary censorship on all programs on radio and television. Citizens' right to religious freedom was also infringed on. Actions by the repressive regime contradicted the initial perception citizens had of their country as a garden of freedom, equality, collaboration, hospitality, and justice for all.

Religious leaders and the cognoscenti of Nineb dreamed of a republic that respected human rights and needs, a country that safeguarded the freedom of beliefs and the freedom of expression for all citizens, but Oga's oppressive regime offered a harsh alternative that violated basic human rights. Many civilian leaders and political opposition groups projected a nation where political pluralism was a right. They expected all citizens to enjoy the freedom of affiliation to political groups of their choice, but the regime presented them with only one option: a single-party rule for all.

Citizens saw Nineb as a paradise where basic human needs and rights were equally accessible to all—in a participatory democracy. All such goals collided with the program of the authoritarian government. The regime militarily imposed its single-party rule and its Marxist ideology upon all citizens without exception. At that defining moment of the radical change, Oga enforced a ban on political opposition. With the ban on political opposition and their freedom of expression taken away, citizens were not happy. Many citizens suffered from a high blood pressure, heart attack, and depression in that period. Iya's depression occurred in that period. Prominent leaders of opposition parties went in exile, but ordinary citizens who did not have the means to run away consented to facing the regime's contradictions eyeball to eyeball and day after day.

Growing up, Suru watched some disturbing dynamics of such contradictions speechlessly. Citizens were not allowed to express their opinions, yet they did publicly. They were not allowed to demonstrate, yet they did it. As a result, they often clashed with the authoritarian ruling party. And the price they paid for disobeying authoritarian rules was often very high. The repressive regime threatened and tried to silence its critics and voices of freedom by using kidnapping, arbitrary detentions, incarcerations within infernal conditions, and horrendous tortures. Some citizens even paid the price with their lives. As the killing of citizens became routine, so was the reign of a lack of transparency and accountability. Suru witnessed the rule of the jungle in the reign of a chaos in Nineb.

The Marxist ideology added insult to the damage Nineb sustained with successive military coups. The ideology further endangered any chances of economic success and political peace in the nation. The contradiction was clear. A big gap appeared between promises and reality. Using pompous slogans, the autocratic regime pretended its Marxist agenda would prevent and eradicate the scourges of inequality, injustice, and poverty from the republic. Yet the actions of the government highlighted practices of inequality, injustice, and the reign of mismanagement and poverty. The regime fell short of its promises. The rise of Marxism in Nineb led the regime to nationalize all economic sectors. The nationalization opened the way for negligence, nepotism, and corruption. Public office was perceived as a sinecure. Officers used their position to ransack or ransom citizens openly or under the table. Government officials spent money like water. This would ultimately dump Nineb in a dramatic sinkhole of economic disaster, which ended up breeding political confusion. However, citizens did not throw up their hands; they would not give up on hope at all. They were captives of repressive structures, but they awaited the opportunity of liberty. They were kept in the shadows of oppression, but they awaited the dawn of freedom.

The moment of their redemption would finally come. Nineb would transition toward democracy and peace against all expectations. It all happened in a national gathering. The national conference was a rendezvous for conflict resolution by means of debates on acute issues that entangled the republic of Nineb. That get-together provided a venue for making constructive decisions on the fate of Nineb. Ensnared in political, economic, and social contradictions, citizens of Nineb felt unhappy with the regime and its Marxist dogma. Citizens understood the authoritarian rule with its code of belief was a wrong orientation for Nineb. Such dogmatic orientation alienated the citizens. It enslaved their freedom and dreams for happiness. Unanimously, citizens stood against the oppressive system that kept them in captivity for years. They seized the constructive tools of self-examination and dialogue offered by a national conference to change their political strategies and move on to a better political pathway. They chose the path of democratic freedom and peace. The national conference served as a great opportunity for individual and collective self-examination in Nineb.

Suru would recall detailed contradictions that tangled Nineb and the transformative dynamics of the national conference. Economic breakdown was certainly a significant contributing factor to the contradictions in Nineb. Confronted with harsh economic issues, the ruling party began to reconsider its chosen ideology. Oga slowly began to refrain from Marxism. It felt as if he understood that system was to be blamed for contributing to chaos in Nineb. Oga was certainly aware of his bad reputation in the West because of his ideological stance. He started thinking of ways to address the contradictions in Nineb and repair his image. He moved to initiate negotiations with major Western financial institutions after the deficit of Nineb sent red signals.

Oga accepted the conditions for a structural adjustment program. Such conditions featured the privatization of public enterprises, the reduction of subsidies, the return of freedom of the press, and the removal of the ban on political opposition and the cuts in civil service. Suru was a teenager. He was extremely happy with the clauses about citizens regaining their rights to political opposition and freedom of expression, but some of the required conditions of the structural adjustment program were not good news for citizens. They were not happy with the articles of privatization of public enterprises, the reduction of subsidies, and the cuts in civil service.

Citizens highly anticipated those requirements would not appease the state of economic emergency that entangled the nation. Some of such requirements were not designed to fit living standards in Nineb. They were disconnected from the social reality and context of their country. The austerity measures adopted to respond to contradictions in Nineb were standard recipes for economic crisis. They failed to take into account contextual parameters and local capacities in Nineb. They represented some executive apparatus from the decision-making process of a technocratic system of thinking. Such conditions were crafted by technocrats at the headquarters of financial institutions that did not understand the social reality of Nineb.

Distinguished technocrats from financial institutions quickly made decisions without fully anticipating the social repercussions or spending enough time on thinking of the meaning and costs of such measures for individuals' daily existence within Nineb. The measures ended up doing more harm than good to the citizens of Nineb. The gap between the social costs and the benefits of the structural adjustment program was harmful for ordinary citizens. In the midst of a sharp social and economic crisis, the well-meaning financial institutions put more burdens on citizens with conditions that increased social tensions and misery. Many workers ended up without an income or a job due to compression and cuts in wages; they would disempower all social services.

Scores of public workers went several months without getting their salaries from the state. The state failed to provide health care to its citizens. The credibility of the authoritarian regime plummeted. Suru was an eyewitness to the entire situation. Oga was cursed, demonized, and rejected along with his ruling party.

Across Nineb, hungry and angry families' best wishes for the regime suggested its demise. Citizens could not wait to hear the knell of the regime sound; it was at the top of most citizens' wish lists.

Nearly every citizen wanted Oga's regime to sing its Nunc Dimittis. Suru prayed for the unwanted regime to breathe its last breath.

Iya and Baba struggled to provide their family with basic needs. Suru still remembers those bitter moments of unpaid salaries and high emotions. The social mood was distressing. Scores of social groups took the issue to the street by organizing strikes to push out Oga, but he would not give up. Oga braved the chaotic situation by giving the impression he still had the upper hand with hidden and meager support. Could such a skimpy and cowardly succor come from business associations in those circumstances? Certainly no!

Unable to allocate credits to businesses due to sweeping decreases in the revenues of the national treasury, Oga fell from grace. His regime was in the bad graces of businesses. The ruling party would gradually lose the backing of business associations. Exasperated with the authoritarian regime, they cut ties with Oga and endorsed democratic changes. As a result, they took actions to sponsor strikes across Nineb in an attempt to oust autocracy and make a clean space for democracy.

At worst, the conditions imposed by Western financial institutions as requirements for the structural adjustment program did not help Nineb by any means. As the government launched the privatization of public enterprises, the winds of privatization decimated the revenues of the national treasury. That winds also blew away many jobs. It left many families without jobs and income. Hundreds of public workers lost their jobs in that period.

Scores of jobless fathers and mothers would be crying and complaining on the streets. Again and again, citizens used public sit-ins and demonstrations to block traffic and disrupt social movements to challenge the government on their dire conditions and their children's futures. The scenes started in the main cities, but they would spark interest across the country in no time.

The requirements of the structural-adjustment program reinforced the inability of the state to provide education and other social services. Oga's regime cut down education budgets to meet the conditions required by the structural adjustment program. He cut down salaries, health care, and housing allowances. University students were denied academic scholarships and the assurance of state employment after graduation. Teachers' incomes remained unpaid. Workers' wages were cut down, and citizens were denied access to health care. In reaction to these somber measures by the government, students and teachers across the nation took the streets in strikes. Students fought for their rights to scholarships, and teachers fought for their salaries. They seized the opportunity to call for profound economic and political reforms. Student unions used their intellectual skills to release a clever wish list of requests. They urged the government to reject all antisocial conditions dictated by the structural adjustment program. They requested an increase in education funds, the freedom of expression, and the freedom to strike. They also demanded the termination of authoritarian governing principles for a new constitution that would pave the way for democracy. Oga's authoritarian regime rejected all such demands.

That unflinching rejection ignited conflict escalation. Prominent non-state actors publicly came out to bitterly express their dissatisfaction with the government. They assigned themselves the difficult task of putting an end to political exclusion and violations of human rights in Nineb.

A popular union of public workers stood up again the regime and decided to join the movement for change at the top of the state. They were frustrated that the government excluded them from its negotiations with financial institutions. They were dissatisfied with the outcomes of those negotiations. They were not happy with antisocial requirements. The measures resulted in terrible financial damages to public workers and ordinary citizens, including Iya and Baba.

Groundbreaking initiatives from civil society emerged in the fight for public workers' rights. One teachers' union movement began to coordinate strikes by students and workers against the authoritarian regime. The telecommunication union joined the movement for change. *Tout le monde* in Nineb observed a striking resurgence in demonstrations. Street protests gained momentum. Thousands of students and workers were marching on the streets every day. Nineb became impossible to govern.

Suru and his fellow students joined forces to partake in demonstrations that supported the movement for change. Many students saw a well-timed opportunity to take a break from hostile school environments. For many students in Nineb, being at school or in the classroom was like being in hell. Students hated their teachers' authoritarian approaches to teaching and their practice of corporal punishment.

Under the authoritarian regime, a new school system was designed to serve the scary agenda of the regime. The new school system was called Uzu School. Uzu School would promote the Marxist ideology and advocate for the hegemony of the single ruling party. Uzu School wielded overpowering authority over all students and teachers. Teachers and students had no choice but to follow the oppressive rules dictated by a controlling system. Uzu School treated teachers and students as objects.

Suru was a student in that system. The national curriculum was crafted to shape students' minds to fit Marxist standards and ultimately serve the interests of Oga's regime. The teacher was hired to teach in accordance with Marxist guidelines. Such guidelines tightly controlled and predicted teaching outcomes. Teachers had no scope to infuse their personal views. They would rather reflect the view of the system and echo its voice. Suru's teachers had no academic freedom. The system would expel teachers who showed resistance. Within Uzu School, the teacher's subjectivity ran the risk of a destructive identity crisis.

Prior to the national conference in Nineb, Uzu School trained students to perceive leaders as strong authorities. You were required to fully obey any order that came from them. You were brainwashed to believe authorities were always right. You were trained to be a toady or bribe authorities to gain favors. Students were coached to venerate their teachers in some cases to get what they wanted.

At Uzu School, students were required to learn and sing songs that praised all actions of the authoritarian regime and its autocratic leader. Teachers were hired, trained, and directed to help implement the government programs in the school system. The mood at school was often tense for students. Many did not feel relaxed at school. They were often afraid of their teachers.

Teachers would quickly punish and spank students for disobeying their authority or not following authoritarian rules. Corporal punishment was fully integrated and enforced in the school system. Teachers were using corporal punishment as a weapon to enforce their authority over students. Students did not trust their teachers, and a number of them did not like their teachers.

Suru was spanked by teachers on the buttocks, the palms of his hands, or the back. Such mistreatments traumatized Suru time and again. Some teachers believed they had the authority to spank him whenever Suru was late, when he failed to give the right answer, or when his behavior was not good. The teachers were not spanking him for the sake of doing so. They believed spanking Suru would help him improve his behavior, and they would let Suru know their intention as they spanked him.

In some cases, spanking deterred Suru from bad behaviors, but did it help him mentally and emotionally? Suru still has to respond to that question. The system did not protect children in their right to grow up and learn. Kids were not allowed to make mistakes or be children. It did not seem like child abuse was a crime. The concept was not even commonly used in Nineb. It was not part of most people's vocabulary. It was unwanted or unknown. The practice was common and despicable in the school system and in many households.

Some of Suru's friends complained to their parents about how their teachers spanked them bitterly at school. The parents did not report the teachers or file complaints against them. Most parents went to school to congratulate the teachers for doing a good job of spanking their stubborn children. Some parents would thank the teachers for helping them educate and raise difficult children. Other parents added spanking at home when their children complained about the treatments of their teachers.

Suru's parents were not very different from the other parents. The few times Suru told his mother that he got spanked by his teachers, Iya did not express any serious concern or worry about it. She did not take any actions against those teachers. She trusted Suru's teachers to be reasonable educators who certainly had good reasons to punish him. At times, Iya even urged her son to respect and obey his teachers. Suru's mother was much less interested in understanding the issues. She was focused on making sure her son followed directions to do well at school.

Suru could not blame Iya. She was also a victim of the structure. Across Nineb, traditions and rules said that spanking was good for educating a child. Actually, traditions said that a good spanking may save a child's life if worse comes to worst. Suru thought he deserved to be spanked for bad behavior, but had no clue of his rights as a child. They were all products of their social environments.

Structures can be compelling to humankind. How could Suru know they were all trapped within a system? At times, Iya's family seemed cognizant of the structure they were all caught in. In those times, Iya's home seemed to be on alert. Intense prayers poured in daily. Suru's parents and their children were praying a lot for Nineb. They prayed and hoped for a better future for the country. They yearned for the arrival of a system that would bring back freedom. Coercive systems can dictate our behaviors without our full consent. They can paralyze our judgment and destroy our personalities. Systems have the potential to jeopardize our freedom. We need some of them to regulate social interactions since systems can also be fairly constructive. In the period of Uzu School, spanking was accepted and embraced as a tool for education at home and at school. The kids were powerless victims of a repressive culture. Without knowing that child abuse was a crime, abusers and their victims were all guilty of ignorance. Suru was not happy in that school environment which was a fallout of Oga's regime.

Carried by the strong wind blowing for structural changes in Nineb, waves of protests churned the country and took violent turns in some cities. Students threw stones at government officials, and they damaged public infrastructures and goods. Tensions between the ruling party and the demonstrators reached their highest point. The schools in Nineb were closed for several months. Students, teachers, and workers organized marches on strategic streets in the key cities. The police and the army used tear gas to disband them. The tear gas did not intimidate or deter the crowds.

Oga's government made massive arrests. The regime also tried to strengthen decrees that banned public meetings and strikes, but none of the actions stopped the protestors from pursuing their ultimate goals. The masses were unwavering in confronting the ruling party. They wanted to get back their civil and political rights.

Overwhelmed by the intensity and scope of the demonstrations, Oga's government took harsher repressive measures against the strikers. The regime ordered the army to stop the movements by any means necessary. Scores of protesters faced bloody results. In attempts to disperse the crowds, the army shot and killed demonstrators. In those circumstances, some strikers lost their lives. Others were wounded. The strikes continued and mutated into a political cataclysm.

A large number of protestors defied the shootings with sustained street parades and sit-ins. They chanted and called on Oga to step down. Such social mobilizations set a general tone of turmoil in the nation. Oga's regime slowly began to understand the message, but the regime did not back down quickly. The army continued to shoot citizens. Innocent citizens were killed in the streets as they fought for their rights to civil and political liberty. The shootings did not deter the manifestations.

The demonstrators opted to listen to their inner voices of freedom and bravery. They marched for freedom and exhibited their willpower to put an end to the yoke of the regime and snatch back their rights. Marchers also displayed their readiness for the ultimate sacrifice. They were set to give up their lives, which worked wonders for Nineb. Activists were aware that the sacrifice of their lives would echo their patriotism. They saw this as a noble requirement for altering the cruel structures that had ensnared Nineb for so long.

In response to the citizens' resolve to perish for structural changes in Nineb, the army began to slow down. Besides, the soldiers were irked by increasing cuts in military spending since the cuts affected their wages. The discontent within the military hurt the ruling party and benefited the uproar. Some soldiers started siding with the protesters. They started guarding the marchers instead of killing them.

The demonstrators perceived this as some sort of tacit endorsement from the armed forces. This boosted the movement for change in Nineb. The situation got out of hand. The regime lost control. They did not anticipate such developments. Oga came to his senses and decided to do a self-examination and face up to his citizens.

When a leader or a government refuses to serve or listen to its people, it no longer represents them. The people will ultimately stand against any government that does not stand for them. The people will take to the streets and call for change. People can change any government that does not represent them. When citizens demand change—if they really want transformations in policies or governance or government—they become unstoppable. They take all good actions to bring about change.

Empowered and coordinated by a spirited civil society, citizens can strategically and successfully use nonviolent demonstrations, including economic boycotts, to paralyze a nation and bring about structural and systemic changes. Citizens who deeply wish for structural changes cannot be deterred by arrests, detentions, or death. If leaders were to kill all their citizens, who would they govern? In the case of Nineb, Oga would eventually open his eyes to the citizens' misery. He would unclog his ears to listen to his people. He would realize the size of the issues. He would humbly talk and negotiate with the citizens over the fate of Nineb. He would show remorse, apologize to the nation, and ask citizens to forgive his mistakes. He would voice his readiness to change and do wonders for Nineb. At the time, he did not promise a regime change, but his subsequent actions would lead to it.

To please the protestors, Oga would agree to remove the ban on the freedom of press as a condition for stability. As soon as this happened, it was as if Oga opened a Pandora's box. In no time, Nineb recorded a resurgence of newspapers. The newly liberated media churned Nineb and stirred turmoil. The press daily criticized the ruling party and empowered the protesters. The press thoroughly clarified all issues and parties involved in the contradictions in Nineb. Newspapers raised citizens' awareness about the issues both nationally and globally. The independent press was hasty to unveil and decry corruptions condoned or hidden by state officials. Most newscasters became vocal about political transgressions in violating human rights. Suru enjoyed reading the newspapers during that period. The involvement of the press fueled citizens' aversion toward single-party rule; they would join forces for political change in Nineb.

Oga had no choice but to lift the ban on political opposition to meet citizens' demands. That move turned the tables for all parties. Renowned opposition leaders seized that opportunity to resurface. They came out to reheat opposition parties to enable the agents of change and put pressures on the single-party rule. Freshly molded opposition parties granted citizens encouraging political alternatives to the ruling party.

Leaders of the newly formed opposition parties eventually joined forces and called for widespread strikes across the entire republic. Their call was heeded instantaneously. The demonstrations were irresistible. Citizens marched and chanted in every corner of Nineb. Citizens took pride in demonstrating on the streets instead of being in class or the workplace; most students, teachers, and workers spent their days on the streets instead of their homes.

The streets became homes for many people during that period. They spent their days demonizing the ruling party and calling for a new political era. In the same breath, new opposition parties called for free democratic elections to unseat the authoritarian ruling party.

Suru witnessed an extremely unstable republic of Nineb in those hard months. The scope and level of the unrest became daunting for ordinary life. The unrest paralyzed any social life in the entire country.

Nineb was isolated and cut from the international community. A number of businesses shut down. Citizens scarcely had basic goods. Existence across Nineb became unbearable. How could one except to sustain life in a chaos for so long without getting hurt?

Nineb grew into an ungovernable hell. Could anyone govern anarchy successfully? How long can you govern chaos without getting hurt? At the climax of the contradictions, the autocratic regime felt a deadlock, a fallout which sent a clear signal of its breakdown. Citizens understood that they needed to fold up their sleeves, flex their muscles, and work together to get rid of that deadlock so that Nineb could have access to political and economic health and social happiness. In that moment of collaborative efforts, the idea of a national conference slowly emerged as a turning point to rescue the republic of Nineb.

Oga would continue testing the waters. He sought advice from the scholars of Nineb. He called in academics to enlighten him on issues and their potential solutions. Those intellectuals would consult with leaders of political parties and trade unions for negotiation. Political leaders would touch base with their respective constituencies to factor the grass roots in the equation of consultations.

The noble cognoscenti wanted to ensure their recommendations resounded the alarms and expectations of the masses. In due course, they would instruct Oga to make sweeping structural changes to accommodate citizens' needs and requests. At the same time, the idea of a national conference started bubbling in Oga's mind and stirring his heart. In good time, he would discuss his thought with members his cabinet in a meeting. In that venue, he told the high-powered members of the ruling party to do a self-examination over their political attainments and governance in Nineb.

Behind closed doors, partakers in the meeting lent themselves to a process of self-examination. By the end of their meeting, the self-examination process resulted in tangible outcomes. Participants decided to get rid of the Marxist ideology. The breakaway mood would spill over and contaminate most members of the ruling party. More importantly, they decided swiftly to call forth a national conference with the intention of bringing democracy back in Nineb.

Following that critical meeting, Oga made the good news public. He clearly unveiled to the general public his intention to convene a nationwide conference that would rely on local capacities in the republic of Nineb for problem-solving. The nation welcomed the news with happiness. At the sound of the news, citizens happily exploded with joy in all corners of Nineb.

Suru remembers the excitement on the streets. Citizens in his neighborhood were all jubilant, but the protesters remained vigilant. They could not believe it, and they no longer wanted to be fooled or bewitched. They were fully aware of the tendency the ruling party had to manipulate citizens for its own gains. Opposition leaders also cautioned all agents of freedom and change to remain on alert. They warned all citizens to wait and see. They cautioned everyone to watch the regime translate its words into actions before believing what was said. It was hard to believe, but Oga would not disappoint on his promise of holding a national conference.

In good time, the proceedings of the conference opened in a fabulous hotel. That hotel was located on a breezy beach in the capital. The location was selected to help participants relax in times of stress. That setting would appease participants in moments of tension or heated debates.

For days, hundreds of men and women from all social ranks and political groups negotiated over the issues facing Nineb. There were national and international actors; there were state actors and non-state actors. National actors at the conference included reps of the ruling party and the military hierarchy. Other national actors included leaders of opposition parties and former heads of state. There were also delegates from local NGOs, religious leaders, leaders of trade unions, prominent businessmen, civil servants, academics, student organizations, and farmers. International actors included NGOs and a remarkable cohort of foreign diplomats.

Suru delightedly listened to everything on the radio and happily watched some of the scenes on national television. The mood was incredible.

In the joint assembly, Oga would briefly emerge for his opening statement. He urged the entire gathering to focus on addressing the structural and systemic issues facing Nineb. The audience responded to Oga's exhortation with sustained ovations inside the conference hall and beyond.

Such scenes of cheering were visible in Suru's neighborhood. Suru could not resist applauding for Oga's courage in that defining moment. Crowds in the conference hall hailed Oga with their hands and their voices. Loud voices in the audience praised him for initiating the gathering. Visibly empowered by citizens' ovations, Oga went on to make a few procedural suggestions.

Following Oga's persuasive opening statement, the delegates engaged in negotiations under the watch of a beloved religious leader named Dotu. The delegates in unison selected Dotu to facilitate their negotiations due to his integrity and strength of character. Dotu carefully approached his role of facilitator as a servant. He did not exert any coercion in the process. He was a humble spiritual leader. Dotu would constantly ask citizens to pray intensively for a successful conference. He avoided putting pressure on participants in the process of decision-making. He used charismatic tactics of negotiation, facilitation, and meditation. Under his humble and well-favored leadership, the conference would agree on a clear agenda with sound ground rules. They carefully unveiled details of the schedule of meetings.

Dotu encouraged all participants to share information. He empowered delegates to exercise their right of free speech. Again and again, Dotu would remind them to listen to one another with mutual respect. Dotu tactfully enforced the ground rules. The distribution of tasks at the gathering was democratic. The meeting set up a number of committees to thoroughly examine all the issues.

The delegates' objective was to conduct a diagnosis of the contradictions in order to design a decent treatment strategy for Nineb. Delegates were eager to shed light on the past and do wonders for Nineb. The participants broke down into small groups with clearly assigned responsibilities. The get-togethers dynamically fluctuated between long hearings in the assembly of all delegates and short consultations in small groups.

The long sessions brought together all the small groups to adjust their undertakings for the common goals of the conference. Participants slowly tackled fundamental economic, ideological, and political issues. They labeled the Marxist ideology as a devilish or ruinous political disorientation that should be a no-no for Nineb. They argued that the ideology bewildered the single party and brought all sorts of economic, political, and social outrage upon the republic of Nineb. Participants denounced the corruption and nepotism in the hierarchy of the state. They decried the ample violations of human rights by the ruling party in Nineb.

The hearings got intense and emotional when some delegates expressed their frustrations with gruesome kidnappings, arbitrary detentions, torture, and killings under Oga's watch. A number of delegates questioned Oga's ability to be a leader. Suru cried as he listened to some of the stories on the radio. A number of delegates seized that moment to call out for justice. As partakers in the meeting took turns bringing up issues at the table of negotiations, discussions over the issues turned cogent and meaningful.

Suru enjoyed every aspect of the debates. The structure and content of the discussions lucidly blended consistency and substance. Suru was ecstatic as he listened to the delegates on the radio and watched the discussions on television. The coherence of the debates galvanized Suru. The conference was a like a showdown of talks, but it showed how negotiation or dialogue could uniquely honor words and grant them meaning. At first sight, words are meaningful and persuasive. They can convince their users to shape and reshape structures and systems. Thus, we ought to be mindful to never lose sight of their meaning. Human beings should be mindful to make sense while negotiating. Suru watched the national conference illustrate how words can serve as resourceful munitions for peacemaking.

The conference slowly and consistently unfolded day after day with its ups and downs. Participants had high hopes that the gatherings would end up doing wonders for Nineb, but some reps were anxious. Their anxiety was justified by negative feelings in the light of the deceiving tactics the authoritarian regime was notorious for using. The ruling party was known for its false and empty promises.

Government officials sounded loud noises to captivate citizens' attention by promising them an arm and a leg, to move heaven and earth, or other big promises. Citizens would find out the noises came from empty vessels. With that in mind, participants at the national conference called into question the honesty of the single party. They also questioned the legality of the conference and all decisions it would bear. They wondered what would happen if the ruling party were to reject all decisions reached at the conference on the basis that they had no legitimacy. Participants forecasted the worst and proactively tooled the conference to prevent it or counter it.

The conference reached a breakaway moment when the participants unanimously decided all decisions adopted in the gatherings would be binding. That action was taken out of the fear that the ruling party might refuse to implement all would-be decisions of the national conference. That breakaway development electrified the mood of the conference. Participants felt reassured and happy. It was a turning point with boiling tensions.

At first sight, the ruling party did not welcome the move, but confronted with omnidirectional pressures from all citizens and the international community, the regime eventually endorsed the citizens' request and recognized the legality of the conference and its acts. That was a major step forward in achieving the reign of democratic freedom in the republic of Nineb.

Suru witnessed that unique moment with satisfaction. He could feel democratic freedom was on its way. You could feel structural changes were in the air for Nineb to breathe. From that moment on, the country marched boldly toward democracy.

Happy with the official recognition of the statute of the conference as legal and binding, the participants carefully crafted a series of recommendations. They would diligently vote on such recommendations and ultimately pass the final decisions of the conference under citizens' watch. It was a day of joy and celebration in Nineb. The national conference terminated the controversial Marxist Constitution of Nineb. It disbanded a revolutionary legislative branch. It set up a provisional high counsel of the republic. That counsel was tasked with drafting a new constitution and serving as the provisional legislature until the democratic elections of a new legislature.

The gatherings also granted political immunity to Oga in

recognition of his courageous act of patriotism in calling forth the national conference. The conference strategically preserved Oga as the head of state, but it dissolved the rest of the government. Oga was trimmed of his executive power. The conference handed all executive power to a freshly nominated acting prime minister named Eki. Participants elected Eki to wield executive power for a transition of one year. To further enact a system of balance of power, the conference took a ruling to reinstate the independence of judicial power for equal justice for all citizens. In due course, the conference set a clear schedule for presidential and legislative elections.

All such decisions were the outcomes of dedicated patriotism from highly motivated citizens. Motivated by the common good of Nineb, they braved differences and mixed feelings to consult and collaborate successfully for the advent of democratic freedom in a land of oppressive authority. The moment Oga solemnly welcomed the decisions of the conference, the entire country radiated with positive energy. Suru felt peace and happiness within his heart and mind, and beyond, around him. The vox populi had the upper hand.

At the conclusion of the conference, Oga accepted and endorsed all decisions reached at the conference. In a final speech, he promised to respect all such decisions. Suru still remembers exactly where he was when it all happened. Suru was thrilled to watch such incredible events on television. The city hosting Suru was also exultant. The sky certainly did not fall upon them, but it was a great day of joy for all citizens of Nineb. Out of the darkness of repression, the country widely opened its doors to embrace and experience democratic freedom. That deserved celebrations. All citizens of Nineb welcomed democracy with open arms.

Following the conference, Suru witnessed a smooth implementation of its decisions. The first act of recovery of citizens' lost civil and political rights would quickly follow. Citizens were able to freely express their vote in a national referendum to approve a new constitution for the republic of Nineb. They did not take it for granted. For the first time in his life, Suru was able and happy to cast a vote in national elections. The new constitution won massive support from citizens, and it became the law of the land.

The freshly adopted constitution triggered the emergence of a number of new political parties. All emerged political parties competed for seats in a newly elected parliament. In good time, they also participated in the presidential elections. That period of transition recorded a resurgence in independent media and civil society to allow all citizens of Nineb to enjoy their freedom of expression. Municipal elections and a constitutional court would follow. Other major structural reforms would take place, including reform of the school system. As a student, Suru was happy to see positive changes to the school system in the era of democratic freedom.

School became a place for education and not indoctrination. It became a setting where students learned to be in relation with their natural and social environments. They learned to collaborate in constructive ways for the welfare of society and humankind. The school environment was designed to educate and lead students in the socialization process. By providing students with important life skills, such as listening and respect for the dignity of other people, new school programs were openly aimed at human education and socialization. They were no longer aimed at brainwashing students with Marxist and authoritarian principles. Instead, students learned how to get along in spite of ontological and social differences. Most schools in Nineb were made up of diverse ethnic groups. In that context, students worked to develop skills for managing ethnic and social differences. The new system understood the challenges of shaping generations that perceive leadership not as authority but as an opportunity to serve through collaboration with everyone.

The positive outcomes of such changes in the school curriculum did not take long to see. Students started working together within political organizations to demonstrate their ability to get along. They began to participate in the democratic process of their country through student unions and other political associations. As a political system in which citizens ultimately hold the ruling power, democracy is a meaningful expression of the art of getting along. In the period after the national conference in Nineb, students understood just that. They saw citizenship as a common denominator of people partaking in the management of public affairs and finding a way to get along in the process.

The schools became reliable settings for nurturing democratic behaviors. They educated students by highlighting academic learning and exposing them to valuable social skills. In such circumstances, students like Suru were no longer nervous at the thought of engaging their teachers. Suru became open-minded and open-mouthed in the classroom and beyond. He was not afraid of his teachers anymore. He no longer saw them as authorities but as public servants. He understood they were at the service of his learning process. He trusted them to lead him through his learning process. Suru was eager to learn from his teachers. He was happy to be a student. Suru was free. The light of democratic freedom shined upon him. It shined upon the land of darkness where he once dwelt. It felt so different from the authoritarian regime! It was hard for Suru to even endorse any thought of comparing the two systems.

The conference transformed Nineb into a peaceful heaven. Democratic traditions became rooted in the political culture of Nineb. The country has kept on honoring its tradition of hosting free democratic elections every five years. Through the national conference, the small republic of Nineb became a modest model of democracy. The country remains poor per global standards and indicators, but its political stability allows its citizens some peace of heart and mind.

The experience made citizens grasp the sense and value of democratic freedom. For the time being, citizens enjoy freedom and political participation. Public workers are timely remunerated for their labor. Business seems to be booming in Nineb with imports and exports. Farming and entrepreneurship flourish as well. Students acquire a valuable and dignifying education. Suru remains a happy product of Nineb's remodeled education system. Suru feels indebted to that education system for the favor received in his social skills. He has faith in the future of Nineb. He dreams of a happy economic future for that nation. Nineb is a vibrant nation, full of talent and human potential. The national conference demonstrated how Nineb has yet to be fully developed.

The national conference was an earnest opportunity for self-examination. It allowed leaders of Nineb to achieve self-examination. In the end, they bravely rejected social and political misconduct and chose to head in a direction that made citizens happy and their country stable. Self-examination usually results in a good outcome for people and for social environments. That was the case for Oga and its people.

CHAPTER 14

Wandering between Greed and Generosity

From reading previous chapters, you would think that Suru's experience with collaboration had pulled him out of resistance and competition. Thinking so would be relevant. Suru would fully agree with you on that account. By all odds, Suru slipped out of some adversarial traps. It was a powerful and transformative learning opportunity for him. However, such an experience was only a small step on his path to transformation and peace. Suru quickly realized that he was still at the beginning of a long journey. His road to transformation was long. There were still many steps ahead. Suru did not take long to figure out that his heart and mind were still ensnared in other existential contradictions. In the next steps of his journey, Suru would face the struggle between greed and generosity. It was not easy.

After his years of study at D Seminary of Rako, Suru moved on to the next level of training toward priesthood. He was sent to P Seminary of Rete for a year of intense spiritual experience. Rete is a small city in Nineb. Its remote location makes it fit for the goal of nurturing seminarians with intense spiritual training. Such spiritual experiences would allow Suru to get some good, smooth, and hands-on transition toward the last straightaway on the track of immediate or straight-out preparation for priesthood.

Due to the spiritual nature and orientation of P Seminary, its students' daily activities revolved predominantly around meditation, prayer, community building, and selected courses on spirituality, methodology, ethics, Bible, catechism, and French. The curriculum was designed to emphasize spiritual discernment. The daily schedule was arranged in ways that assigned enough time for silent prayer and spiritual examination of conscience. Suru saw such moments of prayer as great opportunities for self-examination. He would seize them to examine himself and contemplate existential struggles that often entangled his mind and heart. One memorable struggle was between greed and generosity. Greed and generosity were often at odds in Suru's existence. Suru was often wandering between greed and generosity and tossed between both.

Suru remains mindful of one scene he is not proud of. That scene occurred in the refectory of the P Seminary. It was time for lunch on a sunny day. The seminarians stood into groups of eight around rectangular tables. One of them led a short prayer for blessing the meal they were about to enjoy.

They sat down for lunch. As usual, the meal was served in limited amounts from hand to mouth. In needy countries, food scarcity can become daunting. The amount of food served was for all tablemates to share equally. It was served in a common pot for everyone at the table. The pot would go around the table, and everyone took turns getting their portions of food.

As the pot went around, everybody helped themselves by putting just what they needed on their plates. On that day, Suru was starving. When the pot of beef stew reached Suru, he took time to serve his plate, but he took a little bit more food than he needed. As a result, there was not enough beef stew for the last two tablemates after Suru. Their names were Umu and Ahi. Umu and Ahi were not happy with that behavior—not by a long sight. How could they be? Suru only needed to fleetingly look at their straight faces to understand their negative feelings.

Umu and Ahi seemed to be blaming Suru for not having enough for their lunch. Suru could see they were frustrated with him for depriving them. They were frustrated with his selfish behavior. Other tablemates quickly noticed the dynamic of frustration. Nearly everybody at the table became silent. Some tablemates could no longer stand Suru's look. They could not cope with his greed. For a while, the mood was difficult for Suru and them to bear. Even so, it did not occur to Suru to cut down the ration on his plate to share with tablemates who did not get enough. Instead, Suru went around the lunchroom desperately to check if there was any table with leftovers he could gratefully retrieve for his deprived tablemates. Thankfully, his search was successful. Suru was able to get some leftovers from another table.

Upon getting the leftovers on their plates, Umu and Ahi smiled. In no time, their faces became nearly glittery. To some degree, the ambience around the table felt calmer at that moment. Some tablemates even used the opportunity to joke and laugh at what they called Suru's voracious assets.

Suru joked that they should be aware that he had a lot of hungry cells to feed in his small body.

They all laughed about it.

Suru thought, *If there were no leftovers available from that generous table, Umu and Ahi would suffer deprivation and frustration because of my senseless act of gluttony.* For a second, Suru imagined how people around the world could easily get deprived and frustrated due to other people's greed. Greed did not allow Suru to think of his tablemates when he took his portion. He just thought the beef was cut into too small pieces, and he needed to fish out enough of it to satisfy his appetite. Suru still feels embarrassed and ashamed of that behavior when he thinks of it. He took as much as he wanted without thinking of others.

Suru was aware that there were eight students around that table, but he ignored his conscience—and he felt badly later on. Suru had problems digesting the food. He was not able to take a good nap that afternoon. He was not able to sleep at all. His stomach bothered him all through his nap time. It was too full and took Suru to the lavatory again and again. He was very uncomfortable with abdominal cramps.

It started with minor burps and hiccups immediately after lunch. Suru did not care much about them and went to bed anyway for the regular nap period. Before he knew it, the issue was serious, escalating into stomachaches and vomiting. Suru's stomach ended up forcing out some of what he ate to make some space of its own. What he put in his stomach exceeded its natural capacity. He put too much in it, and it could not handle it. Suru's greed ended up in waste.

Suru would learn time after time that greed often ends up in waste. The greedy often end up wasting what they have been tightly holding onto. Suru's conscience would also bother him throughout his nap time. It relentlessly asked him why he had such a greedy attitude and behavior vis-à-vis Umu and Ahi.

Suru felt guilty and restless for a long time about his greedy behavior. That evening, his guilt would inspire his attitude and behavior at dinner. Instead of rushing to be among the first to serve his dinner, Suru kindly allowed everybody else to go before him. His tablemates were not displeased with that manner. His appetite was unparalleled. Suru was blessed with a metabolism that made him eat a lot. The food he ate never showed up on his body in the form of any weight gain. His tablemates were satisfied with his decision to go last.

After everybody helped themselves, Suru put a small portion of food on his plate and enjoyed it. Unexpectedly, there was still enough food for anyone interested in a second round. As he ate his food and chatted with his tablemates, Suru noticed smiles on all faces. They seemed relaxed and happy. The mood was better than it was at lunch. Suru could tell his tablemates felt good, and he felt good as well.

Before going to bed, Suru spent his time of self-examination contemplating his behaviors at lunch and dinner. There were two behaviors with different outcomes for him and those around him. At lunch, he was greedy. As a result, he was unhappy and made others unhappy. At dinner, he was generous. As a result, he was happy and made others happy. Suru decided to keep on being the last person to get food at the dining table. He also resolved to always be mindful of others and to be generous to all.

Following his self-examination, Suru had a very good night's sleep. His sleep was so deep that it even took him into the kingdom of Morpheus, the good god of dreams. That night, Suru had an awesome dream, the best dream he could wish for after such a tormenting day. Suru found himself in the paradise of generosity. In that place, nature was so generous toward everyone. Milk and honey were running for all. The sun shined on everyone, and the rain fell down for all. Light was available to all, and no one needed to pay for it. Water was free for all, and nobody had to pay for it.

The land belonged to all, and there was no private property. It was all for the public good. All the inhabitants were delighted to share their living space and time. Everyone owned something and was glad to share it with others. It was a world of sharing. Everybody was happily sharing what they had. They shared their possessions and their talents. They gave without expecting anything in return. They lent money without asking for interest. They were not interested in profit. It felt exceptionally good in that world of Suru's dream. Everybody was happy. Suru was happy.

Quite impressed with what he saw, Suru decided to settle down in that world of his dream. Suru was still in an ecstasy of delight when he felt the need to use the restroom. It was the signal that brought him back the real world. Suru checked the alarm clock by his bed. It was five o'clock, almost time to get up. He went to use the restroom and went back to his bed. Suru was not able to go back to sleep, and he thought about his wonderful dream. He imagined a happy world where the rich shared their riches with the poor without expecting anything in return.

Suru began to long for a world where people lend without expecting interest in return. He wondered what it would take to make such a dream become reality. He became mindful of Iya's lessons about dreaming. Suru thought he could try to make that dream real by allowing his thoughts and actions to reflect it in his daily life.

Suru was a poor seminarian. He thought he did not necessarily have to give away his financial or material assets. Sharing what we have could certainly take the form of making a generous financial or material gift to those who are in need if we have the means, but it could also imply giving our time by volunteering, giving our energy to serving others in need, or giving a smile when it is needed. It could also mean giving credit to people when they deserve it and giving thanks.

Suru thought he could start learning to give and share the little he had to make the world a happier place. If he could do it, others would be able to do it too—and society would be able to do it somehow. Suru imagined society would be a peaceful place if we were able to give and share what we had. We would transform the world into a happy heaven if we gave to one another without expecting anything in return. The ability to share makes the giver and the receiver happy.

Soon after that thought, it was time for the seminarians to wake up for their daily activities. Suru was refreshed and ready for the new day. From that time on, he started implementing his decision to lean on generosity toward others in the dining hall and beyond. And it felt good. He felt good, and his social environment also felt good. Out of that experience, Suru learned about the persistent dynamics of greed and generosity within the self and within society. He would grasp the sense of existential contradictions at the heart of greed and generosity.

His personal adventures helped Suru understand and conceptualize the dynamics of greed and generosity and their implications on human society and happiness. Suru learned that greed makes us miserable inside and out. Greed creates a malaise within the internal environment of the greedy, inside the gluttonous body, as well as within its external environment, outside the greedy body.

We should always be on guard against greed. For greed is deceitful in how it presents itself to all greedy people. It is tempting and flattering, but it actually destroys our happiness. Greed comes to us with enticing feelings; it shows up disguised as a good friend, but it is one of the nastiest enemies of our peace of mind and heart. At first sight, it seems to console our greedy senses. However, it creates troubles inside our hearts and minds. It also creates troubles within the hearts and minds in the social environment of the greedy.

We can easily get caught up in greed. It can be hard to resist greed at times, but our hearts cannot rest until they give up on greed. At its worst, greed has the potential to suffocate its victim. Keeping too much or more than enough stresses your heart and mind. Greed can make us blow up physically and mentally. When you eat more than you should, you either vomit, increase your waistline, or get sick. When you try to keep everything in your mind, you may crash or lose your mind. It is sane to forget; it is also sane to forgive instead of keeping all inside your mind.

Greed creates deprivation and conflict in your social environment. By being greedy, you deprive others from getting what they need. As a result, they are frustrated. They may try to fight back to get what they rightfully need or deserve. Such interactions may occur in situations of greedy individuals, groups, or organizations. They also occur in cases of nation-states that are too greedy in the international system. An honest look of the history of human society reveals that greed triggers conflicts among individuals, groups, organizations, and nations. We need to share with others for our peace of mind and heart. We need to share for global peace. What a precious lesson Suru learned!

Greed usually ends up in waste. Suru's vomiting of the extra food he consumed was a meaningful illustration of this. Another eloquent illustration comes from Suru's experience as a student worker in the cafeteria at a major institution of higher education. During the course of his graduate studies, Suru worked as a dishwasher in the school cafeteria. That position allowed him to earn some much-needed cash. He was a poor student. He struggled to pay for his tuition and fees. He had to work very hard on campus every day, and he did not regret it.

The small amount of money he was making on campus contributed to paying his rent and tuition. Suru was able to manage his meager earnings, but his position as a dishwasher granted Suru a golden opportunity. Dishwashing stood him in a good stead to observe how greed can end up in waste. Every day, as he washed the dishes, pots, and pans, Suru observed how much leftover food was dumped down the drain. It was a tremendous amount of sustenance. Suru did not like the food dumping scenes he witnessed. He observed the scenes again and again and wondered why it was so. He actively sought to understand the issue.

Suru ended up understanding that the cafeteria was not allowed to save leftovers for a long period. The policies did not permit the cafeteria to keep some leftovers for reuse. It seemed to be more of a tradition. The motivation for such a tradition was not bad. It aimed at serving fresh and healthy food, but it did not satisfy Suru's thirst for meaning. He was not able to grasp the sense of that tradition.

Suru remained frustrated that so much food was being wasted. He decided to visit a series of other similar institutions of higher education. Suru observed the same scenes in most institutions he visited. He also went to a number of restaurants and collected almost the same data. Apparently, the same scene occurs in some of our households as well. It was frustrating. Suru put the blame on greed. He thought society was unfair. He thought it was unfair to dump the food other people desperately needed.

At some point, Suru even felt guilty to be a powerless witness as a student worker. Why couldn't we carefully calculate and cook just what we needed? What if we anticipated and cooked only what we needed with the intention of sharing the surplus with the needy or the poor? Do we really have to disregard and dump the leftover food? Why do we dump and waste so much while so many people are deprived of the basics? What if we found a way to forward the daily leftovers from cafeterias, restaurants, and kitchens to the homeless on our streets and to the poor around the globe? If we have the means to reach the Moon or Mars, we certainly have the means to reach the needy with our leftovers, regardless of the corner of the world they live in. We cannot waste food with the pretense that the needy are too far from our tables. They are not too far; many of them are on our streets, in our neighborhoods, in our communities, our cities, and our countries. Mindful of how many people go without enough food daily around the world, Suru thought there should be a better way to manage leftovers from our kitchens. *Let us all think about it strategically. There ought to be a better way! If we can find a way to share more food out of our abundance with those in need, we will put smiles on more faces and make the world a happier place. The first step in moving into that direction requires learning to stand strong against greed. We should wash our hands of greed. Greediness results in waste.*

Ironically, it did not seem that all the lessons Suru learned from previous greedy experiences were enough to completely purge his heart and mind from their inclination to greed. He would get trapped in greedy tendencies again.

Years after his greedy lunch experience, Suru was teaching online for a major academic institution. All the interactions were online. Suru had to design and teach courses on conflict resolution-related topics. His tasks encompassed course design and delivery as well as grading assignments. In the process, Suru was required to post his syllabus online, create course announcements, discussions, and other assignments. He was required to actively participate in class discussions by logging in more than once every week. He had to respond to student discussions and questions with constructive feedback. He was required to grade all assignments within three days of their submission. In general, Suru was doing well on all accounts. The school and Suru's students appreciated his contribution to teaching and learning, but the position was a part-time position, and Suru was looking for a full-time position. A year after he started teaching online, Suru happily got another teaching position with another major teaching institution. This new position was a full-time one in a residential classroom.

Suru faced a dilemma. He weighed finishing the online courses or focusing only on his residential courses with the new institution. He decided to finish teaching all the courses he had signed up to teach that year. Suru had to balance his part-time online teaching with his regular full-time courses at his new institution. He had his hands full. It was not an easy transition, but Suru was able to navigate through it successfully.

Due to his regular job schedule and family commitments, Suru's days no longer fit the online teaching. He would turn to his nights for online teaching. Suru would stay up quite late at night to make comments on student discussions, grade assignments, and craft and post his announcements and lectures. As a result, his hours for sleep were shortened. That habit affected the quality of his days. He felt stressed out by being here and there on every hand.

Suru was burned out. He did not even have time to make a phone call or check his messages. Suru still did not have the common sense to think it was time to give up his part-time online teaching, but his heart and mind started wrestling with the thought of keeping that extra job. Suru's physical and mental assets were doing everything they could to push him to give up his additional part-teaching position. His psyche was no longer responding to collaborate with him at night when Suru needed it. He had recurrent insomnia and obsessive headaches and stomachaches. He was not happy at all.

Stressed out and drained, Suru spent a few days without logging into his class. Then one night, absorbed in self-examination, he had the courage to listen to his heartbeat. His process of self-examination granted Suru an opportunity for self-education; it helped him measure himself against himself and nobody else. Both his mind and heart called him out. They were straightforward in telling Suru they could no longer survive that rhythm.

Suru asked himself critical questions: Did he really need to keep two jobs? Was that safe for him and his environment? Was it even fair to him and them? Eventually, Suru understood that keeping that extra job was another vivid expression of his inclination for greed. Suru got so attached to the small additional money from teaching online that he was not willing to wash his hands of it.

The faces of his children also appeared in the mirror during Suru's self-evaluation. With a mixture of sadness and a smile, Suru's children wondered why their father was damaging his health and theirs. Suru understood the symbolic message coded in their facial expressions. Their sad faces were to alert Suru that he was being greedy in keeping his additional online teaching. Their happy faces were to urge Suru to find refuge within generosity.

By the end of his self-examination, Suru decided to give up his online teaching. His decision was clear, and before even sharing it with Lafia, Suru felt some peace in his heart and mind.

Upon getting the news, Lafia joyfully welcomed the decision as a good one for Suru and their family.

Suru added that it was also good for his students and others. That night, Suru slept so well. The next morning, he woke up strong and happy. He tried to log in online to let the school officials know about his decision. Suru was unable to log in successfully. He did not have any access to his classes. He thought it was due to a technical issue. He tried to get in over three days without success. Suru called the school to let them know the technical issue he was experiencing, but the process Suru was invited to follow to recover access was only going to add to his stress and trap him. He decided to leave things as they were.

Suru used that opportunity to give up that extra job. He felt relieved after that job was no longer part of his life. After Suru left that job, somebody else he did not know—someone who needed that job more than Suru did—probably got that opportunity and had more time to commit to it fully. That person was certainly happier with it than Suru was. To some degree, giving up a job you do not need to allow another person in need to get it reflects an act of generosity.

When he bought his first house with his wife, Suru decided to do most of the basic maintenance by himself. His goal was to save some money. That decision implied Suru would be doing all the basic repairs and cutting the grass around the house. He planned to cut the grass by himself. For some time, Suru was able to find his way around with some tools and maintain his house. He bought a lawnmower, but he was stressed out and discouraged after the first weeks. He contacted a gardener, and Oda agreed to cut Suru's grass biweekly for a fee. Oda offered to trim the bushes around Suru's house whenever they needed to be trimmed for some more money, but Suru thought it would cost him an arm and a leg.

Suru trimmed the bushes on his own twice a year. He was able to trim his bushes for a few years, but he got tired of trimming the bushes in addition to the regular work, domestic, and extracurricular activities he was involved in. He went back to his gardener and renegotiated with him to trim the bushes for some extra money. Oda graciously accepted. Suru could not just do it alone. He would prefer to give away some money and reduce his stress level and feel relaxed and happy. Sooner or later, greed ends up giving you stress, which makes you unhappy.

Why do we have to be stressing ourselves out with so many hours of work? Why do we work under pressure for long or extra hours? Why can't companies or corporations recruit more workers to get the job done without the workers being frazzled? Why do we work several jobs? Why can't businesses pay workers decent wages to cover their needs? One word may sum up Suru's answer to all such questions. That word would be greed.

Greed is a vicious human inclination. In the case of Suru's questions, it could be greed on the part of workers or on the part of their employers. Some employers could be greedy for not hiring more workers. They want the biggest share to remain in their pockets. What they could use to employ additional labor would become bonuses for themselves or their CEOs.

In other cases, the employees could be greedy. They load their shoulders with too many hours of work because they want more money. Some employees even work two or more jobs. Regardless of the case, the price you pay for greed is stress. Working too many hours stresses your heart just as eating too much food does. Working hard does not mean stressing yourself out by taking several jobs or putting an unreasonable number of hours into work. You could be working yourself to death. Hard work requires finding a healthy balance. Working hard requires developing your talents to achieve your modest and generous contribution to society without risking your wellness and well-being.

His personal experience would not authorize Suru to advise anyone to keep more than one job or work too many extra hours. Suru thinks his experience put him in a good position to speak to this issue. Keeping more than one job or working too many extra hours will give you a headache and stress you out. It would also stress your immediate environment of relatives and friends.

If we work more than one job or many extra hours for financial reasons, greed could also find its hideout in some of our motives. A bigger picture would reveal that we load ourselves with several jobs or many extra hours of work due to personal greed, structural greed, or systemic greed. Personal greed refers to an individual's natural or existential inclination to greediness. Structural greed associates with the voracious tendency a structure or an organization has to exploit or extort its workers. Organizations inclined to structural greed would hire far less staff than they should. Their cherished intention is to spend less money by using a minimum amount of people and exhausting them in the process. After wearing you to the point of breaking you down, they are quick to throw you away and replace you.

You may die of cardiovascular or other life-threatening diseases. If you do not die of a heart attack, the odds are that you will get sick with a terminal condition. The greedy organization will put you on the sidelines, replace you, and move on. Nobody wants to be a victim of such a sad scenario, but it is easy for some organizations to entangle many of us with similar scenarios. Structural greed can also be called organizational greed because it is deployed by organizations against the people they employ.

Last but not least, systemic greed relates to policymaking. Systemic greed alludes to policies or laws that are intentionally designed to favor only a few people or groups. Those policies or laws do not serve the interests of the general public. Instead, they promote the specific interests or agendas of a few individuals. For instance, systemic greed would tacitly endorse gun violence with policies or laws that protect guns on the streets but jeopardize people's lives. Some political or economic systems endorse or foster such avaricious policies or laws.

The implementation of such policies and laws allows a few people to take advantage of social and natural assets to the detriment of the majority. Their implementation process puts too much financial burden on the underprivileged and less fortunate of society. Such systems immerse some people with enormous bills. You must pay for everything, including the water that nature graciously grants to all living creatures, to survive.

Because of a lack of adequate health insurance, you are required to pay expensive medical bills you cannot afford. In some cases, medical bills wait for you at home while you are still fighting for your life in the hospital. Systemic greed does not care whether you are sick or whether you are able to work to pay for your medical bills. It does not want to know whether you remain in a coma or on life support. You may still be bedridden or agonizing at the hospital, but systemic greed takes no pity on you.

Sadly, it is a shameless system that shows no compassion. It forcefully demands that you pay your bills while you are still sick in bed, unable to move or suffering terribly. Moreover, systemic greed constrains you to pay your rent or a mortgage that requires you keep more than a job or work many extra hours. The system does not even allow you to sleep or spend time in the apartment or house you pay for. It makes you work day and night to pay your bills. You spend your days and nights working for the system.

We might not be aware of it, but many of us are victims of systemic greed. Once we become aware of systemic or structural greed, we should stay on guard against it. We need to learn to live up to our means and live by taking into account what we can afford. We could live well without living high. We should certainly live and let live in accordance with our means. More importantly, we need to find time to actively participate in the elections of our policymakers. As we vote for them, we should be mindful of people-centered servants or humble leaders. Every single vote counts in the decision to counter systemic greed.

Suru would learn a lot more about the implications and social dynamics of greed in human existence and society. Greed could make you run the risk of obesity and expose others in your environment to high risks of malnutrition and poverty. Suru is certainly not an economist, and he has no specific training in finance, but he tends to think of greed as a cradle, a source, and justification of the notion of interest rates in our banking systems. You may want to forgive Suru's naïve mind. To some extent, greed motivates banks to lend you money with high interest rates. If you get a big student loan to complete your studies, be prepared to spend the rest of your life paying high interest rates on that loan. When you borrow from a bank to buy a house, be ready to spend the next thirty years paying your principal plus interest. You become one of those slaves who spend their entire existence working to pay back powerful lending masters. You could get frustrated in the process, but you are required to pay them back. Otherwise, they will mess up your credit and make your life miserable. By the time you finish making your payment, your life is about to end.

Some dramatic conflict dynamics that greed fosters in the international system are obvious. Due to greed, only a tiny percentage of people, groups, and nations tightly hold the wealth that could serve to feed or take care of the entire global population. Owing to greed, some developed countries save or preserve their natural resources such as crude oil by keeping them as strategic reserves while they exploit raw resources of other countries. In some cases, businesses from developed countries extort, compete, and even fight over oil, diamonds, and gold in those developing countries. The main victims of such fighting in developing countries are primarily the local populations.

Greed triggers senseless tariff conflicts and trade wars in the international system. In international trade, greed inspires multinational corporations and developed countries to impose a price on the cotton, coffee, cocoa, and other goods produced in developing countries. As a result, poor farmers in countries such as Nineb and others work very hard to earn a living, but they remain poor because of unfair dynamics of greed in international trade. They produce the goods, but they have no say in pricing their goods. The buyers set the price of goods for the sellers. Such dynamics of greed deprive the poor farmers of fair rewards for their hard labor. They barely get enough to take care of their families. They do not get any subsidies from their governments, and they have to sell their products at subsided prices. In some cases, for a kilogram of coffee beans, they get less than what a cup of coffee would cost in any Uncle Sam's coffee store. Their goods make big corporations wealthier.

Workers in developing countries work in despicably insane conditions to make shirts and trousers that are very expensive in the nice stores of big corporations around the globe. Meanwhile, those factory workers barely make enough to provide for their families. In some cases, they make much less than the cost of a shirt or a pair of trousers.

Greed also affects how we want others to share the opportunities in our countries and how we talk about building walls between us and them that they would have to pay for. Greed generates frustration, conflict, and unhappiness in others and in you. It makes everyone unhappy. In contrast, generosity anoints everyone with happiness. Generosity makes you develop friendships with others.

How could Suru grasp the sense of his repeated experiences with greed? Philosophy would put the blame on human nature. Without getting into the instinctive game of blaming, Suru would agree that human nature certainly has something to do with it. Human nature is inclined to greed, but human nature is also inclined to generosity and peace.

A cost-and-benefit analysis would make Suru side with generosity and peace, but how could he turn away from greed for good? It could be difficult to escape greed completely for the rest of his existence, but it is possible to transcend greedy behaviors if Suru commits to trying to escape greed. Thank God for self-examination! Self-examination has the potential to alert Suru to such greedy traps. It often makes him wash his hands of greed. Suru's self-examination allows him to turn away from greed to knock at the door of generosity again and again. When he does so, Miss Generosity widely opens her doors to warmly welcome Suru into the heaven of peace and happiness. Suru has to keep his eyes on the ultimate goal of peace in his heart and mind.

Suru sees generosity as a consciously activated disposition of the heart and mind that stimulates you to happily share with others what you could chose to keep only for yourself. Generosity translates some active willingness of ego to share something with the alter ego. Generosity challenges Suru daily. He always wants to be generous, but he often finds reasons or excuses not to be generous.

Suru keeps trying to reach Miss Generosity to possess her sense of unselfishness, but every time he thinks he has reached her, she escapes and challenges him to keep on trying. Anytime Suru partakes in generosity, it feels good. Every time he is able to run away from greed, Suru takes shelter in the warm armpits of generosity and finds refuge in her dwelling. How good does it feel to dwell in the shadow of generosity! It feels really good staying under her supervision. It certainly feels good sharing what you have with those in need.

Wouldn't you feel good sharing the little you have to assist innocent children who are struggling with cancer or other deadly diseases? Yes, you would! Suru can assure you that you always feel good by being generous. He knows generosity is sharing what you have and who you are. Generosity means giving without asking for or expecting anything in return.

Generosity inspires us to share the little we have—even if it is not enough for us. We can give tangible or intangible assets. Tangible gifts include our presence, time, money or materials goods. Intangible gifts include our emotions and thoughts. When we are generous, we help feed those who are hungry. We give a drink to the thirsty. We seek shelter for the homeless. We welcome refugees and strangers into our nations and homes. We provide clothes to those who are naked and health care for the sick. We pay attention to those who are marginalized. We visit those who are in prison.

What you give or share might not be material. What we give could also be spiritual. In that sense, we all have something to share. You can certainly share your talents, your time, your gratitude, your smile, your services, your thoughts, your prayers, and even your attention. You can donate some of your time by volunteering in the community. Sharing a smile with others or giving them a smile reflects an act of generosity. Giving a smile can be twofold. When you give a smile to people, you either show them your smile or you make them smile. Gratitude also epitomizes generosity to some extent. Learning to appreciate yourself and others or learning to appreciate this given moment in time and space reflects generosity. Every *thank you* you give to others is a blessing you send to them. Every *thank you* you receive from them is a blessing they send to you. Generosity can also help in giving hospitality. Whenever we open our doors or borders to others who need a safe haven, we show them generosity. Giving or sharing a refuge with those who need one makes everyone happy to some degree. You can also show generosity by being present or by paying attention to others or listening to them.

As an adventurous teenager, Suru once had a meaningful encounter in his neighborhood with an old man in his eighties. The man's name was Ata. Ata's house was by a road Suru was using nearly every day. Every morning, Ata would sit on an armchair by the gate of this house. Every time Suru was passing by his house, Ata would try to wave his right hand at Suru, but Suru would not pay attention to him. Suru would not respond to Ata. Suru did not know him. Suru was always rushing.

One day, as Suru was passing by, Ata limped over to him.

Suru stopped suddenly.

Ata started purring like a cat and buzzing like a bumblebee.

Suru was scared. He had no clue what Ata was saying or trying to do. At some point, Suru thought that Ata was dumb. Suru did not know Ata was pretending. Suru did not try to run away because the old man looked nice, smiled, and had nothing harmful in his hands. Suru tried to give Ata a coin to get rid of him, but the old man shook his head and smiled to indicate that he did not need Suru's money. Ata took out his wallet and gave Suru the equivalent of five dollars.

Suru took the money and thanked Ata because it was a lot of money for Suru. Ata started talking sense; he spoke to Suru in a clear language. Suru was baffled. Ata explained how he just wanted Suru to pay attention to his morning greeting and waving.

Suru apologized to Ata for neglecting his greetings. He thanked Ata for letting him know about it in such a meaningful way.

The old man waved his right hand as if he were testing Suru, and Suru responded by waving back at Ata.

The old man slowly returned to his armchair and let Suru continue his way.

Upon returning home, Suru told his mother the whole story.

Iya made Suru sit down and told him the old man's life story. Ata was happily married, but his wife passed away. Her name was Owo. Their two children, Ale and Odi, moved out and lived in different cities. Ata's grandson was the only one living with his grandfather. His name was Uka. Uka would leave early in the morning for work, spend most of his day at work, and come home in the evening. Ata would spend most of his day by himself in his armchair. Ata had been known in the neighborhood as a workaholic. He spent fifty-five years working hard in the public and private sectors, but after a massive stroke, he retired. Following his retirement, Ata elected to spend his mornings and evenings waving at people passing by. He enjoyed it. Ata once explained to Suru's mother that he spent nearly his entire life paying attention to working and not to people. Ata's retirement granted him the opportunity and time to pay some attention to people. Waving to people was making him happier than he felt in all the years he spent working. Ata felt good waving at people. He felt even better when people waved back at him.

Suru felt guilty for failing to wave to Ata. A few days later, a neighbor would share the awful news of Ata's death. Suru felt terrible and regretted the missed opportunity to further engage with Ata. Suru wept, but he was grateful for the clear lesson the old man taught him.

Sometimes, the only thing people need is our attention in a greeting, in a smile, or in time dedicated to listening to them. People may not need our money, but they always yearn for our attention. Generosity means attention to people. We should seize every opportunity we have to pay attention to people since we do not know if we will ever get the opportunity again. We should never miss any chance to ride on the wings of generosity. Let us make sure we do not miss any opportunities to be generous.

Generosity often challenges societal standards of justice and endorses equal treatment as a norm. Hopefully, the reader still remembers how Tunde was so generous to Suru's mother at the farmer market. Inspired by a biblical parable from Matthew 20:1–15, Tunde demonstrated how generosity transcends certain standards of justice. Tunde once needed some extra help to harvest his corn. On a Saturday morning, Suru was playing catch with a friend on the playground.

Suru and Loa were waiting for more friends to join them so they could play volleyball. Suru noticed Tunde passing by and ran to greet him.

Tunde let Suru and Loa know that he needed some help harvesting corn. If Suru and Loa were interested, he would pay each of them the equivalent of five dollars at the end of the day.

Loa and Suru gladly agreed on the wage. It was a lot of money for teenagers, especially for the context they lived in. Suru and Loa followed Tunde to his field. It was about half past nine in the morning.

They immediately joined forces to help Tunde's wife and children. Tunde's wife was named Yala. Their children were Feli and Kere. Yala, Feli, and Kere were tirelessly harvesting the corn. Suru and Loa joined them and sang with them happily while working hard with them.

Around twelve o'clock, they all took a well-deserved break for a decent farmhouse lunch of roasted corn and fish. Suru enjoyed eating the roasted corn. Loa and Suru also took the opportunity to alert their parents on their whereabouts. They came back to the farm at one thirty to resume the harvest. It was an impressively large cornfield, and it was a hot day. The farmworkers worked hard in the hot sun, yet there was still a lot of corn to harvest. The harvest was large, and there were only few workers.

Around two o'clock in the afternoon, Tunde saw four more teenagers on the playground. He invited Obu, Keba, Aso, and Pupa to help in his farm for the same wage. They gleefully accepted the invitation. At four o'clock in the afternoon, Tunde did the same thing to maximize his chances of completing the harvest before sunset. He went to the marketplace and saw three men doing nothing. He invited them to come help in the farm for the same wage. They gaily accepted his invitation. Their names were Abo, Ochu, and Ufe.

At six o'clock in the evening, the farmhands cheerfully completed the harvest. All the laborers were proud of such a great achievement, but Loa and Suru were worn out. As Suru awaited his wage, he yearned for long hours of rest and sleep. He was even yawning while standing. Very satisfied with his harvesters' performance, Tunde enthusiastically called them to gather under a tree for their wages. They were nine workers, excluding Tunde's wife and two children.

Suru and Loa expected to be the first people to get their wages since they were the first workers Tunde recruited.

Tunde decided to start with those who were recruited last and end with those who came in first. At first, Suru thought Tunde's decision was unfair, but he thought Tunde might pay them more than the other harvesters and did not want to reward them in other workers' presence.

The men who joined the harvest at four thirty got the equivalent of five dollars each. The teenagers who arrived at the farm at about two thirty also received five dollars each.

Suru and Loa had joined the harvest at nine thirty—long before the other workers—but they were also paid the equivalent of five dollars each. Suru and Loa were not happy with Tunde. They thought he was unfair. They took the money and started grumbling.

Suru did not want to confront Tunde, mindful of the farmer's previous act of kindness to Iya.

Loa said, "We deserve more money than the other workers. These men who were recruited last worked less than two hours. We put up with work a whole day in the hot sun, yet you paid them the same amount you paid us. We should be getting more!"

As if Tunde literally intended to mimic the biblical parable, the farmer patiently answered Loa, "My son, you agreed to work for a day for the equivalent of five dollars. Now take your pay and go home rest. I want to give the people I recruited last as much as I gave you. Do I not have the freedom to spend my money as I wish? Are you jealous because of my sense of generosity?"

Tunde mimicked a parable from Matthew 20:1–15 in the New Testament.

Tunde's answer silenced Loa. The good farmer's answer made Suru think. He thought Tunde was right, fair, and even generous. If Tunde were to follow common standards of social perceptions of justice, he would do the math and pay the other workers less money. He would calculate and pay them for just the hours they had worked. Instead, he decided to be fair to Suru and Loa and generous to the other farmhands. As a result, Tunde made those workers happy, and he felt good.

Maybe it was not those men's fault that they did not get recruited early. They were not as lucky as Suru and Loa were to be recruited early. What would they do if nobody recruited them? They were certainly willing to work. They did not throw up their hands. They even decided to stand by the marketplace, hoping someone would see them and recruit them. Thankfully, a good farmer generously recruited them. Even though it was late in the day, the men were delighted to accept Tunde's offer. They went and worked hard on the farm. Some people are lucky to get opportunities earlier than others. Existence would make some people get their way early, and others would get it later. Regardless of when we get our way, generosity grants us equal respect and treatment as long as we are willing to collaborate with existence.

Suru pulled Loa's hand forward. Suru's friend was speechless. They both politely expressed their gratitude to Tunde for recruiting them in the first place. They politely bid farewell to him and his family.

Tunde walked and talked with them through the paths of the farmland and around the farmstead. When they reached the roadway, he said goodbye to them, urging Suru to greet Iya and Baba. Tunde went back to join his family in the farmhouse.

As Loa and Suru started pulling away from the farmland, Yala and her son Feli reached out to them with two bags of roasted corn. Yala was carrying one bag, and Feli was carrying the other one. Yala gave to Suru the bag in her right hand and asked him to give it to Iya. She took the bag Feli was carrying and gave it to Loa, telling him it was a gift for Ako, Loa's mother. Surprised by Yala's act of kindness, Loa and Suru were grateful. They both left the farmstead happy. Iya was happy with her bag of roasted corn. In Suru's family, nearly everybody was fond of eating roasted corn.

Though generosity neither expects nor asks for anything in return, whatever you give comes back to you in one way or another way sooner or later. Ido, Eke's Muslim boyfriend, gave up his seat at the banquet and sat on a broken piece of wood. The host of the banquet invited him and his girlfriend to sit with the guests of honor. Ido's humble and generous act earned him honor and greatness in the eyes of all the other guests.

Greatness springs from humbleness and generosity. After Tunde loaded Suru's mother with bags of fresh vegetables, he recorded a high turnout in customers.

Suru was at a fish market when an elderly woman came in to purchase a considerable amount of fish and crabs. Her name was Naga. Due to the quantity of her purchase, Suru assumed Naga was buying it for a big group. When her order was ready, Naga was faced with the dilemma of carrying the big bag of seafood by herself or asking for help. The fish market was extremely busy and crowded. With a long line of customers waiting, the staff forgot to find out if Naga needed help to get her bag to her car.

Suru understood that Naga needed someone to help her and volunteered to carry Naga's bag of fish to her car. Suru was glad to assist her. Naga was very grateful and happy. A few minutes later, Suru's own order of black bass was ready. Suru paid for it, picked it up, went to another grocery store. Surprisingly, all the items Suru needed to get at the store were on sale. Suru ended up paying half of the money he expected to pay for items he needed. Suru had never experienced anything of that magnitude before that day. He thought it was a miracle. He did not plan to go visit that store; he did not have to go to that grocery store on that day because he did not need the items right away. Suru would hypothesize that his act of kindness at the fish market generated positive energy to drive him to that grocery store that day. You do not have to agree with Suru. He believes that every act of generosity radiates into positive energy. In a way, Suru seems to lean on quantum theory or some pillars of quantum physics.

Day and night, Suru implores Lady Generosity to remind him to be generous to himself and to others. Suru beseeches her to help him be grateful for his existence in time and space. Suru supplicates her to grant him the courage to open his heart and mind when he wants them closed. Suru prays that he can open his hands to others when he wants them closed. He prays for the strength to donate when he feels he should keep everything for himself. He prays so he can happily share with others who he is and what he has, including his presence, his talents, his time, his gratitude, his smile, his services, his thoughts, and his prayers. Suru prays that he is able to reward with good those who do him bad. He prays that he is able to send blessings to those who send him curses or insults. He prays so he can welcome those who reject him. He prays so he can be merciful to those who show no mercy to him. He prays so he can become an instrument of generosity, its ambassador, a messenger who spreads generosity in the social environment.

We enter existence with empty hands, and we exit with empty hands. We should be sharing whatever existence puts in our hands with other citizens of the world. Nothing truly belongs to any of us forever. What we think belongs to us today will belong to other people in the future. We are today, but tomorrow, we are no longer. We leave everything behind.

In that existential perspective, let us pause for a moment and ask ourselves some existential questions. What are we really trying to gain by saving all the riches of the world for ourselves? Why are we piling up riches? From an existential perspective, there is no point in amassing the riches of the world for ourselves while others next door lack the basics. Our existence is not what we own. We exist to share global riches with all the citizens of the world.

In the final analysis, the survival of humankind depends on generosity. Let us guard ourselves from every kind of greed. Greed breeds selfishness and violence. Generosity nurtures kindness and gentleness, and it feeds compassion and happiness.

CHAPTER 15

Religion of Heart and Mind

Following his year of spiritual training at P Seminary of Rete, Suru was admitted to the next round of training at G Seminary of Dah in the last trimester of 1993. His first two years at G Seminary allowed him to get both grounded and rounded in the study of philosophy. Suru's philosophical studies quickly erupted in existential questioning. He called into question such things as the meaning of human existence, religion, conflict, and violence. It would not take him long to figure out that all such questions were existential and relevant to all social contexts across time and space.

In 1994, with a genocide in the nation of Wan, Suru's questions became even more relevant. While delving in the love of wisdom with philosophical interrogations, Suru was appalled and disgruntled by the news of the 1994 tragedy in Wan. It was despicable. It was heartless and mindless.

As he watched the horrific events unfolding, Suru raised questions about the human heart and mind time and again. His questions would often remain without answers. Whenever Suru thought he had an answer for a question, the so-called answer mutated into a new question.

The cycle of questions went on endlessly, but Suru did not panic or throw up his hands over the lack of answers. He was not dismayed by his lack of understanding of the nature of human violence. As an initiate in philosophy, Suru knew it was the nature of philosophy. Philosophical wisdom keeps challenging the human mind and heart with unanswered questions. He learned that every tentative answer becomes a new question in philosophy and in existence. It was not easy to grasp the sense of this puzzle, but philosophy translates to daily life. Life is an endless cycle of questions that are never fully answered. Life is a series of unanswered questions. There seem to be more unanswered questions in life than answered ones. This may be hard to accept, but it is reality. Parts of that reality unfolded during the 1994 genocide in Wan.

As Suru watched and questioned the events in Wan, he observed the dynamics of a critical variable in their midst. The variable of religion caught his attention. Wan was a mainly Christian country. Citizens of Wan were mostly Roman Catholic. Suru's attention to that variable hardly ever helped solve the puzzle of his questions. He could not understand how some Christians could be so devoted to killing other Christians and human beings.

Suru's heart deeply despised the tragic images, and his mind experienced a wave of shocks while thinking about the whole tragedy. He was traumatized. It was horrifying. As a devoted Christian, Suru was aware that the message of love at the heart of the Christian faith prohibited killing. What contradictions!

As a Catholic, Suru seized that opportunity to settle down for a set of self-examinations over the deployment of his Christian faith in practice. He was saddened by the many challenges his actions were faced with. In the process of his self-examinations, Suru understood how he was trapped and how many human beings could be ensnared by structural religion. The concept of structural religion is used here to depict religion as it is commonly understood, perceived, or conceived.

In the mainstream, religion is often associated with structures. Self-examination enlightened Suru about the danger of hosting such a perception of religion. Once entangled by structural religion, the likelihood is that we discriminate against others. The traps of structural religion have the potential to fail our ability to love others. Our failure in loving other human beings had triggered massacres in Wan and elsewhere.

As Suru looked at the genocide in Wan through philosophical lenses, he became aware of how structural religion could run the risk of inadvertently incubating hatred while preaching love. Suru was disgruntled by such contradictions. He was stunned to discover how a structure aimed at sowing seeds of love and peace could also unintentionally spread weeds of hatred and violence in the same process. At the sight of such existential contradictions, Suru's peace of heart and mind fainted away.

The scenes of the 1994 genocide in Wan shocked Suru deeply. He was devastated to see the horrific images. People were killed in their places of worship and inside their churches. Many of their killers were fellow Christian worshipers. As Suru watched the violence the Christian fellows waged against their peers in such a great Christian nation, he questioned the benefits of structural religion for social interactions. His questions triggered a process of self-examination on structural religion.

In his process of self-reflection, Suru contemplated the images of the 1994 genocide in Wan again and again. He felt ashamed about how Christians massacred their fellow Christians, including within church settings. Suru thought of other religious violence between Catholics and Protestants. Suru's mind opened up historical records of the Jihad, the Crusades, and other religious violence carried out in the Ottoman Empire and the Roman Empire.

Suru mentally reviewed the hideous tension and violence between Hindus and Muslims and between Christians and Muslims in other countries around the globe. In the process of that contemplation, Suru felt as if structural religion was not connecting people for peace. Like many people, Suru felt structural religion was sometimes divisive.

On an intrapersonal level, Suru felt trapped in his religious perspectives and their contradictions. He felt his religious denomination enslaved his worldviews and determined how he perceived others and interacted with his alter ego or alter idem, but those feelings were often counterbalanced by his awareness of constructive religious deeds as he continued his contemplation. The two faces of structural religion Suru contemplated were at odds.

Suru's contemplation also opened his eyes to some good achievements of structural religion in building peace and reconciling people around the world. He thought of many good deeds by religious organizations such as Misereor, the Catholic Charities, the Catholic Relief Services, the Jesuit Refugee Service, World Vision, the Mennonite Central Committee, and other well-thought-of religious organizations.

Suru thought of the constructive roles religious monasteries played in the history of global development. He thought of beloved religious leaders tirelessly committed to educating children in religious schools, caring for the sick in religious hospitals, sheltering and feeding the homeless, visiting prisoners, preaching nonviolence, or helping the poor around the world. Suru thought of charismatic religious leaders like Mahatma Gandhi, Martin Luther King, Mother Teresa, and others. Those observations portrayed religion as a force of good and peace.

Structural religion certainly holds seeds of peace, yet Suru remained frustrated by the genocide in Wan. As miserable and unjust conditions made people victims in part due to structural religion, crucial questions kept waving in Suru's mind and heart: How can we be so religious and wicked at the same time? How can human beings be religious and selfish at the same time? How do we associate religion and hatred?

Some readers might want to remind Suru that political and ethnic factors were the main contributors to the violence in Wan and elsewhere. Suru was aware of such contributing factors, but why was structural religion—with all the preaching on love and its assets for peace—unable to keep the citizens of Wan from killing their brothers and sisters in humanity and faith, including innocent people? Suru's doubts nearly obliterated his faith. In the quest for an answer to such unyielding questions, Suru decided to contemplate the roots of religion in the heart and mind since we all have a common religion in the heart and mind.

Fortunately, Suru's self-examinations opened his heart and mind to a golden perception of religion. He came to understand there is a religion that comes from within the self. That religion deploys from within our hearts and minds. It is inherent to humankind. It is within all human beings.

Suru coined the phrase "religion of heart and mind" to identify that religion. Religion of heart and mind emerges from the self and focuses more on people than on structures. It finds the face of God in people. It displays compassion to connect and serve people. Unlike structural religion, which seems to come to the self by adoption from outside, religion of heart and mind is inherent to the self and comes from within us.

When adopted, religion has the potential to lead its subjects to division and violence. When innate, religion erupts in love, compassion, and tolerance. That new understanding of religion shed some light of peace on Suru's heart and mind. He felt a shift in the midst of his self-examination. Suru grasped the sense of that shift clearly. His primary religion was in his heart and mind. The one religion we all have in common became the focus of Suru's attention. Yes! We have one religion in common—regardless of our structural religious denominations and conventional religious belonging.

To substantiate his epiphany on religion of heart and mind, Suru decided to conduct surveys that would confirm the results of his self-examination. He went to a shopping mall and randomly selected a sample of one hundred adult shoppers from a relatively diverse population of people with different religious backgrounds. Participants in the surveys were fifty women and fifty men of twenty years in age or older. Participants' religions included Hinduism, Buddhism, Daoism, indigenous belief, voodoo, Judaism, Christianity, and Islam. Suru presented them with a survey that included the following set of closed-ended questions: Do you worship in a temple? Do you worship in a synagogue? Do you worship in a church? Do you worship in a mosque? Do you love or experience love from others?

The goal of the survey was to examine how each participant responded to those questions and where the participants stood in general. About forty-five of the people worshiped in a temple (a Hindu temple, a Buddhist temple, a Daoist temple, a voodoo temple, or in a setting of indigenous belief). About five of the people worshiped in a synagogue. About twenty-five worshiped in a church. About twenty-five worshiped in a mosque.

Interestingly, all hundred participants indicated that they loved or experienced love. Suru used techniques of independent t-test to compare how men and women differ in rating the question of love. There was no difference with the variable of gender. We all love and experience love regardless of gender or religion. Those results are meaningful.

The reader may still be wondering what that religion of heart and mind is. Suru would reiterate that our common religion is that of the heart and the mind. Our common religion is in the deployment and delightfulness of our heart with self and others; it is in the radiation of our minds. How so? This requires clarification.

We are all aware of the vital role the heart plays in our bodies. There is no need to take a course in biology to understand that. The heart irrigates our organs with blood to keep them alive and healthy. The heart connects all the parts of our bodies and binds them altogether. The mind energizes our bodies and generates a field of energy that affects the internal as well as the external environment of our bodies.

The internal environment of our bodies is that of self. Its external environment is that of others, our social and natural environment. Per its etymological definition, religion binds us together or connects us with ourselves and others. We should be mindful of the Latin root of the word *religion*. Religion comes from the Latin word *religare*, which means "something that binds us together" or "something that creates links and connections."

Our hearts do the same job. They bind our bodies together, creating links and connections between all parts of our bodies. Our hearts connect us to other people in our social environment and beyond. Our minds also connect us to ourselves and to others in the perspective of energy fields as understood in quantum physics. Our hearts and minds are critical in connecting our bodies to ego, to alter ego or alter idem, to ourselves, and to others. If we reason on the premise that religion connects us to ourselves and to others, our hearts and minds become our basic inherent religion. Somehow, we all become religious as long as we have hearts and minds. The religion of heart and mind becomes our common religious denomination, but what should we understand by the religion of heart and mind? That question remains.

The religion of heart and mind is that of love, compassion, and tolerance. The heart and mind connects us to ourselves and others through love, compassion, and tolerance. What is love? It is that ability to open the self to the subject or object of our positive feelings. We open the self to make room in the self for another self, the subject or object of our love. We open our egos to welcome and host our alter egos. We dilate our hearts to share our feelings with them and welcome their feelings. When you love people, your heart beats for them. You connect with them, you trust them, you admire them, you embrace them, you want to be with them, you want to live with them, and you have compassion for them. What is compassion then?

Compassion is the ability to feel with and for alter ego as you feel for ego. Compassion implies communion of heart in spirit. The Latin root of the concept is meaningful: *Cum* (with, together) and *passio* (feelings of suffering or sorrow, but also feelings of joy). Passion is certainly suffering, but passion is also positive feelings or incentives in a desire that drive a person to achieve something. When your heart beats with compassion for them, you suffer with them when they suffer, but you also rejoice with them in times of joy. Compassion makes us expand our hearts to them with generosity. It makes us sympathize with them in times of sorrow and happiness. It makes us share their feelings in a dynamic sense of solidarity. When our hearts beat with compassion, we are ready to help them. When our hearts beat with compassion, we put ourselves in their shoes and treat them as we wish to be treated. When we have compassion, we respect them and accept them as different from us. Compassion echoes a keen sense of tolerance. What is tolerance then?

Tolerance is the ability to accept others as different. It is the sense of open-mindedness that makes us patient with others. It is that broadmindedness that welcomes and hosts the alter ego into the vicinity of the ego. It is a fine fruit of love and compassion. When you love, you understand that you need her or him so that you may become complete as much as she or he needs you.

Compassion further enhances this. When you show compassion, you understand that you are because they are. Compassion makes us contemplate us and them like the colors of a rainbow. All the colors are needed for the rainbow to be a rainbow—and to be beautiful. Compassion makes us beautiful together and attractive to one another. If we have compassion, we tolerate and respect our denominational religious differences and transcend them constructively. We understand that we are all looking at the same truth from different angles.

Eventually, love, compassion, and tolerance allow us to focus on our common religion: the heart and the mind. A heart of love, compassion, and tolerance drags the mind into positive thinking. Positive thinking contaminates our energy fields in ways that constructively irrigate our behaviors and actions. This radiates in our social environments and makes us recognize others and treat them with respect—just as we wish to be treated.

Ultimately, our religion of heart and mind seems to be what binds humankind together, regardless of color, ethnicity, gender, religious denomination, or nationality. That religion of heart and mind removes denominational barriers from the large family of God. In the perspective of that religion of heart and mind, love for self and for others becomes the main criterion for belonging to God's family. The benchmark of love extends God's family beyond denominational frontiers to all people. Developing the religion of heart and mind requires us to clean our hearts and minds to make room for others next to self. That is the key message all religious traditions strive to convey or operationalize in categories of love, compassion, and tolerance.

Buddhism raises our awareness about the importance of cultivating peace with self and others through meditation. Hinduism alerts us on the principle of *ahimsa* (do no harm), which implies tolerance and nonviolence. The Hindu greetings of *Namaste* meaningfully recognizes God in everyone: "I bow to the God in you; the Spirit in me salutes the Spirit in you." The notion of totality and reciprocity conveyed in the principle of Karma is meaningful here. In Daoism, we learn how the necessary contradictions between the yin and the yang create a balance that contributes to harmony in the oneness that generates everything in the universe. Indigenous beliefs and voodoo remind us of our duty to care for nature. Judaism reminds us to show compassion for self and others. *Shalom* is a wish of peace to others. Christianity enhances that God is Spirit of love and compassion. From a Christian perspective, we worship God by the power of that Spirit within each one of us. For our bodies are the temple of the Holy Spirit as Saint Paul indicated. This implies that our hearts and minds are the tabernacle of our religion. In Islam, we learn about forgiveness and reconciliation with others. *Salamalekoun* is a wish of peace to others.

In the house of existence, we all look at the same Truth or God, but we observe or see that Truth from various positions or corners of existence. From our isolated corners, we cannot pretend to see the front and back of Truth at the same time. We either see the front or the back or the right side or the left side. As a result, the face of Truth we see only represents one face among many others. Other faces of Truth are hidden to us. Those faces that are hidden to us are seen by others who are trying to see the same Truth from a different position.

Suru would think here of an analogy about the differences we record in telling time. He would contemplate the differences between the twelve-hour system of time and the twenty-four-hour system of time. Let us assume you read time in the twelve-hour system. When it is four o'clock in the afternoon, you could tell everyone who asks you that it is four o'clock post meridiem, and you all understand what you mean as correct. Somebody else could select to mean the same thing by reading that time as sixteen hours. That reading would also be correct. That other person is following the twenty-four-hour system of time and is not wrong. Both you and that person mean the same time, the same truth, but you follow two different systems of time, depending on your respective culture or traditions. That could be how Suru would observe the Truth of God through different religious denominations.

Suru would also bring forward another similar analogy. In general, a day is made of twenty-four hours irrespective of the corner of existence you live in, but the day does not start at the same moment everywhere. Whenever it is 6:00 a.m. in New York, it is 3:00 a.m. in California. The time is not the same in Washington as it is in Paris, London, Berlin, Rome, Madrid, New Delhi, Bombay, Mecca, Nairobi, Lagos, Accra, Abidjan, Kigali, Kinshasa, Johannesburg, Cairo, Tel Aviv, Mexico City, San Paolo, Beijing, Hong Kong, or Tokyo, but the truth about time is that time is time everywhere. Suru has even more meaningful stories to serve the purpose of this perspective on religion.

Wahala, Suru's aunt, was involved in a bitter conflict with her daughter for not accepting the daughter's boyfriend. Wahala eventually accepted the deep-rooted love between Eke and Ido. A few weeks after that notable family reunion, Wahala suffered a major stroke. Fortunately, the stroke did not take her away for good. She did not die. However, some parts of her body were paralyzed as a result of the stroke.

Prior to the stroke, Wahala had a battery of health issues, including uncontrolled diabetes. Her diabetic condition was not an asset to her paralysis. To maximize her chances of survival, Wahala had to face the challenges of diabetes and high blood pressure. That required good care and frequent checkups. Good care implies paying hospital bills among other things. Paying hospital bills required money. Wahala was a poor woman. She struggled financially to take care of herself and raise her daughter and support other dependents. She was the main breadwinner for her family. Ebu, her husband, was unemployed and depended on Wahala's small business for living.

Wahala needed financial assistance to pay her hospital bills. She did not seem to have anyone to turn to for help. She decided to talk to Iya and Baba. Suru's parents tried to help her, but it was not much because of their own financial struggles. Their aid to Wahala was parish-pump. Wahala desperately needed assistance, but she was not sure what to do or who to resort to for rescue. Not even her children were able to help her since they also had major financial lacks.

Unexpectedly, Eke's boyfriend stood up to the challenge. Ido rose to the occasion against all the odds. At the news of Wahala's stoke, Ido quickly showed up at the hospital. He offered to pay all the hospital bills out of his pocket, and he did it without asking for anything in return.

Ido's generous move was a pleasant surprise for Eke. They were not even married; Ido was just her boyfriend. Wahala could not believe it. In addition to paying the hospital bills, Ido paid for all the prescriptions and medications Wahala needed. He bought all the refills for a year. Moreover, Ido bought a wheelchair to alleviate Wahala's handicap and facilitate her movements.

Wahala's mobility had dropped to zero. She needed a wheelchair to move around her house. She was overwhelmed with joy and wonder at the sight of the new wheelchair from Ido. Upon seeing the wheelchair, Wahala was speechless. Bursting into tears, she went on with emotional words of thanks.

Somehow, everyone witnessing the scene understood her feelings.

Sometimes words can be poor in expressing how you feel. In those moments, emotions speak louder than concepts. For concepts can be too weak to express emotions. Even more so than emotions, our actions speak so profoundly. Everyone who witnessed Ido's acts of kindness was amazed. His actions eloquently spoke what his mind and heart were full of. Ido meaningfully exemplified what Suru would call religion of heart and mind by showing compassion and kindness to Wahala.

When Suru was traveling from the southern part of Nineb to its northern part, he was reading the Bible. Suru enjoys reading the Bible because it reminds him our daily human stories. The Bible presents him with daily contradictions in human existence. Reading the Bible reminds Suru that he is not alone in facing existential contradictions. It reminds him that he is not the first and will not be the last to face such contradictions. Reading inspirational biblical stories grants him hope. As Suru kept on reading his Bible on that trip, the passenger sitting next to him asked Suru what he was reading. That passenger was named Iri. Suru responded that he was reading about God. Iri smiled. Suru noticed Iri was also reading a book. He inquired about what Iri was reading. Suru was surprised when Iri indicated that he was also reading about God.

Excited, Suru asked Iri what church he attended. From where Suru was, he could not tell Iri was reading the Koran.

Iri smiled again and replied that he was a Muslim.

Suru realized his query about the church Iri attended was wrong. His question did not seem appropriate in that situation, but he smiled at Iri. His heart and mind exulted at his sudden awareness that Iri's notion of God and Suru's notion of God reflected different understandings or faces of the same God. In that moment, Suru and Iri became friends. They took a break from reading their holy books and spent the rest of their trip chatting enthusiastically in what could be called a very decent interreligious dialogue.

Suru carefully listened as Iri presented his perspective on religion and faith. Iri explained the Islamic rituals of forgiveness and reconciliation for peace. He stressed the importance of fasting as a ritual of purification of the heart and the mind in Islam. Iri indicated how he understood Islamic Jihad in his existence as a spiritual effort to redeem his own heart and mind from negative thinking and wrongdoing. He implied Jihad should not be a war against other people or groups—but a spiritual war over the self.

Suru learned a lot about peace in Islam from listening to Iri's views, and he got to know Iri better. It turned out that Iri, the deeply spiritual and down-to-earth man, was an imam. Suru felt so humble and peaceful while listening to Iri.

After he stopped talking about his faith, Iri asked Suru to tell him about his own faith. Suru delightfully shared his views on Christianity and peace.

Iri humbly and politely listened to Suru. Iri expressed his admiration and respect for Jesus and the Christian faith. Beyond their religious differences, their hearts and minds connected and energized their communication to be loving, compassionate, and tolerant—from both Suru and Iri. Their communication was constructive.

Upon arriving at their destination, Iri whispered that Suru was a good boy. He promised to pray to Allah to help Suru remain a good Christian. Suru marveled at those compliments and words. He thought Allah was another name for God—the God that welcomes and listens to all. Suru left Iri with a good impression. Iri was a good man. He was a holy man. He was good to Suru. Their discussions demonstrated that we can have a civil dialogue and get along regardless of religious differences since we all worship the same God in the religion of heart and mind.

The good impression that Iri left with Suru brought back to Suru's mind another pleasant experience he had with another Muslim friend. His name was Ijo. While growing up, Suru enjoyed playing soccer. He was once playing soccer with friends after school. In the excitement, Ako kicked the ball straight into Suru's face.

Suru collapsed on the ground with a bleeding nose. After that accident, the game ended instantly. Suru's house was next door. A group of friends, including Ako, carried him home. Iya took care of Suru's wounds and did what was necessary to address her son's needs. Suru had to spend the following week in bed without going to school. It was a tough week in pain, in bed, and away from all his friends. Suru did not see any of his friends around. Only one of them visited, and it was not even Ako who had kicked the ball that hit Suru.

The only friend who came to visit Suru was a Muslim friend. Ijo was one of the friends Suru was playing soccer with. He showed up every evening in Suru's house to check on him. After school, on his way to his house, Ijo would stop by Suru's house to check how he was doing. It was usually a quick visit for ten minutes, but Suru liked it and found it so meaningful for some reasons.

Out of all of them playing soccer that evening, Ijo was the only Muslim in the group. Everybody else was Christian, including Suru. Suru respected his Christian friends tremendously. Most of them lived in his neighborhood. After school, they would usually walk home together, and Suru's house was the first house on their way home. Suru wondered why none of them could stop to check on him except his Muslim friend. Perhaps they were very busy with schoolwork. Maybe they just did not think of it. Suru certainly grappled with understanding their behaviors. He did not make it a big issue, but he knew Ijo was very kind to him. Suru would seize a well-timed opportunity to show his appreciation and gratitude to Ijo.

In the same perspective of how the heart and mind connect us beyond religious denominations, Suru would shed light on another meaningful story. In addition to the judge who officiated their marriage, the only witnesses of Suru's court wedding with Lafia was a Hindu couple. Their names were Pasi and Mapa. Pasi and Mapa remain good friends of Suru and Lafia. Mindful that Lafia and Suru are Christian, you may wonder why there were no Christian friends at their wedding—not even any Christian relatives or family members. If you were to ask Suru that question, your query would be very pertinent, but Suru would only give you a short answer. All he would tell you would be that it was due to existential contradictions! Details of that answer would be too long to fit in this section. Suru would rather save them for another volume, but he will certainly tell you more about the context of those existential contradictions on a different occasion.

Over the years, across time and space, Suru has encountered many other people of good faith in the heart and mind, Muslims, Jews, Buddhists, Hindus, Daoists, indigenous believers, voodoo practitioners, and others whose lives exemplify the love Jesus Christ preached. Without calling themselves Christian, many of them challenge Suru on his Christian duty on the grounds of loving thy neighbor. They remind Suru of what it means to love your neighbor without expecting anything in return. Baba's mother was a Voodoo practitioner. Her name was Vedo. Vedo was one of the most caring people in the universe. She was loving, compassionate, and tolerant. Suru owes Vedo some of his passion for peace and equal justice for every human being. May she rest in eternal peace!

We should be mindful that we are religious first and foremost in our hearts and minds. The input of our heart in religion is essential. The heart seasons and spices up what the mind cooks to make it tasty and healthy to the ego and alter ego or alter idem. A mind without heart is vapid or tasteless, and it ends up dying. Let us practice the religion of heart and mind. The ultimate worship happens in your heart and your mind. Your heart and mind are the ultimate tabernacles of God. Your heart and mind are your ultimate temple, synagogue, church, and mosque. Your heart and mind are your actual worship places. If we embody the religion of heart and mind, the world will be a safer place for everyone.

Religion of heart and mind would inspire a Catholic pope to travel to Myanmar (Burma), a predominantly Buddhist country, to call for peace and respect for every ethnic group at a time when Buddhist nationalists waged violence against the Muslim Rohingya community. Religion of heart and mind inspired Christian organizations to intervene and help Muslim and Hindu communities during riots in India. Religion of heart and mind allowed Jewish leaders to raise money to rebuild a mosque set on fire in Texas and repair another mosque set on fire in Tampa, Florida. Religion of heart and mind also made Muslim leaders raise money to repair decimated Jewish headstones in Saint Louis, Missouri, at about the same time.

Religion of heart and mind inspires every act of kindness we perform. It makes us take care of the poor. It urges us to provide health care for the sick, shelters for the homeless, and clothes for the naked in our communities. It leads us to feed the hungry and give a drink to the thirsty. It allows us to welcome refugees and strangers in our countries. It makes us visit prisoners. If we exemplify the religion of heart and mind, the world will be a better place for all.

Religion of heart and mind blossoms in beatifying social interactions. Religion of heart and mind triggers effective communication with others. It allows effective communication to spring up, flourish, and spread in your house, community, workplace, country, and the international relations. Religion of heart and mind sprays the mist of effective communication in our relationships. Effective communication requires that we communicate with others from the heart and the mind.

Communication with the heart and mind implies compassion. We show compassion in communication by feeling with others while we communicate with them. Our communication feels and reckons with their pains. It also feels their joy and takes it into account. When we communicate with compassion, we recognize them as they are.

Compassionate communication implies identity recognition. Identity recognition implies respect for alter ego or alter idem. As we respect them, we learn to put ourselves in their shoes in the communication process. Once we are able to put ourselves in their shoes, we treat them as we wish to be treated. The process eventually empowers them and us. Compassionate communication is the springboard of love. It generates tolerance. When we communicate with compassion, we love and tolerate others.

This approach to religion does not put any rigid line between religion and spirituality. Many people often observe a dichotomy between religion and spirituality. It is common to hear people say they are spiritual but not religious. Suru's perspective on religion challenges that commonly accepted knowledge that ensnares religion into structural categories.

Per its etymology, religion goes beyond structures. No structure can pretend to contain religion. Actually, before being structural, religion is first and foremost a human attribute; it is that disposition within us to connect to ourselves and others. If we stick to the etymological definition of religion, we understand that all human beings are religious to some degree by a natural design. We are also spiritual because we are body and spirit. There seems to be a contradiction in pretending that we are spiritual but not religious. The words we use are certainly meaningful, but our narrow understanding of concepts can create confusion and conflict where there should not be any.

We are all spiritual by our human nature. We all have spirit within us. Our degree of attention to the spirit within us might be different. There are people who pay more attention to the spirit than others. There are people who are more committed to the spirit than others, but we are all spiritual regardless of our level of awareness of the spirit within us.

Suru would suggest an analogy for understanding what is meant here. His analogy is that we all swim constantly in a refreshing river of spirit. Some of us select to float and remain on the surface of the water. Others often dive in and out of the depths of that river. Some others dive deeper inside the river and settle down under its refreshing waters. We are all immersed in the waters. We are all wet. We all live by the spirit of the water, and it touches and refreshes every one of us. We are all spiritual irrespective of where we select to be in that water. As long as we are in it, we are spiritual.

By analogy, the depth or degree of our spirituality might be different, depending how deeply immersed we are in the spirit, but we are all spiritual. Those of us who are diving deeply under the waters have a higher level of spirituality. They pay more attention to the spirit living within us. They dedicate their time and lives listening to the spirit through meditation and living by its inspiration.

Those who dive in and out often experience highs and lows in their spiritual levels. Those who constantly float and remain on the surface have lower spiritual levels, but they are all spiritual—whether they are aware of it or not. We all live in the circle of the spirit. Some are closer to the epicenter of the circle. Others are on the outer edge on the circumference of the circle. Those who are closer to the center experience a higher spiritual experience than those who remain on the outer edge.

In the same analogical perspective, we all drink water because it is vital to our existence. We cannot live without drinking water. However, some of us are more aware of the importance of water in our lives. We tend to drink a lot of water daily. Others are less aware of the importance of water in life. They tend to drink less water. Instead, they drink other beverages and alcohol. Regardless of how much water we drink, we are all made of water—and we need it to live. Our intake of water might be different, but we all live by water. In the same way, we all live by the spirit regardless of the awareness we have of it.

We are all religious because we are all social beings. We all relate to each other. We are all connected to one another. If we understand religion in the Latin roots of the concept as *religare* (to bind together, to connect), then it becomes obvious that we are all religious. We all connect to somebody or something. We connect to a mother, a father, a wife, a husband, a child, a relative, a friend, a boyfriend, a girlfriend, a partner, a roommate, or a coworker. We could also connect with money, a house, a dress, a car, a country, a land, or God. Our hearts and minds connect us to ourselves and to others. As a result, we are all religious in the strict sense of the word. Obviously, our levels of religiosity might be different.

The news of the genocide in Wan was heartbreaking and depressing for Suru, but his perspective on the religion of heart and mind brought him some peace of heart and mind. Besides, in the midst of Suru's exposure to the bad news of the genocide, spiritual music would often pacify his heart and rescue his mind from the negative news. Thankfully, the beautiful liturgy of G Seminary often radiated positive energy to revitalize Suru's heart and mind. The positive energy Suru was getting from singing or listening to spiritual music safely countered the negative energy he was receiving from watching the events unfold in Wan.

Negative news certainly has the potential to destroy our happiness. By loading us with negativity, such news can poison or contaminate our energy levels or energy fields. In that process, they create vapid and raspy zones of turbulence in our hearts and minds. If our peace of heart and mind is jeopardized, we can counter or limit the destructive impact of negative news. One way is to sing or listen to spiritual music.

Spiritual music translates any music that springs up from the heart and mind to galvanize our spirit. Spiritual music lifts up our hearts and minds. It has a great potential to counter and even annihilate the poison negative energy injects into our hearts and minds. Suru felt the positive effects of spiritual music as he sang alongside his fellows during the liturgical rituals of matins, lauds, vespers, and Masses at G Seminary of Dah. The liturgy felt like a holy place where heaven and earth congregated in the euphoria of a symbiotic meeting.

As they sang in unison, and as Suru listened to the humming of their giant organ, he felt lifted up in spirit. His heart savored the stout melody of the organ. Suru's mind was delighted with the rumble of the drums. The jingling tambourines, the ringing gongs, and the creaking clarinets and clarions all echoed in a spiritually delectable concert. That mixture of sounds galvanized Suru's heart and mind with peace. The echo resounded in his soul. The harmony often triggered Suru's soul to rejoice with happiness. It felt so good. It felt like he was in the divine presence at the celestial court.

With resounding voices and instruments, Suru and his fellow seminarians happily worshiped God in the presence of angels. Their hearts and minds praised the divine majesty. They tried to approach the God they were not worthy of approaching. They sang for the God they could never sing enough for. They venerated the God they were poorly skilled to worship. They contemplated the God they could not fully see. They tried to grasp the sense of the God they would never understand plainly. They tried to understand the mystery of God in the divine presence and under the holy and divine watch of Eucharistic Sacrament. They contemplated and even experienced heavenly felicity on earth. Spiritual music has the potential to launch our ascension and access to the divine altar. Spiritual music takes us to the top of our spiritual mountain.

However, such moments of spiritual ascension interfere with daily earthbound realities. Earthly realities would regulate Suru's spiritual ascensions with frequent descents into realism. That sharp contrast would certainly fit in the logic of existential contradictions. Human existence is filled with moments of consolation and desolation. Human existence often reflects and oversees a perpetual cycle of consolations and desolations. Periods of consolation always alternate with periods of desolation in every human existence. They come and go and come back again.

The time Suru spent at G Seminary was so regulated. Suru's days and years at G Seminary rhythmed with existential contradictions. His happy periods of consolation would collide with depressing and vapid moments of desolation. Some of the velvety periods of consolation culminated in the Eucharistic liturgy as Suru contemplated the holy mystery of the Eucharist in songs.

Suru met other moments of consolation in physical activities such as sports and manual activities. Every weekend, Suru would find one hour to play soccer, handball, ping-pong, or volleyball. He also dedicated an hour to gardening daily. G Seminary had gardens of flowers and fruit trees. The beautiful gardens of flowers displayed exuberant families of roses, tulips, frangipani, sunflowers, and other types of flowers. The fruit trees included orange trees, lemon trees, grapefruit trees, mango trees, papaya trees, avocado trees, guava trees, banana trees, and others. Every evening, Suru would spend his time trimming, weeding, and watering plants when he was not involved in other housekeeping activities. All such activities flooded him with positive energy. Suru felt good doing them. As philosophy was enlightening his mind and heart, gardening was refreshing and appeasing them. The fragrance of flowers and fruits pacifies the mind and the heart as much as music and prayer do.

In contrast, Suru also experienced moments of desolation getting the tragic news of the genocide in Wan. The time he spent at G Seminary nestled other moments of desolation. Such critical periods of desolation were mainly triggered by Suru's philosophical questioning about the goal of his existence and his vocation in life. Suru kept asking himself existential questions about the orientation of his life. Was he indeed called to become a priest or was he just pretending? Why did he want to be a priest? Did he have the potential to embrace and live by all the requirements of the priesthood? Suru was mindful of how human beings can sometimes pretend to be or do something instead of actually being who they are or doing what they exist to do. For we can give the impression to be instead of just being. We can try to do what we are not called to do or predisposed to do.

Suru's answers to such questions were not clear. All such questions and Suru's lack of clear answers made existence nearly vapid during that period. As a result, Suru experienced severe and persistent moments of doubts about his vocation. Time and again, he felt he did not belong on that path. At times, he felt anxious at the thought of becoming a priest. More than once, Suru thought he would be happier in the vocation of marriage. Becoming a Catholic priest would imply that he would not get married.

Suru often felt uncomfortable at the thought of spending his life without a wife and children of his own. It slowly became obvious that Suru would enjoy having a wife and children. Nevertheless, the doubts were often transcended by the consolation Suru felt at the thought of dedicating his life to loving and serving God in all people through priesthood. He kept on thinking that the priesthood would provide him with the best opportunity to achieve that dream of loving and serving God by loving and serving people.

Suru was confused, and he grappled with understanding what he really wanted to do with his life. In that process, he was often entrapped in that game of cost-and-benefit analysis. He would admire the benefits of the priesthood. They would console him to some degree, but he did not feel he was ready to accept the costs.

Suru often felt sad about the costs of the priesthood. In his heart and mind, the costs of priesthood started outweighing its benefits. Suru considered quitting the training toward priesthood after the completion of his cycle of philosophy at G Seminary. The thought of that option did not grant him peace either. Suru was worried and afraid of social and peer pressures. The thought of what people in his entourage would say or think about him tremendously tormented Suru and deterred him from quitting.

Suru was so concerned with pleasing everyone else. Like a slave, he was allowing his social environment to dictate his behavior to his heart and mind. Suru was also troubled by the fear of the unknown. So far, things seemed to be going well for him in the seminary. Suru was a good seminarian by all odds. There was no complaint about his behavior. In general, Suru's colleagues appreciated his presence among them. He was a good companion to have around. All his teachers and trainers thought of him highly. Suru's parents, his parishioners, and his parish priest were all proud of his scholarly performances. His bishop was caring, understanding, and good to him. Suru was up for a great career in the priesthood if he were to become a priest.

He was not so sure how life would be after he abandoned the

vocation. Suru did not want to make a mistake he would regret for the rest of his life. He was listening to society instead of paying attention to his heart and mind. It can be cumbersome to experience how society contradicts the cry of our hearts and minds.

It is sad how we harshly silence the voice of truth in self by mimicking society. We tend to try to please our social entourage instead of seeking to also please our hearts and minds. In doing so, we can easily become victims of society and its structures. Adjacent to Suru's option of leaving the priesthood was another option. He called it his plan B.

Suru's alternative to quitting the priesthood for good and all would be to join the Jesuit order. He felt attracted to the Jesuits, a religious order of priests and brothers, founded by St. Ignatius Loyola in 1534. The Jesuits are actively dedicated to loving and serving God by loving and serving people. Their love and service of God is rooted in the principles of a book written by their founder, the *Spiritual Exercises of St. Ignatius of Loyola*. Theirs is an extremely inspiring spiritual tradition. That tradition is tooled with techniques for spiritual discernment.

Spiritual discernment holds the potential to allow human beings to identify and distinguish different motions or energies crossing their minds and hearts. It helps identify and distinguish negative energy and positive energy. It allows us to identify and enjoy moments of consolation. It alerts us to times of desolation. It prepares us to confront and handle desolation. Spiritual discernment ultimately serves as a tool for good decision-making.

By the time he completed his cycle of philosophy, it slowly became clear that the Jesuit spiritual discernment was the tool Suru needed in his toolbox to make the right decision about his vocation and future. The thought of that alternative made his heart and mind nestle in peace. Suru thought it was his best option, but he would put his decision to join the Jesuits on hold for another year.

Prior to joining the Jesuit order, Suru would spend a year of service at Jat Seminary in Nineb. The next volume will let you know what happened during that year of service and beyond.

INDEX

T

U

V

W

X

Y

Z

ABOUT THE AUTHOR

Dr. Jacques L. Koko is an associate professor of conflict analysis and dispute resolution at Salisbury University in Maryland. His focus includes organizational conflict resolution and leadership development, cross-cultural conflict resolution, religion and conflict resolution, conflict coaching, effective communication in the workplace, group facilitation, family therapy, peacemaking (meditation, self-examination, negotiation and mediation), peacekeeping, peacebuilding, and research methods in conflict resolution. He is married and has three children.

CPSIA information can be obtained
at www.ICGtesting.com
Printed in the USA
LVHW030517060122
707947LV00006B/781

9 781982 208875